A NAP SYSTEMS PUBLICATION

Answers:

A parents' guidebook for solving problems.

Paul W. Robinson, Ph.D.

Leo D. Hall, M.Ed.

LION HOUSE PRESS • CANBY, OREGON 97013

Dedicated to:

Carol Robinson and		Charlotte Hall and	
	Michael	Greg	Tom
	Kit	Darcy	Amy
	Shawn	Karly	Julie
	Brooke	Shari	Chris
	Marta	Alan	

A NAP SYSTEMS PUBLICATION

Drawings by Ron Kingsley
Cover design by David E. Canaan

Library of Congress Cataloging in Publication Data:

Robinson, Paul W., 1942-
    Answers: A parents' guidebook for solving problems.

    Includes index.
    1. Parenting—Handbooks, manuals, etc. I. Hall, Leo D.,
1932-   . II. Title.   III. Title: Answers: A parents'
guidebook for solving problems.
HQ755.8.R622   1983   649'.1   83-17538

ISBN 0-914107-00-3

LION HOUSE PRESS, P.O. Box 791, Canby, Oregon 97013

TABLE OF CONTENTS

FORWARD

After living in Europe for many years, and having several children become teenagers, I decided to return to the U.S. and further my graduate training in psychology. While at Brigham Young University I met experimental psychologist Dr. Paul Robinson and saw things done with children of all ages that I previously thought not possible. In June of 1982 I saw a thirteen-year-old boy who weighed a mere 43 pounds brought to Dr. Robinson. This boy messed his pants repeatedly every day, was somewhat autistic, could not read or write, and showed no signs of emotional joy. Having been fed only soup and milk all his life, he was like a child raised by animals. For the last few years prior to going to Dr. Robinson he had been worked with in special schools and hospitals with no success. One year later the boy ate normally, did not mess his pants, would read books by himself and write, and in addition, laughed and played like most young children.

I worked with Dr. Robinson in his "Controlled Living Program," a program for teenagers who were sluffing school, on drugs, promiscuous, smoking, drinking, and no longer controllable by their parents. A representative case was that of twin girls, referred to by the high school principal as the "local mafia." After one and a half years of straight F's in school and doing whatever they pleased, their parents placed them in the Controlled Living Program. Four months later both girls had an above C average. One year later both girls were doing better than B+ work in their own home. Their parents couldn't be more pleased with their two loving daughters.

Not only has Dr. Robinson helped change the exterior behavior of these girls, but also he has somehow helped restore their inner values, especially those of self-esteem.

Dr. Robinson has shown me that loving children really means caring enough to discipline them when you would rather not. It means disciplining when it is needed and being there with affection and support when children act positively. The NAP System for raising children really works!

Nancy Passeretti
School Psychologist

I have learned more from working with Dr. Robinson in three months than in the ten years I worked at the State Youth Center (or the more than 14 years as a faculty member of a state hospital). Dr. Robinson not only changes children, but helps their parents develop effective parenting skills. I was very excited to learn he had decided to put this valuable information in the NAP Guidebook and share his methods with fellow professionals and parents.

Leon Duncan
Utah State Hospital

Several years ago, while a Dean at a university in Thailand, I read one of Dr. Robinson's books. My government sent me to the United States, where I lived in Dr. Robinson's home for over a year watching and learning the methods he uses. Although he and his wife, Carol, have only two children of their own, the fewest number of children present while I lived with their family was ten. Most of the children in their charge were referred from agencies who could no longer handle them. The parenting system in their home is based on that of this Guidebook and is one all parents can benefit from, once they understand and use the principles involved.

Basically, the NAP System is a combination of the close-to-nature method of raising children combined with principles of scientific behavior management. Too many people are running away from natural principles toward new scientific technologies, later to find out the hazards involved. This is not the case with the NAP System. Dr. Robinson has combined his skills in behavior management and the "old-fashioned" approach of our grandparents day into an approach to parenting that balances love and discipline. I have seen children acquire a self-control through firm discipline in a home where there was always a warm and loving relationship between the parents and the children.

Implementing the principles of this NAP Guidebook has the potential of doing the same for your family. I recommend it be a part of your parenting responsibilities.

Sitichoke Waranusuntikule
Bangkok, Thailand

We are using the NAP Guidebook as the basis for all our parent training. We find this program to be the most effective approach possible to help adults across the country deal with the challenges of being a parent. Much of our training is with parents from diverse cultural backgrounds and with parents of juveniles who have been arrested or have been in trouble with the law or at school. These techniques have been effective in helping them to improve very difficult situations. This program really does work for all parents, regardless of the age or circumstances of their children.

Darryl R. Townsend, Ph.D.
Training Director
National Corrective Training Institute
Austin, Texas

The "Natural Approach to Parenting" as reflected in the work and writing of Dr. Paul Robinson has the virtue of translating the most reliable, scientifically-validated methodologies into down-to-earth, practical action steps that parents can begin to use immediately. Dr. Robinson's latest book, *Answers: A Parents' Guidebook for Solving Problems,* is the most comprehensive and dynamic parenting resourcebook available today. It is a must for all parents who are seriously interested in solving family problems or having a more positive impact on the lives of their children.

Richard J. Allen, Ph.D.
Educator, author, consultant
Former developer and administrator
of graduate programs in Applied Behavioral
Science and Change Management at
The Johns Hopkins University,
Baltimore, Maryland

As a clinical psycholigist who spends much of my time working with troubled families, I am continually searching for effective ways to help discouraged parents influence and change their children's behavior. Frustrated parents who come to my office are not looking for complicated theories which will explain away their children's problems. They want to know, and they have the right to know, practical solutions to these problems. They want to know what works!

I had been counseling a discouraged couple, in whose charge an extremely agressive four-year-old had been placed. I referred them to a facility specializing in the evaluation and treatment of such children. I was shocked to learn several months and many thousands of dollars later that the child had been returned to the couple and was seemingly in worse shape than before. At this point I felt it was time to ask for assistance from my colleague, Dr. Paul Robinson. Dr. Robinson will tell you that he enjoys a challenge and thus agreed to to talk with the couple and to take the boy into his own home in a "Controlled Living Program." Within six weeks Dr. Robinson had discovered the techniques that would effectively bring this child's behavior under control. The next step was to teach the parents how to structure their own home environment and utilize the powerful tools of "natural parenting."

Answers: A Parents' Guidebook for Solving Problems is one of the most exciting and valuable guidebooks I have seen today. In it Dr. Robinson describes *practical, effective* methods parents, teachers, school counselors, and therapists alike can use to help children they live and work with. I highly recommend it to anyone who loves children and has an interest in working with them.

Sherry Lynn Aronoff, Ph.D.
Clinical Psychologist
Private Practice

PREFACE

In the 1950's the world renowned naturalist Konrad Lorenz wrote a book entitled *King Solomon's Ring* in which he recounted the experiences he and his wife had had in their attempts to better understand the laws of behavior by allowing a variety of animals to roam freely in their home. Lorenz acknowledged that his way of studying animal behavior seemed a bit strange and eccentric. In *King Solomon's Ring*, he notes:

> For who else would dare ask his wife to allow a tame rat to run free around the house, gnawing neat little circular pieces out of the sheets to furnish her nests, which she built in even more awkward places than men's Sunday hats?
>
> Or what other wife would tolerate a cockatoo who bit off all the buttons from the washing hung up to dry in the garden, or allow a graylag goose to spend the night in the bedroom and leave in the morning by the window? (Graylag geese cannot be house-trained.) And what would she say when she found out that the nice little blue spots with which song birds, after a repast of elderberries, decorate all the furniture and curtains, just will not come out in the wash? . . .

By allowing these animals into his home Lorenz discovered principles of behavior that could be described as no less than amazing. His findings rocked the field of animal behavior. But was it necessary to let animals in his home to accomplish this? To this question Lorenz responded: "Yes, quite definitely yes! Of course, one can keep animals in cages fit for the drawing room, but one can only get to know the higher and mentally active animals by letting them move about freely."

Touched by the success of Lorenz's approach (and the emphasis on observing children by such men as Jean Piaget and B. F. Skinner) my wife, Carol, and I opened our home to problem children of all ages. Against the advice of friends and colleagues we began taking in problem teenagers whose parents could no longer handle them. We took in teenagers who were flunking school, on drugs, agressive, suicidal, promiscuous, and noncompliant to parental authority that wanted no part of an adult-run world. We took in a somewhat bizarre five-year-old who almost strangled a two-year-old. We took in a thirteen-year-old boy who weighed only 43 pounds and who had eaten nothing but soup and milk all his deprived life. Among many such unusual cases came dozens of children with much more "normal" problems.

Have you ever interacted with a teenager who has great parents, but lives in pain because he or she has a distorted perception of mom and dad? Have you seen an aggressive, afraid-of-nothing, fifteen-year-old cry at night because his mother gave him away at age eight and told him she did not want him any more? Have you heard a four-year-old dark-skinned girl from India whose father tried to drown her kneel and ask God to let her get back in her new white mother's tummy so she could come out white and not be teased by other children?

Such experiences gave Carol and me greater resolve to take in even more children to try to get a better understanding of human behavior. We observed, experimented, and observed again. We searched for answers to questions like "What do you do when children don't negotiate fairly in conflict situations?" "What do you do when children don't want to listen?" "What are the best ways of reprimanding children, when you really care about them?" "Do the laws of human behavior work the same for 'problem' children as for 'normal' children?" "How do you get children to do things for the *right* reason?"

The first lesson we learned from our experiences is that the advice we psychologists give across a desk falls dismally short of meeting the needs of parents and children alike. Some "sounds-good" psychological theories are leading parents who are searching for family improvement down the wrong roads. We found that parents need to preside in the family and *can* do so with mutual respect for all family members. We found that parents need to discipline on occasions, and will receive a child's love and appreciation when it is done properly.

Like Lorenz, we began to see there is an important and powerful natural plan of life that many scientific areas have violated with attempts to solve problems quickly. In the book *Manipulating Parents* I wrote about tactics children use to manipulate parents. I told short stories about what children have done. I received stacks of letters asking to hear more about the children and what was done to help them. I also received scores of requests for more information on exactly what parents can do to better raise their children.

The NAP Guidebook was written to give parents more specific information about what they can do to improve their parenting skills. The NAP Guidebook does not have the stories in it that *Manipulating Parents* does. It was designed to be a sourcebook. It includes the things we have learned over the past twenty years to help both parent and child be more successful. I hope you enjoy *Answers: A Parents' Guidebook for Solving Problems*. I enjoy hearing from you and apologize for being unable to reply to many of the letters I receive because of the volume of mail. Please be assured that I have personally read every letter sent to me.

Paul W. Robinson
September, 1983

INTRODUCTION

We believe you will find the NAP Guidebook one of the most important resources available today in assisting you in your parenting role and helping you and your child experience what parent/child relationships should be—enjoyable and rewarding. The NAP Guidebook is different in two ways: in its content and in the manner in which it can and should be used.

Its major difference is in its contents and the concepts upon which it is based. These you will note especially in Unit One, with more detailed information in the following units.

However, it is more than just a book full of helpful information. It has been designed so that that information can be used, analyzed (with reference to a particular child), adjusted and used again. The NAP System works if it is "worked" and followed. Most of the units have exercises at the end. You won't just read about how to solve a problem or strengthen a weakness in your child's behavior—you'll find some definite processes to follow, worksheets (Outlines for Action) to use in analyzing what you need to do, and charts to record what's happening. So, the Guidebook doesn't just suggest **what** to do—it provides help and support in **how** to do it.

What, then, is the best way to use the NAP Guidebook?

We suggest you first read Unit One completely through. It provides the basis for the rest of the Guidebook. Then, browse through the remainder of the book, unit by unit. Read the boxed preview information at the upper right of the first page of each unit; then read the major headings; finally, in your quick overview, read the information in bold-type in the outer margins of each page. These small segments of information can either be used as a preview of what you will read in the lengthier, adjacent material or they can be used later as a review of what you have read earlier. In either case, they become a sort of outline of the contents of the Guidebook.

To make the Guidebook of real benefit to you and your family, do those exercises that are at the end of most of the units. You may want to use some of the exercises (especially the Outlines for Action) more than once—depending upon the size of your family or the number of "problems" you wish to work on. In that case you either may make copies on a local print-shop's copying machine or you can order extra copies. (A price list is available upon request. Ordering information is on the last page of the Guidebook.)

Is the Guidebook written so any parent can understand it or is it full of "two-dollar" words—words than only professionals use and understand?

It is written so that anyone can understand it. However, we have not attempted to over-simplify it. We have included, with explanations and examples, words such as *consequation, attribution, sets, consequential focusing,* and others. Some parents using the NAP Guidebook may also be meeting with professional counselors in family and social service agencies. An understanding of some of their terminology and language in such situations would, we believe, be helpful to parents.

Successful parenting is not easy—it takes time and effort. Your success with NAP will be determined by how much action you put into the material you find in this Guidebook. We have attempted to write and arrange it to help you in whatever way your particular parenting situation warrants.

Isn't this Guidebook really for those parents with younger children?

No! We believe the principles of the NAP System are valuable for any adult who has an involvement with another person—and not just children. That would seem to include just about everyone.

While it is written with a parenting emphasis, we believe the information in the Guidebook also has value for improving husband/wife, employee/employer, and student/teacher relationships.

In the area of parenting, this Guidebook can benefit anyone from the young couple planning marriage and a family, to those with children (infants through teens), plus those whose children have left the "nest"—those parents who now are or may become grandparents. Today, grandparents have a greater potential for positive influence than ever before because of split marriages or situations where both parents work.

Many others in child-tending, -rearing, or -counseling positions will find this Handbook invaluable. School teachers, counselors, and psychologists, day-care center personnel, instructors of high school and university family living and parenting courses, family counselors in social service and family service agencies, foster parents and foster parenting agencies should find valuable information in this Guidebook and other materials available in the NAP System of parenting.

So, there are other materials available that support or supplement the NAP Guidebook?

Yes. The NAP Guidebook provides the basic information of the NAP System. Additional material is available on cassette tapes and in smaller booklets. The tapes—30-45 minutes per side—contain additional information and explain in more detail the material in the Guidebook. Additional materials are available, such as loose sheets of various Outlines for Action, chore charts, family meeting agendas, etc.

What if I have a particular problem that I need more help with?

Also available is a series of tapes and booklets titled *The Practical Problem Series*. Each tape or booklet covers a specific topic such as *Lying and Stealing, Indolence, Reaction-Seeking Misbehaviors, Fears,* and so on.

Another program, designed to help you with special parenting problems you might have is called the NAP Audio-cassette Counseling Service. This program allows you to communicate your particular problem to Dr. Robinson via cassette-tape and receive a reply back also via tape.

Are there other ways of learning more about the NAP System besides the books and tapes?

Yes. Parenting workshops and seminars are being conducted. If you are not aware of any in your area and you are interested, write to the Lion House Press address—Attention: NAP Workshops.

We will be glad to let you know if there are any scheduled in you area. If not, we will try to set one up. You may be interested in organizing and conducting a workshop yourself. We are prepared to train and certify instructors in the NAP System and will make every effort to help you and others in your area.

Leo Hall
September, 1983

The Natural Approach to Parenting: Five Basic Principles

> The Natural Approach to Parenting is based on five basic principles—*presiding structure, value development, association, consequation, and individuality.* Children apprentice in a home where parents preside. Because Mother Nature has given mankind freedom of choice, a family may develp its own value system. We become what we are through our associations. A child's actions can be influenced by the consequences—rewards or penalties—of those actions. NAP recognizes the value of the individual and the importance of the development of the self.

ANOTHER YELLOW BRICK ROAD?

Well, here you are—reading another one of those parenting books, still searching for some answers on how to be a successful parent with happy, well-adjusted children. Do you even feel you're headed down another yellow-brick road, trying to find the real Wizard of Parenting—someone or some method that will help you correct problems and weaknesses in your parent/child relationships?

If you think about your situation for a moment, you may find that you have a lot in common with the tin man, the scarecrow, and the cowardly lion in the classic story, *The Wizard of Oz*. As you recall, all three had specific **desires** and **weaknesses** that they wanted transformed into **accomplishments** and **strengths.** They were searching, perhaps as you are now, for the Wizard, who, it was said, had the power to fulfill their wishes.

Just look at all those authors of parenting books—the current Wizards of Parenting. In *The Wizard of Oz* the main characters had only **one** wizard to seek help from. But parents have **many.** Aren't we parents fortunate? **Or are we?** How come there are so many? And how come they advocate different philosopplies? And why is it that some don't seem to work?

I'M TAKING YOU TO SEE THE WIZARD!

WE ALL WISH TO CHANGE DESIRES INTO ACCOMPLISHMENTS, WEAKNESSES INTO STRENGTHS.

BEWARE OF THE WIZARDS OF PARENTING

It's natural to assume that the philosophies of the Wizards of Parenting should work, since they seem to be spoken with authority. But many parents fail when they try using certain philosophies on their children. Why? There are at least two possible explanations why they don't:

1) Parents fail to implement them properly
2) The philosophy is wrong

Now every parent knows how wise psychological wizards are, so the problem must be that parents are applying the parenting philosophies incorrectly. Right?

Wrong!

Perhaps it is time that parents began to question (just as Dorothy questioned the Wizard of Oz) the parenting advice given them and quit blaming themselves for their lack of success.

A MAZE OF METHODS:

AUTHORITARIAN?
DEMOCRATIC?
TALK PROBLEMS AWAY?
NOTHING NEGATIVE?
DON'T PUNISH?
GOBBLEDYGOOK?

Perhaps there is something wrong with the current parenting philosophies. Each year a different method seems to be in fashion. One suggests that all family members should have equal vote in family matters. Another advocates that *talking* about problems, rather than *doing* something, is sufficient. Also, everything must be positive—no punishment, no unpleasantness. And each year new words are added to the parenting vocabulary— *bonding, patterning, behavioral dysfunction, schizophrenia, logical consequences, active listening, Id,* and *hyperactive* are just a few.

To the everyday parent, all this parenting advice, supported by a special vocabulary, would appear sensible and valid. Dorothy and her three friends thought the same thing—wizards are wise, wizards are to be followed. "Star Wars," another popular, more up-to-date story, has its heroes in a similar search—looking for a power or force to help them turn weakness into strength.

The desire people have to find some special source of help and strength seems to be timeless. For centuries we mortals have looked for some supernatural solution to our problems. Isn't it nice to see movie audiences today satisfied to find the solution is really within our natural capabilities? The theme behind both *The Wizard of Oz* and "Star Wars" is that the force or power being sought is really within each individual and that it's available to everyone. The key is to build upon the natural qualities each person already has. As you remember, our heroes from Oz found that the Wizard's claims of super-power were false and that the key to their reaching **accomplishments** and developing **strengths** came from within themselves. Using their own **natural** talents and the experiences encountered during their search brought them the goals they had been seeking.

The power to succeed does not come from supernatural or plastic psychological philosophies. The force is indeed within you. Just as your friends from Oz used their **natural** capabilities to reach their goals and find success, so can you as parents. The key to parenting success is within you, and better than help from any wizard, you have a special guide to follow—*Mother Nature*. Her plan for parenting has been around a long, long time and is as sensible and valid today as it has always been in centuries past.

For years, using scientific technology, we have raced on from one "success" to another. More effective cleaning detergents were developed. Powerful chemical insecticides were created that were wholeheartedly welcomed as important contributions to our lives.

But now our mistakes begin to show up. Those effective cleansers were not biodegradable—they have become an eternal poison to life. Those insecticides created resilient strains of insects, destroyed important balances in nature, and in many cases will remain for years and years as poisonous residues left in our environment. Using science, we tried to improve on Mother Nature's work, without fully realizing the rhyme or reason behind her ways. We failed to respect her guidelines and grabbed for achievements without realizing the potentially harmful side-effects our creations would cause.

IT DOESN'T PAY TO FOOL WITH MOTHER NATURE.

In the natural sciences, scientists have seen the error of their ways. Now they try to work within Mother Nature's guidelines. For example, they are focusing more on getting rid of insects through the use of natural enemies or are developing naturally occurring compounds that confuse the mating tendencies in insects, so they will not multiply. Now science focuses more wisely on learning the basic, natural principles and then builds upon those principles with scientific advancements that are compatible with Mother Nature's basic, daily procedures.

In the realm of parenting, social scientists have also changed Mother Nature's course. Children have been given equal decision making power along with parents in the family. Punishment and adversity are labeled as being primitive and problem-causing factors in Mother Nature's plan. Love and firmness are considered contradictory in family management. Some parental plans say that misbehaving children are a fact of life we must live with. Children will grow out of their inconsiderateness, so parents should not intervene. Claims are made that love is all a child needs to develop in a positive way.

Families, where parents are following such words from these Wizards of Parenting, are failing—one after another. And parents are blaming themselves for not correctly following such philosophies, rather than questioning the validity of those philosophies.

The pendulum is swinging back. Just as in the natural sciences, we see that the proper methods of parenting need to follow the guidelines of a **natural** system. Mother Nature has all along provided a basically sound parent/child system in which parents should preside in the family. She has given us free choice.

She has included things in our world so that we could learn to build upon her beautifully simple but effective system. There are many things parents can do to better guide children without destroying Mother Nature's natural way. And that is what the Natural Approach to Parenting (NAP) system is all about—parenting based on incorporating scientific findings into the basic plan of nature.

Our basic needs and those of our children have not changed over the centuries. Granted, our environment and modern life style are different today and those differences have not only introduced some new problems to consider, but have also obscurred the best way to solve them—Mother Nature's way. Just as the physical maladies and ailments of today require the help of medical doctors and lab technicians to supplement Mother Nature's healing processes, so does this time in which we live require some extra help in understanding and implementing Mother Nature's plan. And that's what the Natural Approach to Parenting is all about—doing what comes naturally and making it work in today's changing world.

So, how can parents guide their children toward a successful future? First, by understanding the natural reasons for a child's actions and then using Mother Nature's principles to direct those actions. This handbook shows a very **powerful** system for successful parenting. It contains no supernatural forces or methods. The potential for success is in nature and you! The power in this handbook is your power. As you implement and work with Mother Nature's plan as outlined in the Natural Approach to Parenting, you will find the strength, the power, and the satisfaction of successful parenting.

MOTHER NATURE'S WAY:

THE BEST APPROACH, PROVEN AND TIME-TESTED

THE NATURAL APPROACH TO PARENTING:
Five Basic Principles

The key or combination that unlocks this natural parenting plan and makes it work consists of five principles. These principles include *presiding structure, value development, association, consequation,* and *individuality.*

Presiding Structure
WHO'S DRIVING THE FAMILY BUS?

It is popular nowadays to talk about a family system where each family member has an equal vote. With this philosophy the child is told his opinions and wants have equal weight with those of the parent. The dishonesty of such claims is felt when little Johnny finds himself stopped from walking through mud puddles or big Johnny is not allowed to smoke pot in the home or do many other things that often "drive parents up the wall." And few children can ever recall being seriously asked how the family income should be spent. This popular family system, in its attempt at equality, often seems most inequitable to the child.

That grand old lady, Mother Nature, never intended a family system based on such "equality." Children are not born with a well-developed library of correct decisions in their minds. Experience and maturity are ingredients children gain over the years. When properly aged, such ingredients can be thrown into the family decision-making pot.

Mother Nature's family plan calls for a *Presiding Structure.* Under such a plan, parents, who are travelling a different part of the same road their children are travelling, preside over the home and what happens in it. Children are apprenticing, learning from parents who have travelled that part of the road earlier. As little Johnny learns to take the responsibility for his own actions, he is given more. Gradually he is able to make more and more decisions for himself and participate in family decisions. Eventually he will be of an age to leave the family, hopefully then prepared to make it on his own.

Where children are now, Parents once were. Where parents are now, Children soon will be.

Here are the finer points of the Presiding Structure family plan:

1. It is an apprenticeship plan where the young child spends the first one-fifth of his life under the caring eye of the parent.

2. The child is not owned by the parent. When the child reaches the legal age of adulthood, the parent no longer has any right to supervise the child's life.

3. Both parent and child should be continuing to grow in mind, body, and spirit during these child-rearing years. Each is simply at different points on life's continuum. The growth of the parent is as important as the growth of the child.

PARENTS AND CHILDREN SHOULD GROW TOGETHER.

4. Both parent and child are of equal value in the family. However, each has different roles and responsibilities. That allocation of responsibilities requires the parent to provide security and take the burden of major decisions off the shoulders of the child while he or she trains on simpler, less severe decisions. In turn, the child accepts the guidance of the parent.

5. Having reached adulthood, new parents are given the right to set up a home environment based on their own individual values. It is the right of adults to create their private little corner of the world based on their beliefs of right and wrong. Neither their parents nor their children have the right to take that opportunity away from them. Children do not, but will when they reach adulthood, have the right to establish their new corner in the world.

PRINCIPLE OF PRESIDING STRUCTURE:

Mother Nature's family plan places parents in a presiding position with children apprenticing toward increased responsibility as they become prepared for adult living.

6. The Presiding Structure is based on parents having the ultimate responsibility for decisions concerning the child with the parent treating the child with the dignity and mutual respect parents want for themselves.

7. Children are given greater responsibilities as they reach the legal age of adult accountability. The end result is total responsibility for one's self by legal adulthood.

Value Development

DIGGING FOR DIAMONDS OR DIGGING FOR WORMS?

Jimmy is in the garden digging his eighth hole, young radish plants scattered all around him. His mother looks out the kitchen window, notices his activity for the first time, and dashes outside.

"James! What in the world are you doing?" She can barely control her anger and frustration.

"Gee, Mom. Just diggin' for diamonds."

"But look what you've done to my radishes," she moans.

"But Mom, diamonds are more important than radishes."

Indeed, diamonds are valuable. But so are radishes, if you're hungry. Most everything in this world has value or worth to one individual or another depending upon the circumstances. Our actions or goals are determined by the value obtained from pursuing them.

Unlike animals, we are not born with instincts that control our thoughts and actions. Most of Mother Nature's creatures are endowed with instincts that cause them to behave in certain ways and follow certain patterns. A bear, for example, is required (whether he wants to or not) to hibernate during the winter. Man, on the other hand, may choose to get up at four a.m. to go fishing or sleep until noon, depending upon whether he places more worth or value on going fishing or sleeping in.

We humans, as intelligent beings, have been given the ability to make choices, to chart the direction of our lives. We do have within us a rather mild but persistent need system which motivates us to grow and develop. But the standards, guidelines and procedures we follow in meeting these needs of growth and development are ours to choose. We are given the ability to develop our own unique values and they determine our actions. We can learn to prefer fishing and hunting, art and culture. We can learn to enjoy sports, either as spectators or participants. We can learn to value books and the pursuit of knowledge. We can learn to enjoy the company of good friends at a backyard barbeque. One teenager may develop an overwhelming desire to cruise main street with friends, while another teenager might have a goal of Olympic competition and devote hours of practice and training at ice skating. Not only can individuals have different goals but the goals and values of an individual may change. Neither parents nor their children are locked forever into any set of values that have been developed.

The Natural Approach to Parenting recognizes that people do not automatically develop positive values. Children can learn to enjoy antisocial activities. Teenagers can find a value in joining gangs, stealing, and taking drugs. NAP also recognizes that values can be changed, that children can find association with their family worthwhile, that teenagers can find value in school activities, and that parents have the right to establish family rules, guidelines, and standards. They have the right to encourage family members to follow them. Unit Ten shows how values are developed, how they can be changed, and how they can be made of worth to the child.

Perhaps little Jimmy will be digging holes again tomorrow (in a more appropriate place)—but this time, looking for worms. He's going fishing with his dad.

CHILDREN DON'T JUST AUTOMATICALLY DEVELOP POSITIVE VALUES.

PRINCIPLE OF VALUE DEVELOPMENT:

Not being limited by instinct, and having freedom of choice, parents are allowed to develop and encourage adherance of their own system of values in the home.

Association

IF YOU DON'T WANT THE MEASLES, YOU'D BETTER READ THE QUARANTINE SIGN

Mary Lou, in her recently washed pale yellow dress, runs into the house to show her mother her latest discovery. "Hey, Mom! Look what I found!" She holds out a lump of coal to her mother, who sees only the black streaks on her dress and the coal dust on her hands.

Perhaps Mary Lou had never seen a piece of coal before and hadn't yet learned that part of the coal might leave itself on her dress or her hand. She didn't know that her hand could become black by *associating* with the piece of coal. If you stick a piece of chalk into a bottle of ink, it will automatically begin absorbing the ink. If you place a troubled foster child in a well-balanced family, some of the positive qualities of the family can't help but become absorbed by the child. Did you ever notice how some elementary school teachers begin to talk a bit like the children they deal with every day? Would you be surprised to learn that people working in the psychological and psychiatric profession who deal with mentally disturbed individuals have a higher than average rate of developing mental problems?

"You are what you eat." "Hang around with that crowd and you will get a bad name." Often heard statements like these remind us of a principle of life that even the ancient Greek scholars understood: **We become what we are through our associations.** A teenager whose friends and associates use drugs is more likely to use them also, than one whose friends don't have such habits. If Michaels's mind is filled with thoughts of flying and becoming an airline pilot, he is more likely to become one than if he dreamed daily of joy riding, pulling pranks, and sluffing school.

Each of us is like a piece of chalk that absorbs part of those things and people we associate with. Mother Nature made it so. It is through this process that we become who we are. A bit of Aunt Jane, some of Grandfather Johnson, a part of our best friend in the third grade, a lot of our parents and current friends—these are what make us who we are today. And next week we will be different, for better or for worse, because of our associations.

The effect of our environment and the people around us, this associative process, has been around from the beginning of time. Today, however, we understand more about it and how it works. We know how to arrange conditions to increase the likelihood that a child will pick up positive traits and values rather than bad ones through association.

The Natural Approach to Parenting helps parents understand the process of *association* and provides methods parents can use to get that process to work in helping the Mary Lous and Michaels become the best they can. (Units Three, Four, Ten and Eleven explain more fully and give examples of how the association process works.)

WE BECOME WHAT WE ARE THROUGH OUR ASSOCIATIONS.

PRINCIPLE OF ASSOCIATION:

The value of an object, an action, or a person takes on the value of other objects, actions, or persons that are associated with it.

Consequation
TOUCHED ANY HOT STOVES LATELY?

Why do children do the things they do?

Did Mother Nature pre-program them to automatically behave as a biological robot?

Are they guided by mysterious instinctual psychological forces deep within their minds?

The actual forces governing the way we behave are quite interesting. Mother Nature designed us to be guided by making choices and experiencing the consequences of those choices. A child is not born with an instinct which has him avoid touching hot stoves. If little Albert touches one, he will decide from the result or consequence of his action, whether touching hot stoves will be something done again in the future. If saying such things as "Thank you," "Please," and "I'm sorry" produce positive consequences from others, using such words will become a part of our way of acting. If you want a young infant to smile, show enthusiasm and affection when he smiles.

According to one dictionary definition, a *consequence* is "something produced by or resulting from a previous condition." The infant, having smiled, receives attention and affection and soon learns that if more attention and affection are desired, smiles will bring them on.

WE DO THINGS BECAUSE OF THE CONSEQUENCES OF OUR DOING.

Since we do not behave instinctually, why do we behave the way we do? More specifically, why do children behave the way they do? What guides their actions? **Everything a child does is because of the results or consequences he receives for his actions.** A child rides a tricycle because of the consequence—enjoyment. An infant with a soiled diaper cries because in the past crying produced a desired result: mother came and changed the diaper. A parent works at a job for, perhaps, two consequences: (1) the money received, and (2) personal satisfaction. We do things because of the consequences of our doing.

Natural consequences are a major part of Mother Nature's plan for human motivation. We learn that touching a hot stove causes pain; we learn that the result of wearing a heavy coat in the wintertime is warmth and comfort; we learn that if we don't eat enough at mealtime, we will soon become hungry again. We learn that there are natural laws that produce natural results—results determined by our obedience or disobedience to them. By following these natural laws, a person could develop in a satisfactory manner without parents having to do anything special. But sometimes special parental help is needed.

Natural consequences are a part of Mother Nature's plan, but sometimes she needs extra help.

Doctors and medicine mend broken bones and help the sick.

Parents and others can help mend "broken" behavior.

To draw a parallel, imagine that someone has developed a thyroid gland malfunction or someone else has been in an automobile accident. Mother Nature's natural healing processes are not sufficient to restore full health to such individuals. Therefore, unlike her other animal creatures, she has endowed man with the thinking ability and skills to develop medicines and to become doctors. The sick and injured can then be helped to a point where the natural healing processes can take over.

In the home parents provide much the same assistance to Mother Nature that doctors provide in the hospital. While the natural consequences of our lives are usually sufficient to move us happily along life's path, there are situations that arise where extra help is needed. And so parents can learn to help change and influence actions and adjust behavior when natural consequences are not enough to get the child back on a healthy and normal mental track.

While we live in a land of freedom and choice, there are rules and laws we must obey. Traffic laws do not permit us to run stop signs and experience the natural consequence that might result from an accident—our death or that of another person. The rules and guidelines established by a family are intended to help its members not have to experience the natural consequences that might result from inexperienced decisions. And so Mary Lou and Michael are protected until they are old enough to better handle the natural consequences of their actions.

The Natural Approach to Parenting teaches parents how to use some powerful skills in guiding and influencing actions by adjusting the consequences or results of those actions. This process, referred to as *consequation,* is used throughout this handbook.

Parents can help influence actions and adjust behavior when natural consequences are not enough.

PRINCIPLE OF CONSEQUATION:

Everything we do is because of the consequences which follow our actions. Guide or adjust the consequence and you influence the action.

Individuality
YOU'RE A LIMITED EDITION AND ONE OF A KIND

Name something you always have with you. That's right. It's you. You are the most important thing in your life. Nothing in life will have more influence on you than you, yourself.

But who are **you?** How did the you of today come to be? Is your *self* the same from the day you were born until the day you die? Of course not. We change through life's daily experiences. In fact, that is what life is all about—developing this *self* of ours.

Before we continue, let's get one thing straight. Because we are referring to our *self* and its importance, we are not talking about being self-centered. We are not referring to the "myself," the "I," "me," "mine," the "What's in it for me," and the "I want to do my own thing" approach that has been such a common pursuit in recent years. By *self* we mean all those things that make us what we are, different from any other individual who has lived, who now lives, or will yet live on this earth.

Our *self* is quite changeable. Every experience we have in life has some impact on our *self.* Good habits, such as honesty, cleanliness, and helpfulness are part of *self.* Good attitudes (or poor ones) are a part of *self.* As we have seen already, values, habits, and attitudes are not determined by instincts, they are learned. So we see that the *self* is **learned.** It is something that life helps us develop. A person's *self* can become almost anything. Mother Nature does not restrict us from developing a *bad self* or a *good self*, a *sad self* or a *happy self.* Each person is an individual, each has the freedom to develop in directions of his

HI, SAY HELLO TO YOUR SELF.

WE HAVE THE FREEDOM TO CHOOSE AND DEVELOP WHO WE ARE AND WANT TO BECOME.

YOU'RE ONE OF A KIND!

PRINCIPLE OF INDIVIDUALITY:

The individual is important. What we are—our self— does not just happen. It is learned. And the best place to learn who we are is in the family.

own choosing. As mentioned in the previous paragraph, no two people have *selfs* that are exactly the same, not even identical twins. Definitely, **you're one of a kind!**

Realizing these facts about individuality can help parents develop better parent/child relationships. The *self* of any child is influenced by experiences, so parents can use good experiences to help the child develop a *good self.* In fact, parents can arrange experiences in their own lives to make their own *selfs* even better. The methods for doing both are the same.

The Natural Approach to Parenting can help parents identify more clearly just what their child's *self* is and then learn some ways to help the child develop a better *self.* Helping all the Amys and Andrews, the Jills and Johnathans, and the Sarahs and Solomons feel good about themselves and their places in the home, the school and society, helping them develop self-confidence and self-esteem are some of the most important things parents can assist their children in acquiring. (Unit Nine deals specifically with developing self-worth.)

**FAMILIES ARE FUN.
FAMILIES ARE FOREVER.**

SUMMARY

The Natural Approach to Parenting ststem can best be summarized by the following five articles of belief:

NAP SYSTEM • ARTICLES OF BELIEF

PRESIDING STRUCTURE:

The most effective parenting system consists of a family organization where parents preside. While the mutual respect and equality of parent and child are fundamental, their role and responsibilities differ. Children apprentice for approximately one-fifth of their lives under their parents. Presiding structure emphasizes family unity in the home; teaching accountability, responsibility, and sensitivity; and following words with actions.

VALUE DEVELOPMENT:

Mankind is not ruled by instincts. Given freedom of choice each of us has the ability to develop our own unique values. Our values, rather than instincts, determine our actions. Parents can and should be involved in helping their children develop positive values.

CONSEQUATION:

A person's actions are influenced by consequences. There are natural consequences in life that guide most of our actions. Mother Nature provides things parents can learn so they can increase the effectiveness of natural consequences in guiding a child's actions. Pleasant and unpleasant consequences are a natural part of life. Both are needed in guiding children.

ASSOCIATION:

People learn and become who they are through the process of association. The development of values, of self-worth, and of positive actions (or misbehavior) all come about through association. We are not limited by genetics as to what we can become. We become what we are through association. There are basic principles of association that parents can learn to influence a child's values, self-worth, and actions.

INDIVIDUALITY:

Each person is unique. Just as no two snowflakes are exactly the same—although the natural process which creates snowflakes is standard—so is it that the standard process for producing people is such that no two are physically or psychologically exactly alike. Each person is an individual, an individual that gets his or her meaning in life from being a unique part of something bigger than he or she is.

THE NATURAL APPROACH TO PARENTING
Exercise 1.1

1. List two situations that have happened in your home where your child most likely realized your family was not run on a democratic format.

   Example: *Linda wanted to stay out past midnight on a school night*

   a. _____

   b. _____

2. List two misbehaviors your child does and state what you feel is the consequence that causes each misbehavior to occur.

Misbehavior	**Consequence**
Example: *10 year old pouts when he can't go out and play*	*sometimes his pouting influences me in letting him go*
a.	
b.	

3. List two actions you do every day and write the consequences for them.

Action	**Consequence**
Example: *I cook supper for the family*	*If I do, I feel better If I don't, they complain*
a.	
b.	

4. List two actions you do each week that are not done because of consequences.

Action	**Consequence**
Example: *Can't think of any*	
a.	
b.	

5. List something your child has learned to value that you like and state how you think that value developed in the child.

Value	**Development**
Example: *friendship*	*has had good times with friends*
a.	
b.	

6. List something your child has learned to value that you don't like and state how you think that value developed.

Value	**Development**
Example: *loud rock music*	*friends like it*
a.	
b.	

7. Pick two things in your life where the principle of association played a role.

   Example: *used perfume when going out with Ken*

   a. _____

   b. _____

continued on next page

8. Pick something you could do to help your child, using the principle of association.

Example: *Being with her in the emergency room of hospital when she is hurt*

Example: *Gave David a dollar to weed the garden*

a. _____

b. _____

9. List two likes and two dislikes your child has that are different from other children.

Likes	Dislikes
Example: *carrot and radish sandwiches*	*playing outside*
A.	
b.	

10. List two characteristics of your child that distinguish him/her from other children.

Example: *Julie's nose wiggles when she is mad*

a. _____

b. _____

QUESTIONS and ANSWERS

Q. Does NAP suggest that parents turn to the old ways of running a family?

A. NAP does not advocate parents following the older parenting methods of the past. However, NAP believes many old-fashioned values about parenting are as sound and valuable today as they were years ago. Nature has implemented some solid and effective natural consequences and procedures to guide families. NAP also believes that nature intended mankind to develop and to use additional methods to add to the natural ongoing system. Using scientific technology is important, but it should be employed with an appreciation and consideration of natural processes and laws.

Q. NAP seems to emphasize parents influencing their children. Shouldn't children decide for themselves what they should do?

A. Children make no decisions without being influenced by something or someone. If parents decide not to influence their child's actions because they want their child to "be free to choose" for himself/herself, they are simply allowing other outside forces to have a stronger influence.

Q. Why should children be required to be under the supervision of adults if they don't want to be?

A. Given freedom of choice, children have the ability to make either good or bad decisions. We do not let a child drive a car without first learning from an experienced driver how to do so, because we want him and others around him to be able to live or to live safely while driving. In such a situation a child needs to be protected from himself and from others. In the growing-up process, children need supervision to help keep them from jumping into situations that might hold dangers they cannot see from their vantage point as children. Children should be allowed to benefit from the mistakes and successes of their parents and not be expected to go through many of the same ones over again. Children should be allowed to be "kids" and not expected to make adult-type decisions until supervision and experience warrant such.

Q. Why should parents be allowed to control the lives of their children? Wouldn't government agencies do better? I see many adults who are poor parents.

A. No government agency in any country has come anywhere close to being as effective as parents in raising children. There is no question that some parents do not live up to their responsibilities. Social agencies, however, have never developed any system that comes close to the success ratio of Mother Nature's plan—parents raising children. The answer is not to transfer parental rights to government agencies, but rather to broaden parental rights as a whole, while removing those rights from parents who abuse them.

continued on next page

Questions and Answers continued—

Q. Does NAP believe children go through phases that parents should ignore?

A. No. NAP believes the idea that children go through phases and that they cannot be influenced or changed by parents is wrong. Certainly, children go through physical changes and phases as they grow. But believing that a child who throws a tantrum is simply going through a "stage" he will eventually outgrow is not correct. Such behavior occurs because it pays-off and not because it is a phase the child is going through.

Q. How old does a child have to be before parents can use rewards and penalties to influence actions?

A. Parents should be teaching children about pleasant and unpleasant consequences of life by six months of age.

Q. How does presiding structure differ from a dictatorial family system?

A. Both presiding structure and dictatorial (or authoritarian) family systems are based on parents having the final word. In a presiding structure, however, (1) parents are not considered superior to the child, (2) children are encouraged to provide input in family matters, and (3) children are continually given opportunities to make decisions. Presiding structure encompasses an apprenticing process where the goal is eventual self-rule and self-sufficiency of the child.

Q. The NAP System seems to emphasize parents being firm with children. Isn't understanding the child also important?

A. Absolutely! As you read the NAP Handbook, you will see a great deal about understanding and communication between parent and child. But the need to be firm is a very important factor. Conflicts and confrontations happen in every family. Parents need to know the correct methods for being "firm" with their children. NAP explains how parents can properly use discipline.

Q. NAP seems to emphasize the rights of parents more than other parenting approaches. Why?

A. Parents need the opportunity to grow and develop just as much as children. They should have the right to be individuals, to do things for themselves. They have the right to establish the way they wish their home to be run. They have the right to enjoy the rewards of parenting, to find parenting a satisfying experience. Too many teenagers today do not wish to become parents, because they see no enjoyment or satisfaction in the lives of their parents. They do not see the "fun" of parenting.

Q. The example given in part four of Exercise 1.1, "can't think of any," didn't help much. I couldn't think of any either.

A. Then you answered the question well. Most everything we do is because of some consequence we receive or expect to receive from doing it.

Q. The second example in part eight of Exercise 1.1 seems to be a better example of consequation than it does of association.

A. Indeed, it is an example of both. The consequence of weeding the garden is a dollar. If David values a dollar, then, through association, the weeding of the garden takes on a value sufficient to cause him to do it.

What Motivates a Child?

> What motivates a child to misbehave? Many psychologists claim it is because the child is discouraged. Others say it is because the child is going through stages. What motivates a child to behave properly? Some say encouragement is the key to positive actions in children. Some say children have an inborn tendency to be good. This unit clarifies the natural system that motivates a child to misbehave and behave properly. In this unit parents will learn the key to influencing the desires and actions of their children.

WHEN MOTHER NATURE SAYS, "JUMP" . . .

In Mother Nature's scheme of things, we find a variety of systems for motivating action. For many small creatures the natural motivating and directing forces for action are provided through instincts. Instincts are genetically determined, inborn, motivational forces that demand that an animal act in a certain way when certain environmental conditions prevail. That animal has no choice. If, for example, you had an ant farm in your home and happened to kill one of the ants and then were able to place it down inside the colony, you would find that a fellow ant would pick up the deceased ant and carry it out of the colony. If you replaced that deceased ant back in the colony, the other ant would again pack it back outside. This sequence would continue as long as you continued to return the dead ant. The live ant has no choice. Its instincts require it to act a specific way when finding a dead comrade.

In fact, we know from scientific research that a dead ant secretes a certain substance. If you put that substance on a live ant, other ants will repeatedly remove that wiggling ant from the colony. They have no choice. Their instincts force them to. An additional interesting point is that these ants show no emotion as humans do. Like the famous Mr. Spock in the TV series "Star Trek," they act without emotion. They feel no remorse when losing a co-worker. They do not sit and think about what should be done next. They simply respond in the way their instincts tell them. There is a nice side to their situation, however. They never have to worry.

**MOTHER NATURE
GUIDES AND DIRECTS
THE ANIMAL WORLD
THROUGH INSTINCTS.**

LET GO OF ME YOU FOOL! I'M NOT DEAD. I JUST SMELL THAT WAY.

MOTHER NATURE'S GIFT TO MANKIND— FREEDOM OF CHOICE

Instead of telling people what to do and how to behave in every situation, Mother Nature endowed the human race with a great capacity to learn and to solve problems. She does not tell us what to do. Instead, we are given a *system for action*, which allows us to decide for ourselves what we should do in different situations. People have *freedom of choice*. They, themselves, can decide what to do and when to do it.

MOTHER NATURE GIVES US A SYSTEM FOR ACTION:

FREEDOM OF CHOICE.

But what can influence a person's choices? What can influence how a person acts? Is there anything that can influence which direction a person's actions take? Of course, there is. And that something has to do with what a person *feels*.

People can feel good from doing some things and get an unpleasant feeling from doing other things. People tend to do those things that produce good feelings and avoid actions that produce unpleasantness.

So the key to influencing a child's actions must somehow be linked to influencing a child's feelings.

DIRECTING FREE CHOICE THROUGH DESIRES AND SATISFACTIONS

Desires are those feelings we experience when we want something.

Satisfactions are those feelings we experience when we put a value label on some consequence we received for our actions.

Our feelings can be divided basically into two kinds—*desires* and *satisfactions*. **Desires are those feelings we experience when we want something.** Johnny gets hungry and feels the desire to eat; lonely Mary feels the desire for companionship. **Satisfactions are those feelings we experience when we put a value label on some consequence we received for our actions.** A child whose action leads to food when having the desire for food gets a *positive satisfaction* feeling from those actions. A child having the desire for food gets a *negative satisfaction* feeling if his actions lead to some consequence other than food. Sounds a bit funny to think of some satisfactions as being negative, doesn't it? But that is the case. In a restaurant we may be asked how we were satisfied with the food. We may reply that we were poorly satisfied.

The actions of the blowfly are controlled by instincts. When it gets hungry and needs nourishment its behavior is automatically determined. Its sensory-smell system encounters an odor of sugar and, as if on automatic pilot, it is drawn to the sugar-based honeydew secreted by aphids on leaves. The blowfly does not have a choice as to what his actions are. His instincts automatically determine how the need for sugar will be met. Diagramming the blowfly's action sequence is different from that for a child.

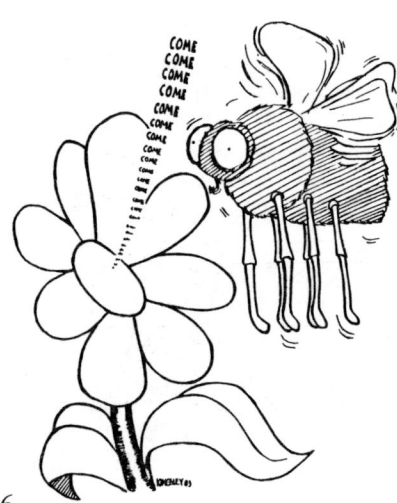

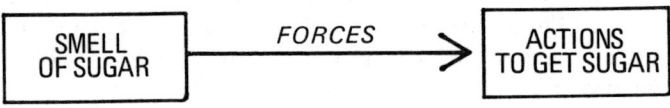

SMELL OF SUGAR	*FORCES* →	ACTIONS TO GET SUGAR

The blowfly has no free choice, so feelings of satisfaction from eating sugar have no influence on further actions.

A child, on the other hand, is not instinctively told how to satisfy the desire for food. He goes through the process of trying several actions to satisfy such a desire. When certain actions produce consequences that positively satisfy the desire for food, then little Andrew has learned to use free choice to satisfy motivational desires. He has also learned that a need for food stimulates him to act. Some of his actions result in food. (Obtaining food is the *consequence* for some of Andrew's actions.) The food results in a feeling of satisfaction. That satisfaction causes him to desire to do certain food-producing acts in the future. Now the picture of what can influence actions begins to take shape. We begin to see that past satisfactions create desires which then can influence a child's choice of action.

NEEDS AND DESIRES MOTIVATE CHILDREN

Desires are those feelings a child has that prompt that child to act. Amy desires a cookie, so she goes to the kitchen to look for one. Brooke desires attention so she throws a tantrum. Desires are very important because they are the motivational forces which stimulate a child to act. But where do a child's desires come from? Understanding how desires develop in a child is important for parents to know, because it provides the key for allowing them to change the actions of their child. **Influence a child's desires and you can influence a child's actions.**

So how do parents go about developing desires in children? To answer that question the two types of motivational forces in children need to be understood—*needs* and *desires*.

DESIRES PROMPT A CHILD TO ACT.

INFLUENCE A CHILD'S DESIRES AND YOU INFLUENCE HIS ACTIONS.

NEEDS. Needs are those genetic forces Mother Nature instilled in us to be active. She did not instill instincts in us which force us to behave in very specific ways. Yet she did not want us to just sit around and expect the world to come to us. She instilled in us a motivational system that prompts us to act, but allows us the freedom of choosing which actions to perform. We are genetically endowed with needs. These needs are a very general type of motivational force. We have needs for things such as food, safety, and companionship. Yet the way each of us fulfills these general needs is left up to each individual's freedom of choice. An American teenager may satisfy his need for food with hot dogs and his need for companionship by cruising main street with his friends. A Chinese teenager may satisfy his need for food with rice and his need for companionship by flying kites with his friends.

We are instilled with general needs to seek food, safety, love and other basics.

DESIRES. Desires are much more specific motivational forces, and they are **learned.** Desires are feelings a child develops to have or do certain things. Desires develop through *consequation.* If Debbie's actions (stimulated by hunger needs) are satisfied by ice cream, she develops a *desire* for ice cream. If Steven's actions

Desires are specific ways we learn to meet these basic needs.

(stimulated by a need for companionship) are satisfied by cruising main street, then he develops a *desire* to cruise main.

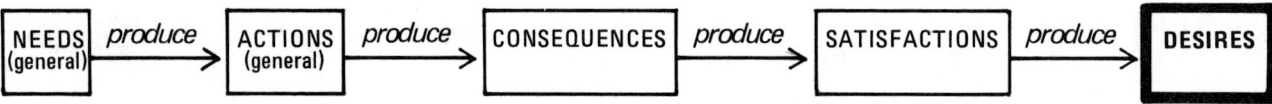

So Mother Nature instilled in each one of us basic, general *needs* which produce general *actions.* Actions eventually produce *consequences* which produce feelings of *satisfaction* which produce *desires* for future actions. Eventually, with repeated occurances, this chain of events shifts and it soon results in *needs* producing *desires* which produce *actions,* and so on.

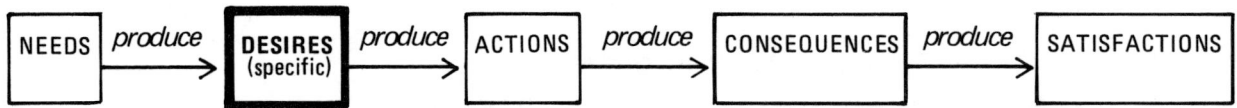

Needs come to make the child think of desires for specific things which are obtained by specific actions. When certain consequences produce certain satisfactions, the child develops specific desires to obtain those certain and specific satisfactions.

What this all boils down to is that children **learn** to desire certain things and they will learn to act in ways to obtain consequences that fulfill those desires. We are not born with a desire to dance, ski, watch football, wear name brand jeans, or run through a mud puddle. We develop these desires by those actions which lead to such satisfying consequences. The more satisfying some consequence is to little Jeffery, the stronger the desire for that consequence and therefore, the stronger Jeffery's tendency to act in a way that will produce the consequence. Sounds simple enough, doesn't it? Well, it is, but there is still a great deal more for parents to know before they can learn to effectively develop desires in their children.

WE ARE MOTIVATED TO ACT, BUT ARE FREE TO CHOOSE OUR ACTIONS.

HIERARCHY OF NEEDS

While Mother Nature did not instill mankind with much in the way of instincts, she did apparently provide us with a bit of direction in which our actions should advance. She gave us great intellectual ability, did not restrict our ability to choose by limiting us with instinctual boundaries, instilled a strong capacity to feel emotions and learn from experience, implanted a vague sense of motivational direction, and sat back to see what heights we could rise to. Restricting man's freedom of choice little, if any, she instilled an inborn hierarchy of needs within us. This hierarchy of needs provides a general motivational force within each of us that stimulates us to act. As those actions pay off, we learn to desire certain satisfying consequences.

Abram Maslow studied the needs of man and concluded there are five basic types of needs we deal with throughout our lifetime.

The first and most fundamental are those relating to meeting nutritional and supportive needs like eating, drinking, and sleeping. These he called the *physiological*. According to Maslow, once man satisfies these, then his need for *safety* is addressed. Once a person's needs for nourishment and protection are met, man's thoughts turn toward a desire for affection and human companionship to fulfill the needs of *love*. After satisfying love needs, man desires such things as human competition and status. Fulfilling *esteem* needs, man then transcends above worldly cares and concerns of self to reach *self-actualization* by placing the value of other's welfare and growth before his own.

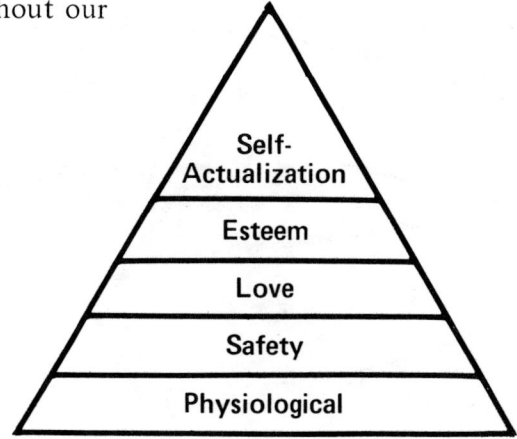

Figure 2.1
Abram Maslow's proposed Hierarchy of Needs in Man

Even though our needs seem to follow a priority or order of importance, we have tremendous latitude on how these needs can be satisfied. The amount and kinds of foods that can satisfy physiological needs are almost endless.The actions people can take to obtain food are also numerous. The same is true about the actions and choices available to satisfy the other four types of needs.

It is important that parents realize all children have basic needs and that these needs were instilled in children by Mother Nature. All children will feel these needs. We cannot change that fact. So, if needs and desires influence actions, and parents cannot influence needs, then they should look towards desires as the way to influence a child's actions.

Parents cannot influence a child's NEED (for food), but can influence the DESIRES a child develops (for certain foods).

THE BASIC MOTIVATIONAL SYSTEM

A basic understanding of the motivational system influencing a child's behavior contains tips about a number of things parents can do to modify a child's undesirable actions. Many of these tips will become evident as we take a closer look at what a motivational system entails.

Practical Relationship Between Motivation, Needs, Desires, Consequences, Satisfactions and Values

When we ask *"Why does a child act the way she does?"* we are in essence asking what motivates the child's action. A child's motivational system can be thought of as having five important parts: *needs, desires, actions, consequences,* and, *satisfactions.* (Figure 2.2 illustrates the relationship.)

19

THE MOTIVATIONAL CYCLE

SATISFACTIONS   CONSEQUENCES

NEEDS

D E S I R E S   A C T I O N S

Figure 2.2

A child's body develops the *need* for food. The child finds himself with the emotion of *desiring* food. He learns to perform certain *actions* to obtain food. Those actions result in the *consequence* of obtaining food, which results in the emotion of positive *satisfaction*. Both desires and satisfactions are feelings of *emotion*. And emotion is the basis for each individual's *value system*.

A child acts in ways that bring him closer to things he holds of positive value (that produce pleasurable emotions) **and acts in ways that move him further away from the things he holds of negative value** (that produce unpleasant emotions).

If a parent wants to get a child to act in a certain way, the solution is to create a desire in the child for that action; then make sure a consequence that produces an internal pleasurable emotion follows the act.

Desires are those feelings which prompt or encourage a child to act in certain ways. And what produces desires? Right, it is satisfying consequences. Now some people argue that encouragement is all that is necessary to get a child to behave. They argue that encouragement from parents will create the desire in Michael to behave. However, suppose you say, *"You can do it, Michael,"* or *"If you don't eat your lunch, Michael, you will get spanked."* Encouragement through promises or threats lose any influence over Michael's actions if consequences do not follow. If a mother repeatedly threatens to spank her child but never follows through, what effect do the threats have in getting the child to act? Right, very little. It is not difficult to look at life and realize that **encouragement influences a child's desires only if consequences follow actions.**

A child acts in ways that bring him closer to things he holds of positive value and acts in ways that move him further away from things he holds of negative value.

I'VE ALREADY TOLD YOU TEN TIMES! I'M GOING TO SPANK YOU IF YOU DON'T GET THAT DONE !!!

A DESIRE DEVELOPS THROUGH THE RESULTS OF OUR ACTIONS.

HOW DESIRES DEVELOP

If a child's actions are directed mainly by learned desires, then how do such desires develop: **A desire develops through consequation.** (We have said this before, but it bears repeating.)

Suppose, for example, a person gets hungry. To satisfy that need for food, a youngster may try an ice cream cone for the first time. The consequence of eating the ice cream cone is a positive satisfaction. The satisfaction produced from eating the ice cream develops a desire for ice cream that increases the likelihood that the next time the child gets hungry, he will satisfy that hunger with ice cream. The more times the child satisfies his hunger with ice cream, the more he feels the desire for ice cream.

Now, ice cream is not the only food that could satisfy hunger. A person can satisfy hunger in a variety of ways. In the Far East rice would most likely be used to fill the need. In Germany sauerkraut and weiners may satisfy the need. In a fishing village a logical choice would be fish. The basic need for food can be satisfied with many different foods. However, the foods used in the past to satisfy a child's hunger are more likely choices he will draw towards to fill future hunger needs. When ice cream is the consequence of a child's food-seeking behavior in the past, **and** that consequence is positively satisfying, then a desire for ice cream develops in the child. **When an object satisfies a person's need, that person develops a desire for the object.**

When something satisfies a person's need, that person develops a desire for it.

As can be seen with the hierarchy of needs, a child also has needs for love and belonging. A child can develop a number of different desires which will direct him toward a consequence which will positively satisfy that need. A child can learn to satisfy the love and belonging need by going to a rock concert or cruising main street with school friends, going on a family picnic, or becoming involved in athletics. For which of these activities will he develop the strongest desire? For the one that in the past has produced the most satisfying consequences!

Can the child develop a desire for rock concerts, cruising main street, family picnics, and athletics? Oh, yes. Then which will he most likely do if given a choice? That depends on which choice has produced the most satisfying consequences in the past. Because each of the five categories of needs can be satisfied in a variety of ways, a *hierarchy of desires* develops in each one of us. Unlike the hierarchy of needs that is fixed, the hierarchy of desires that people develop within each need category is changeable. Figure 2.3 shows two different desire hierarchies for the four previous activities discussed to meet a teenager's need for love and belonging. Desire hierarchies that develop in children can be changed. This means that parents can do things to vary the strength of a child's different desires. Desires do not develop to a certain strength and remain that strength the rest of a child's life. Barbara may have greatly desired playing with dolls at age six, yet at age sixteen has no more interest in them. The value level of desires is changeable. What children like they can learn to dislike and conversely, what they dislike they can learn to like. The secret lies in which type of consequence a parent provides for the child's actions. **Consequences are the key to developing desires.** Parents can arrange consequences to influence their child's desires and actions.

DESIRE HIERARCHIES

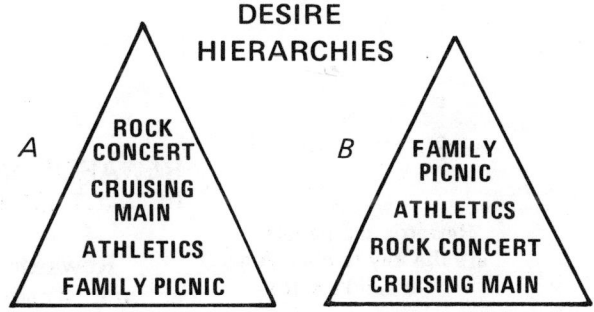

Figure 2.3 Two different hierarchies of desire that could develop in a teenager. In hierarchy A rock concerts are more desirous for the teenager than family picnics. A child could develop one hierarchy and then have it change to another.

CONSEQUENCES ARE THE KEY TO DEVELOPING DESIRES.

ALL RIGHT, SON! GOOD JOB.

CONSEQUENCES HAVING A PLEASANT VALUE ARE CALLED REWARDS.

CONSEQUENCES WITH AN UNPLEASANT VALUE ARE CALLED PENALTIES.

As previously mentioned, **desires develop because of consequences.** If a child's actions are consequated with something that is positively satisfying (in other words, pleasurable), then a desire that motivates that action develops. Now recall that *consequences* are specific things which result from a child's actions. Possible consequences for a child doing her homework could include: receiving candy, receiving a hug and comments of appreciation from dad, receiving an apple, receiving the opportunity to go to the movies, or having an inner feeling of self-satisfaction. All of these are possible results (or consequences, as we call them) of doing homework.

Whenever the mind associates some action with its consequence and forms a memory, it not only records exactly what the consequence was, but also puts a value on that consequence. The consequence will then be remembered as being *pleasant* (a positive satisfaction) or *unpleasant* (a negative satisfaction). The mind not only records a consequence as having a pleasant or unpleasant value, but also records the *degree* of that value. For example, the consequence of receiving two candy bars for mowing the lawn would be registered in the mind with a higher pleasant value than receiving one candy bar.

Consequences, then, come in two basic types: (1) consequences with a pleasant value, and (2) consequences with an unpleasant value. **Consequences having a pleasant value are called rewards, while those with an unpleasant value are called penalties.**

Rewards and penalties are the key to changing a child's actions.

REWARDS INCREASE THE DESIRE TO ACT; PENALTIES DECREASE THE DESIRE TO ACT

Rewards and penalties are the key to changing a child's actions. Actions can change in one of two directions—they can *increase* or *decrease*. A parent is interested in increasing proper actions of the child and decreasing improper actions (misbehavior). When rewards follow actions, such actions increase. When penalties follow actions, then those actions decrease.

The principle behind changing a child's actions is: rewards increase actions and penalties decrease actions.

If you want to *increase* a certain action of a child, follow the child's act with *rewards*. If you want to *decrease* a certain action of a child, follow that action with a *penalty*.

Tom, Tom the piper's son
Stole a pig, and away he run,
The pig was eat,
And Tom was beat,
And Tom ran crying
down the street.

Mother Goose Rhyme

On the following page is a list of both types of consequences—*rewards* and *penalties*.

SUGGESTED LIST OF CONSEQUENCES

REWARDS (likes)	PENALTIES (dislikes)

Social

hugging touching or patting praising peer approval smile tickling kissing	nagging yelling ignoring stern, quiet mom

Activity

free time work puzzles pop balloon, paper bag water plants squirt gun sing a song dance hear story show and tell help prepare dinner talk with parent stay up after bedtime have a party jump from high places parent as slave for 15 minutes choose dinner times pick family activity go to a movie	taking out trash washing dishes vacuuming living room cleaning out car sitting on chair taking away privileges spanking doing task over and over not get to go shopping no TV cannot go to friend's house being left out of game delay dinner go to bed early

Material

masks puzzles money comics fans ribbons use of bean bag	take away toys take away radio give balloon to brother or sister no cookies available no dessert

Edible

penny candy gum nuts apples raisins cookies popcorn soda pop	spinach soup cold pancakes

Figure 2.4

**Provide the consequences
of rewards for good behavior
and penalties for misbehavior.**

There are several things you may have noticed on the list on the previous page (Figure 2.4) that should be explained. First, there are more suggestions listed on the rewards (likes) side than on the penalty (dislikes) side. This suggests that we should always be more concerned with positive approaches to handling any given situation. Not only the child but also the parent benefits when positive solutions are used. Second, some suggestions on the penalty side may not be dislikes to your child—spinach or cold pancakes, washing dishes or vacuuming could be rewards for some, while receiving an apple or nuts may not be considered a reward by others. You'll also find that what was rewarding to your four-year-old no longer means much to that child who is now thirteen. And as children grow older their dislikes sometimes turn to likes. Asparagus, which was "yucky" to the child becomes a gourmet delight to the adult.

Well, there you have it. **The secret to motivating a child's behavior is to provide the consequences of rewards for good behavior and penalties for misbehavior.** That is how the forces of nature influence a child's actions, and that is how parents can do the same.

PROFIT OF ACTION PRINCIPLE

"But when I consequate my child's actions with what he likes or dislikes, it does not change his actions!"

Ever heard a parent say something like that? Many parents have. And all parents at one time or another have had situations where consequating children's actions seems to have no effect. If consequation is such a basic part of changing actions, then why are there times when it does not seem to work?

**WILL YOU LOSE MORE
OR GAIN MORE
FOR YOUR EFFORT?**

The answer to that question lies in the complexity of life. No action produces all rewards or all penalties. A man may receive ten dollars an hour for digging a ditch, and put out a great deal of effort doing it. The results of his effort are both money (a reward) and exhaustion (a penalty). The question as to whether a man will work for ten dollars an hour is really whether that man receives more than he loses for his efforts. In other words, is the money worth the effort? Do the rewards outweigh the penalties?

THE PROFIT OF ACTION PRINCIPLE

A person's actions are determined by whether
he or she receives more than is lost for the effort.

Each child's mind works on this profit of action principle. Every situation and action actually has many pluses and minuses related to it that the mind must consider. If a father says, *"If you keep your room clean for a week, I will give you five dollars,"*

24

the child's mind weighs the pluses and minuses of the situation with a number of unconscious questions such as:

"How much work and effort will I have to put out?"
"How much money do I already have?" (If he already has $1000, he most likely won't be influenced by $5.00.)
"How badly do I need the money?"
"Will dad really follow through with his promise to pay?"
"Can I get $5.00 from dad by doing part of it now and arguing later?"

When a child's mind is in the process of choosing a course of action, it weighs all the possible rewards and penalties. And if there is a potential profit for the child (that is, if the rewards outweigh the penalties) then the child will select that course of action. If there is an alternative course of action that has more rewards and fewer penalties, the child will choose it over another.

When a parent's attempts at consequating a child do not work, it tells us the parent is not aware of all the pluses and minuses the child is considering. Perhaps the parent promises, but does not follow through. Perhaps the parent has not been consistent in the past. Perhaps the child received conflicting signals as to what was really expected. Whatever the case, the child's mind unconsciously determined that the action desired by the parent was not worth the effort. Some of the most common conclusions that children come to for not acting are:

"Dad or mom may promise, but won't fulfill."
"Dad or mom will forget, so I won't have to do it."
"If I don't give in on this, mother will give up and do it herself."
"Mom and Dad give consequences, but give unclear signals about what needs to be done to receive them."
"If I plead or complain, I can get dad to change his mind."
"I can talk dad into giving me the money later, even if I don't do what he wants."

PRINCIPLE OF LEAST EFFORT

Ever notice how your child doesn't make his bed or clean her room? Does your child seem to want to do things the "easy way" rather than the thorough way? Well, don't think your child is much different from other children. You see, that tendency of your child to try to get things done with the least amount of effort is a natural inborn tendency. Mother Nature instilled in each of our minds a kind of *efficiency expert* that prompts each of us to try to get the most out of life for the least effort. Why should Johnny make his bed if mother will do it anyway? Why get up and take out the trash? If David ignores mother's nagging to take out the trash, he may have to put up with some discomfort from her nagging, but he will get to finish watching his favorite TV program, **and** mother will take out the trash herself. So it's really more efficient for David to ignore her request.

IF YOU PROMISE A REWARD OR PENALTY—

FOLLOW THROUGH.

WE ALL (OFTEN UNCONSCIOUSLY) **TRY TO DO THINGS WITH THE LEAST AMOUNT OF EFFORT.**

> ## THE PRINCIPLE OF LEAST EFFORT
>
> **We try to do things to get the most
> out of a situation for the least effort.**

While you may not like some of the ways David acts to conserve his efforts, think what life would be like if all of us did not have that little efficiency expert guiding what we do. We would waste much more time and effort than we do now, **plus** we would have no incentive to invent so many labor saving methods. So don't sit and complain when your child uses tactics to get out of doing work. Just make sure his or her inappropriate attempts to take shortcuts in doing what is asked do not pay off.

SO, WHAT MOTIVATES A CHILD?

So, what motivates a child? Why do they act the way they do? After reading this unit, parents should realize:

- Children's actions are not caused by instinctual forces that parents cannot influence.

- A child has the freedom of choice, and choices are influenced by the consequences that a child receives for his or her actions.

- While Mother Nature endows all of us with the same basic needs, each person develops his or her own ways of meeting those needs.

- Desires prompt actions, and consequences from past actions prompt desires for future actions.

- Children *learn* what to desire, so parents can do things to influence what a child finds desirable.

- *Rewards increase* actions they follow, while *penalties decrease* actions they follow.

- Encouragement without consequences is not enough to motivate a child to act.

- A child's mind operates by two principles:

    THE PRINCIPLE OF PROFIT OF ACTION

    THE PRINCIPLE OF LEAST EFFORT

WHAT MOTIVATES A CHILD?

Exercise 2.1

I. List two *desires* your child has that stimulate him/her to misbehave. Explain how you feel those two desires developed.

2. Explain what needs are met in your child by satisfying the two desires mentioned in question one.

3. Pick a positive action you would like to develop in your child. Explain how you might develop a *desire* in your child to produce that action.

4. Explain the difference between a *need* and a *desire.*

5. Diagram the five parts of a child's motivation system. Illustrate it with a specific need, desire, and action pattern in your child.

6. Identify two types of consequences.

7. Pick two actions your child performs each day; then explain what you feel are the consequences the child could receive that would keep him/her from doing it.

8. Using the Suggested List of Consequences (Figure 2.4), name 10 *likes* and 10 *dislikes* of your particular child. Be sure to include consequences that are special to your child, those perhaps that distinguish him/her from other children.

LIKES	DISLIKES
_____	_____
_____	_____
_____	_____
_____	_____
_____	_____
_____	_____
_____	_____
_____	_____
_____	_____
_____	_____

9. Pick one action you want your child **to do** and one action you want your child **not to do**. Explain how you could influence these two actions using things itemized on the list of likes and dislikes in question eight above.

10. Explain the Profit of Action Principle and how it relates to what you do for a living.

11. Explain the Principle of Least Effort. Examine some of your own actions or activities and write down one where you do (did) something using this principle. Now do the same thing with your child (children).

QUESTIONS and ANSWERS

Q. But aren't many actions of children due to deep psychological problems instead of being due to consequences of actions?

A. The probability that a child's actions are due to deep psychological problems is the same as a child being overweight because of glandular problems. Most parents tend to feel their child's misbehavior has to be due to some psychologically traumatic past experience.

Q. My husband is against giving our son rewards for doing things. He feels we are bribing him. Are we?

A. Bribery is the use of rewards to get someone to do something for your benefit rather than theirs. If a mother wants peace and quiet for herself and tells her child she will give him a cookie if he will be quiet, she is bribing him. If mother gives little Johnny a cookie so he can learn to be quiet, then she has not bribed him. Parents get money for working. Would we call that a bribe? Obviously not. Bribery is the use of rewards to take advantage of others. More is said about this issue later in the NAP Handbook.

Q. If I reward my child, won't he learn to expect payment for everything he does?

A. No. Learning to do things for payment is a necessary step in the development of children doing things for others without getting paid. Who donates more time and money to helping people in need: working people or people on welfare? Busy people who work hard for money are by far the most likely people to donate money and time for the needy. Too many parents fail to reward their children and develop a work ethic in them because they are afraid they will produce "money-grubbing" children. We lose many more children to laziness than to "money-grubbers."

Q. I realized I was inconsistent in rewarding and punishing my child in the past. But when I decided to be consistent, it still did not change my child's actions. What is wrong?

A. Most likely nothing is wrong. Your child has gotten used to your being inconsistent. Keep up being consistent. It will eventually get the job done. If you don't see changes within two weeks, re-evaluate exactly what you are doing. And of course you should read the other material in this handbook.

Putting Motivational Forces to Work in the Family

> Mother Nature's motivational system is based on pleasant and unpleasant consequences for actions. Parents can motivate children to increase their desire to do good by using the application method, the removal method, and the situational planning method. These same three methods can be used to decrease a child's desire to misbehave. Verbal promptings alone do not work. Actions (consequences) give words their motivational power.

MOTHER NATURE'S WORLD OF POSITIVES AND NEGATIVES

The world we live in is strongly based on the principle of positives and negatives. Metal magnets have a positive dimension and a negative dimension. The brain performs its functions through the actions of positively charged and negatively charged electrochemical compounds. Atoms, the basic building unit for all matter in this world, are composed of positively charged and negatively charged parts called protons and electrons. The whole earth itself is polarized with compasses regulated by the North Pole.

Man's motivational system is based on positives and negatives. Each time we behave, our mind evaluates the results (consequences) of that behavior. And that evaluation includes determining whether that consequence was *positively satisfying* (pleasant) or *negatively satisfying* (unpleasant).

So what does all this talk about pleasant conseqences and unpleasant consequences mean to parents wishing to motivate their child? Does it mean parents simply reward a child for being good and punish a child for being bad? Is that all there is to putting motivational forces to work in the family?

Don't sell Mother Nature short. Remember, with only **three** primary colors, she provides all the thousands of colors we see in our daily world. And from the seemingly simple movement of molecules in the air, our sense of hearing is treated to sounds ranging from the threatening crackling of thunder to the rhapsody of a beautiful melody. So now, when you realize that a

THE RESULTS OF OUR ACTIONS ARE JUDGED TO BE EITHER POSITIVELY SATISFYING OR NEGATIVELY SATISFYING

WHAT DO RED, YELLOW, AND BLUE MAKE?

EVERYTHING!

MOTHER NATURE'S WORLD OF SIGHT, SOUND, AND BEHAVIOR—

SIMPLY WONDERFUL, WONDERFULLY SIMPLE

child's motivational system is essentially based on *pleasant* and *unpleasant* consequences for action, be careful you don't underestimate what can be done with this seemingly simplistic idea. As with all of Mother Nature's natural laws and principles, there is more to her motivational system than there, at first, appears to be. To tell parents that Mother Nature intended them to motivate children by rewarding good behavior and punishing bad behavior is like telling us to take the three primary colors and make everything in the world either green or brown.

Parents can use natural ways to influence a child by regulating pleasant and unpleasant consequences.

Let's take a look at **six** things parents can do to motivate children using natural ways of influencing a child's desires by regulating pleasant and unpleasant consequences. Let's focus on **three** things parents can do to motivate children to *increase* the desire to *do good*, and **three** things parents can do to *decrease* the child's desire to *do bad*. Actually there are many more things a parent can do to either increase good actions or decrease bad actions. In fact, Unit Five discusses six methods parents can use to decrease misbehavior in children. But the six methods for influencing a child's desires for action which are discussed in this unit are the fundamental methods upon which most of the other possible methods are based. Once parents understand how to employ these six methods, then they are ready to branch out and try the additional techniques and methods presented in later units. So now, let's look at six ways to influence a child's desires to act.

SIX WAYS TO MOTIVATE

Remember, in Unit Two it was pointed out that *desires* lead to *actions*, actions produce *consequences*, and consequences produce *satisfactions* which in turn influence a child's *desires*. And a child's *desires* are what motivate him to action. The key to motivating Jimmy, then, is to influence his desires. Parents need to do things which **increase** the desire to **do good**, and **decrease** the desire to **misbehave**.

THERE ARE THREE MAJOR WAYS TO MOTIVATE A CHILD TO DO GOOD.

INCREASING A CHILD'S DESIRE TO DO GOOD

There are three main ways this can be accomplished:

1. the application method
2. the removal method
3. the situational planning method

Application Method. Suppose your boss wants you to work overtime on Friday night. How could he increase your desire to stay? One way would be to add something to the situation—such as giving you additional money. He could pay you time-and-one-half or double-time. He could offer you a bonus. He could tie such extra effort on your part to an advancement in

the company. These are all examples of the application method of getting someone to act. **You increase the consequence value by applying positive incentives.** Children will act when the payoff for the act is large enough.

Keep in mind that giving positive consequences only works on children if they perceive the consequence to be of high value. Using the application method, parents often offer consequences that the child (1) doesn't really view as having high value, e.g.: getting to go to relatives, getting a new, but unstylish dress, (2) can get even if she doesn't do what is asked, (3) sees as not of high enough value to offset the effort required, or (4) sees of less value than getting the best of the parent right now.

You can increase the consequence value by applying positive incentives.

Removal Method. Most parents are aware that you can use the application method to reward a child to act, but few realize there is a second way to produce positively satisfying consequences to get someone to act. The removal method is the most popular method children use to get action out of parents. It is based on the principle that **removing something unpleasant increases a person's actions.** An infant cries, and stops crying when picked up. A four-year-old screams and cries until mother buys the ice cream cone at the shopping mall. A teenager pouts and mopes about the house until the home atmosphere is so uncomfortable that mom and dad give in and let her go to her friend's house.

REMOVING SOMETHING UNPLEASANT INCREASES A PERSON'S ACTIONS.

In all three of these instances the child *removes* something *unpleasant* when mom or dad behave as the child wants. The infant gets mother to give attention; the four-year-old gets mom to buy the ice cream; the teenager gets mom and dad to change their minds and let her go.

The removal method can be just as effective in getting a child to behave properly as the application method. And the number of ways this method can be used is limited only by the parents' imagination. Some examples of the removal method are:

1. The mother stands quietly and firmly until the child picks up the toy as requested.
2. The teenage boy wears wrinkled clothes until he starts picking them up so mother is not repeatedly swamped with ironing clothes that he just throws around.
3. The six-year-old eats cold meals until he learns to get to the dinner table on time.
4. A parent sits quietly for an hour or so until the reluctant teenager begins to talk about a problem needing to be dealt with.
5. The six-year-old's toys are taken away until the bedroom is cleaned up.
6. The TV is turned off until Johnny takes the trash out.

The above examples represent unpleasant situations that have been created, later to be removed when the child's behavior changes.

31

The removal method typically involves three parts. First, you create (or let the child create) an unpleasant condition, e.g.: take away attention, turn off television, take away phone privileges. Second, you state what is required to remove that unpleasant condition. Third, the unpleasant condition is terminated when the desired action occurs.

Situational Planning Method. A third way for getting a child to behave as you want is to **select optimum conditions for the task to be performed.** Parents can often get a child to perform some task by requesting it be done when no desirable alternatives are competing. David is more likely to take out the trash if his favorite TV program is not on at the time. A ten-year-old is more likely to do what he's told if he does not have some more satisfying activity as an aternative. With a little thought and planning, parents can increase a child's tendency to do what is desired. The number of ways the Situational Planning Method can be used is almost limitless. A few ideas are listed below:

Select optimum conditions for the task to be performed.

1. Get all house chores done before friends come over.
2. Ask David to take the trash out before or after his favorite TV show rather than during.
3. Schedule household chores so Mary can get them done **and** go with a friend later.
4. Arrange a schedule for baths, hair washing, etc. so brothers and sisters do not argue over who should be using the bathroom.
5. Buy different colors or brands of items to reduce disagreements over ownership.
6. Separate "trouble-makers" from each other around the dinner table.
7. Increase a child's desire to eat dinner by controlling snack availability.
8. Provide fresh fruit and vegetable snacks as alternatives to candy and other sweets.
9. Set up situations where what you want them to do is more satisfying than the alternatives, e.g.: turn off the TV and give them the choice of doing some work, i.e., vacuum or get their school work done.
10. Discuss the rights and wrongs of a child's actions after emotions have died down.

DECREASING A CHILD'S DESIRE TO MISBEHAVE

There are three main ways parents can decrease a child's desire to misbehave. These are:

THERE ARE THREE MAJOR WAYS TO DECREASE A CHILD'S DESIRE TO MISBEHAVE.

1. the application method
2. the removal method
3. the situational planning method

Application Method. Suppose eight-year-old Richard does not come home at the agreed upon time. If he has done this several times after being warned, the parent may decide to spank him. By *applying* something unpleasant for misbehaving, misbehaving will decline, assuming, of course, that what you apply is unpleasant for the child, **and** assuming the child has not learned to talk you out of such applications in the past. Giving (applying) extra chores to sixteen-year-old Gregory for coming home late may help encourage him to be on time in the future.

Misbehavior will decline when misbehavior produces unpleasant consequences.

The secret then for decreasing misbehavior with the application method is based on the very natural principle that **misbehavior will decline when misbehavior produces unpleasant consequences.** Did you ever stop to think that misbehaving is fun for children? Well, it's true. Otherwise children wouldn't misbehave. Misbehaving pays off for them. So, to reduce misbehavior, you must learn how to arrange conditions so the child finds that misbehavior reaps more penalties than payoffs. One of the ways of doing this is for parents to intentionally *apply* unpleasant consequences when the child misbehaves.

What can a parent apply that will be unpleasant? That is a good question and, frankly, it is the key to whether the application method will work or not. Parents need to pick a consequence that is definitely unpleasant to **their** child. Keep in mind that in our world where one child can learn to value something that a second child hates, what is unpleasant to one may be pleasing to another, i.e., doing schoolwork, eating spinach, skating, cleaning things. So the secret to using consequences on little Jeffrey is to **know Jeffrey's specific likes and dislikes.** Applying a spanking may work best on one eight-year-old, while applying extra chores may work better on some other eight-year-old. To effectively use the application method to handle misbehavior, **find what the child dislikes and apply it immediately after the misbehavior.** Figure 3.1 gives several examples for parents.

SULKY SUE

Here's Sulky Sue,
What shall we do?
Turn her face to the wall
Till she come to.

Mother Goose Rhyme

Find out what a child dislikes and apply it immediately after the misbehavior.

Removal Method. If you think about it for a moment you will realize there are two basic types of consequence situations parents can employ to make a child feel unpleasant for misbehaving. The first, as we have just seen, is by *applying* something the child dislikes. A second type of unpleasant conseqence that a parent can manipulate is to **remove something the child likes when the misbehavior occurs.** Parents can remove phone or automobile privileges for a certain length of time, remove toys that are not picked up, or take away money from allowances when a child misbehaves. Such parental actions may (although not automatically) produce unpleasant consequences for the child's misbehavior, **and** decrease the child's desire to repeat that misbehavior in the future.

Remove something the child likes when the misbehavior occurs.

Situational Planning Method. You noticed that the *application method* and the *removal method* are based on the parent applying or removing some specific consequence **after** a

33

child misbehaves. A third method for decreasing a child's desires to misbehave is not so much based on arranging conditions where the parent administers consequences. Instead it it is based on arranging conditions so either the misbehavior is not as apt to occur, or so natural consequences in the situation do not produce payoffs for the misbehaving child.

One example of the *situational planning method* has to do with an elementary school class where third graders are typically seated on both sides of tables in the classroom. In response to the teacher's request for a way to control the children kicking each other under the table, she was advised to place all the tables in a horseshoe arrangement in her room with the children only being seated on one side of the tables.

PLAN SITUATIONS SO MISBEHAVIOR CAN'T HAPPEN.

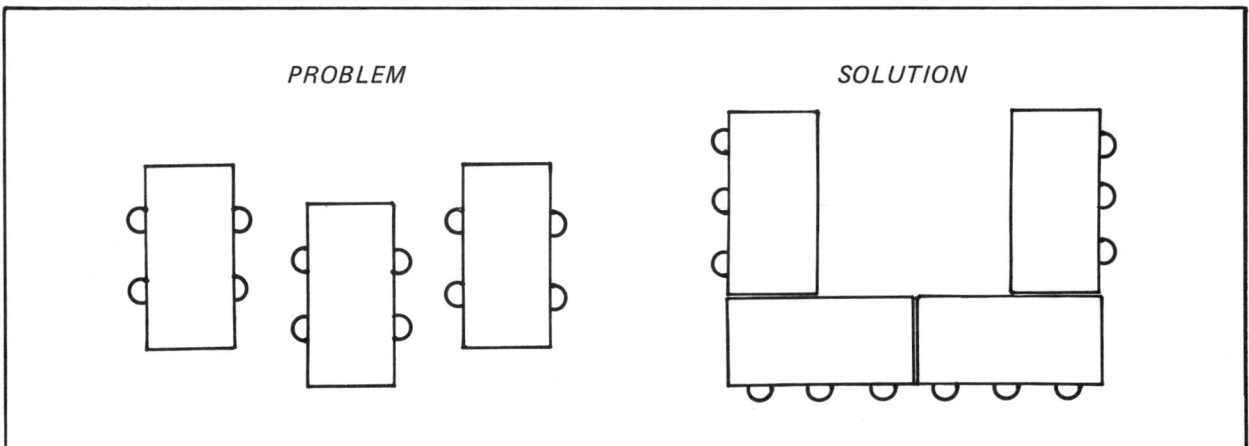

PROBLEM   SOLUTION

Another example of situational planning involves reducing the arguing of two brothers over clothes by having mother buy different colored socks, shirts, and so forth, so it is easy to tell which clothes belong to which boy. In this way, arguing and fighting over clothes is reduced without have to use the application or removal method.

A third illustration of the situational planning method has to do with providing a special time for some things a child wants to do. A child who throws mud pies is misbehaving. But suppose mother says "Each Thursday I will let you make mud pies and throw them at a post." Often times, actions which would otherwise be considered misbehavior are, if done whimsically, appropriate at other controlled times. A third grade girl who repeatedly pesters a teacher may be told, *"If you stay in your seat during the day, then you may come up to my desk after school so we can talk."* With many misbehaviors you can control their occurrence better if you allow some time for them to occur, rather than trying to put a stop to them altogether. Remember, "it is easier to divert a river than dam it up."

The situational planning method is based more on preventing occurrences of misbehavior **before** they start. With a little thought and wisdom most parents can think of several things they can rearrange in their home to prevent some misbehaviors from occurring.

The situational planning method helps prevent problems before they start.

COMPARISON OF THE SIX BASIC MOTIVATION METHODS

Now that all six methods for motivating a child have been presented individually, let's look at all six together and note their similarities and differences. A comparison can help parents better understand how to use them. Figure 3.1 shows all six methods.

FIGURE 3.1
A comparative look at the six methods for motivating children to increase good behavior and decrease misbehavior.

	INCREASE DESIRES TO DO GOOD	DECREASE DESIRES TO MISBEHAVE
APPLICATION METHOD	Say "Thank you" when Amy does her chores. Give treats when David cleans his room. Give money to Kevin who did his work plus cleaned the garage. Tell a story to three-year-old for picking up toys. Robert is given extra time to play video games if he eats supper without any complaining.	Apply spanking when Jeffrey wilfully disobeys. Apply scolding when Lori plays with her food. Apply extra chores when Shawn comes home late. Make Robbie sit on a chair for 15 minutes because he was rowdy. Dump all blankets on floor and empty all drawers when Steven goes to school without cleaning up his room.
REMOVAL METHOD	Early bedtime rule is extended when studies are done. "Nagging" reminders from mom stop when teenager picks up clothes. Cooking and breakfast privileges are restored when Paul cleans his bedroom. Amy must wash and iron own clothes until she learns to put dirty clothes in proper place. Joey may not have after-school snacks or sweets until he learns to eat some vegetables at suppertime.	Take away toys for two days when Billy won't share. Take away phone privileges when teenager does not come home when agreed. Take away radio when child plays it too loudly after being warned. Remove TV privileges when Lisa fails to clean bedroom. Eighteen-year-old Roger may find himself locked out of his house until 7:00 a.m. because he came home after 1:00 a.m.
SITUATIONAL PLANNING METHOD	Put clothes hamper in easy-to-reach location so child is less prone to throw dirty clothes around. Store dishes and glasses at a low enough level so six-year-old Julie can reach them when setting the table. Require less to begin with; then increase what needs to be done. (This is what psychologists call "shaping.")	Arrange conditions so showing off does not result in getting attention. Provide a job so the child who steals can earn the money to buy things. Don't quickly replace toys for a child who breaks them. Buy different colored clothes so children don't argue as to whom something belongs.

Notice that the three methods for increasing good behavior can also be used to decrease misbehavior. And all of them are based on Mother Nature's basic law of natural behavior that **pleasant and unpleasant consequences can be manipulated to influence a child's desire to act.**

Pleasant and unpleasant consequences can be manipulated to influence a child's desire to act.

When the six motivational methods fail, then what?

Is it possible for these six motivational methods to fail? Can some parents apply some of these methods without success? Absolutely! While removing TV privileges for Lori may reduce her misbehavior, that does not mean it will automatically do the same for Shawn. All children's likes and dislikes are not the same. So why would we expect all children to respond to the same rewards and penalties? They won't. The methods of *application, removal,* and *situational planning* are psychologically sound methods. When they don't seem to change a child's actions, there are several possible reasons why:

1. The parent is not manipulating things the child really likes or dislikes.
2. The child has learned that mom or dad is inconsistent.
3. The rewards and penalties the parents manipulate are not strong enough to motivate the child's desires to change his or her actions.
4. The child is not capable of doing what is expected.
5. Clear instructions are not given as to what the child should do.
6. The child knows how to get around mother and dad's consequences.

PRINCIPLE OF PROMPTINGS

Throughout this handbook, it has been said that the consequences of a child's past actions are what motivate a child's present actions. However, it is proposed by some that encouragement and promptings are what actually determine a child's actions.

"Eat your dinner or I will spank you."
"Please don't grab that vase."
"Leave that candy alone."
"Don't get that shirt dirty."
"Stay out of the water."
"If you lie, people won't like you."

Will the preceding list of parental statements influence the child's actions? Does a parent really have to provide consequences for a child's actions? Aren't promptings enough?

It is important to remember that words are simply symbols in our world. They can mean whatever we want them to mean. They have no absolute value.

If a mother threatens a child but never follows through, what does that threat signify to the child? If you tell a child to leave the candy alone, yet nothing unpleasant happens if he doesn't, how do your instructions influence his actions?

As a young boy my mother would call us children six or seven times in the morning before we would get up. On the other hand, we all responded within seconds when our father said, "Kids, rise and shine." Why? Did we love our dad more than our mother? No. It had nothing to do with love. It had to do with consequence.

Mother was easy going, and we knew she would keep breakfast warm until we got up, or until her voice reached a certain octave. Then we knew she was ready to act. Dad, on the other hand, never made his request twice. We all knew that Dad would wait no longer than 15 seconds before his words were followed with action. I don't recall dad ever yelling at us. He would talk in a quiet tone, but not repeat his requests.

Words only stimulate action in children if past experience has given those words the power to stimulate that action.

The *Principle of Promptings* in essence refers to the fact that environmental cues can influence a child's actions. The sight of an ice cream parlor *can prompt* a child to request ice cream. Parental requests *can prompt* the three-year-old to pick up his toys when no thought of picking them up was in his mind prior to the request. Being in the presence of a religious leader *can prompt* reverence in a teenager, while attending a rock concert *can prompt* that same teenager to do wild and exhuberant things.

The sight or sound of some environmental cue *can prompt* a child's actions. The sight of the ice cream stirs the child's desire for ice cream. The words of the parent stirs the child's desires to pick up his toys. These desires are actually the product of the positive feelings resulting from the consequences of past actions in the same situation. Based on past experience, **environmental cues (promptings) can influence a child's actions.**

PROMPTINGS (reminders) CAN INFLUENCE A CHILD'S ACTIONS.

Consequence of Prior Experience →	Environmental Cue →	Desire →	Action →	Consequence →	Satisfaction
eat ice cream →	sight of ice cream parlor →	ice cream →	ask for ice cream →	eat ice cream →	positive feelings
reward from dad → self-satisfaction →	parental request → to pick up toys →	to pick up toys →	pick up toys →	→ reward from dad → self-satisfaction →	positive feeling positive feeling
self-satisfaction →	religious leader →	to be reverent →	reverence →	self-satisfaction →	positive feeling
reaction of peers →	rock concert →	to be exhuberant →	exhuberance →	reaction of peers →	positive feelings

FIGURE 3.2
Environmental cues or promptings, based on past experiences, can influence a child's actions.

USING ENVIRONMENTAL CUES
TO INFLUENCE A CHILD'S ACTIONS

Once parents realize environmental cues can influence actions, they can use the Principle of Promptings to help control the actions of their child. Instead of changing a child's actions through rewards and punishments, an alternative for the parent is to tap into the desires-consequence relationships previously learned by the child. By introducing or removing certain environmental cues, the parent can prompt **increases** in good action or **decreases** in misbehavior. The following list provides some ideas for parents:

ENVIRONMENTAL CUE	prompts	ACTION
candy in dishes, cookies on counter		eating
boisterous three-year-olds		your child to be boisterous
classroom tables back to back		kicking under the table by students
classroom tables arranged in horseshoe		reduced tendency to kick
quiet music		quiet actions
loud music		loud actions
warning about shoplifting		reduction in shoplifting
scheduling bathroom use		reduction in arguing and fighting
chore charts posted in sight		more home chores being completed
picture on fridge of obese person		less unscheduled eating
rock idol saying teenager should finish school		finishing school
parent at teenagers' party		reduction of certain misbehaviors
highway warning signs		accident reduction
mother and dad being courteous		more courtesy from children

FIGURE 3.3
Some actions that are influenced by environmental cues.

There are an almost limitless number of things parents can do to arrange environmental cues to influence the actions of children. With a little thought parents can come up with certain things they can change in their home to prompt certain kinds of actions from them.

Promptings gain their power to influence action from past experiences where consequences for action were given.

It is important to remember that **promptings gain their power to influence action from past experiences where consequences for action were given.** If a parent continues to use prompts without following through with consequences, the prompts will lose their power.

SO, HOW DO PARENTS PUT MOTIVATIONAL FORCES TO WORK?

Keeping in mind Mother Nature's plan based on motivation through pleasant and unpleasant consequences, this unit explained **six** methods for motivating children's actions. Remember— these methods work best with **practice**.

PUTTING MOTIVATIONAL FORCES TO WORK IN THE FAMILY
Exercise 3.1

1. List two actions your child fails to do that you would like done.
   Explain how you might get the child to do them using two of the three methods discussed.

Action	Method	How would you do it?
EXAMPLE:		
Do homework regularly	*Application*	*Monetary reward for each A on report card*
	situational planning	*Specify time and determine place*
a. _____	_____	_____
b. _____	_____	_____

2. Pick two actions you can more effectively get your child to do around the home by using the situational planning method.

Action	What you can do
EX.: *Daily chores*	*to be done before favorite TV programs start*
a. _____	_____
b. _____	_____

3. List two promptings that have been used in your family that have little effect on your child, and explain why you feel they do not work.

Prompting	Why it does not work
EX.: *Extra allowance*	*child has money from paper route*
a. _____	_____
b. _____	_____

4. List two promptings that work for you on children who visit your home although you have never backed up that prompt with a consequence.

Prompting	Why it works though I have not followed through
EX.: *Wipe muddy feet*	*he learned consequences in his own home*
a. _____	_____
b. _____	_____

39

QUESTIONS and ANSWERS

Q. Unit Two strongly suggested that consequences determine what a child's actions will be. Now Unit Three says that cues in our environment can "prompt" a child to act and that such prompts get their power from past consequences. Is that always true? Can you say a little more about promptings so I use them correctly.

A. Recall from Unit Two that instincts **prompt** animals to act in certain ways. The smell of sugar-water strongly prompts (or forces) the blowfly toward the sugar-water because it has an inborn instinct to do so. Too often we parents feel that children should instinctively do something if we just prompt them. Without controlling-instincts, children have no inborn desires which can be prompted to get the child to do things. (Humans do have a few built-in reflexes such as sneezing, eye-blinking, and knee-jerking that can be "prompted" without past experiences of consequences.) But children can develop habits through consequation that can become so strong that certain cues in our environment can prompt a child to do something. An example was a large sixteen-year-old boy who developed a habit of getting mad easily and hitting people. Now, he was not born with an uncontrollable temper. He developed it by being rewarded in the past for getting mad and violent. When he argued with people and became mad, his mind realized people would give in when he got physical. So getting physical **payed off** and eventually produced a strong habit that the boy could no longer control.

So, remember that cues in our world can become powerful prompts to get children to do things, but only if those prompts have been associated with past experiences where good consequences **followed** similar actions that **followed** such prompts. The tinkle of a bell from an ice cream cart in summer prompts many children to ask parents for something. Why will such a sound affect some children differently than others? Why do some children react to parents promptings while other parents are ineffective in being able to prompt their child to act? Think about it.

Q. I understand the idea that consequation influences a child's actions, but why do situational planning methods work? What is it that gets a child to do things if, as the unit says, situational planning methods are not based on arranging consequences?

A. The previous question and answer should answer this question to some degree. But also keep in mind that situational planning ideas often work because of the Principle of Least Effort: *Make things easier to accomplish and more will be accomplished.* Lowering closet rods makes it easier for children to hang up clothes. Giving a child some money-earning opportunities makes alternatives to stealing more realistic avenues of action. Actually the situational planning approach is an *indirect* way of making certain consequences more likely. So, theoretically speaking, situational planning ideas are based (indirectly) on consequences. With the application and removal methods you directly manipulate consequences. With the situational planning method you don't.

Q. In the book *Manipulating Parents*, Chapter 11 talks about four ways to get children to do things. Do those four ways relate to the six ways in this unit?

A. Yes, they do. The four ways mentioned in *Manipulating Parents* are four ways to change a child's actions through consequations. Reading both Chapter 11 in *Manipulating Parents* and this unit in the NAP Handbook should give the reader some good ideas on how to handle a child. You will also find Units Four through Seven in this handbook very helpful.

Developing Positive Thoughts and Actions in Children

Unit Three explained six methods parents can use to motivate children. Three of the methods were to increase good behavior, while three were given to decrease misbehavior. Unit Four focuses on those three methods for developing desirable actions in children and explains how parents can maximize their effectiveness.

ARE YOU RAISING "PLANTS" OR REMOVING "WEEDS"?

In this unit the three major ways to motivate a child (the *application, removal,* and *situational planning* methods—here we'll call them The Big Three) are considered further. However, we will focus on their use in motivating a child to do good, to act and think positively, rather than in changing a child's misbehavior.

"But," you say, "I need help with the problems my child has. Why emphasize the positive?" That's a good question. There are two approaches to dealing with children. We either concentrate on eliminating misbehavior or we direct our attention toward strengthening the child.

Consider the following analogy: When we plant a garden, we first prepare the soil by tilling and fertilizing it, planting the seeds at the appropriate time (temperature), watering it, working the the soil and removing weeds around sprouting plants. Why? So we'll have a clean and weedless garden? No, not really. Our goal should be so we'll have a full harvest of healthy productive plants. Some weeds will crop up in our garden and we'll attempt to keep them to a minimum. But our goal is to raise carrots and beans and corn and flowers and berries—not just to eliminate weeds. Being "weed-oriented" makes gardening a drudgery. "I've got to go **weed** the garden." Because of our emphasis on controlling and eliminating the weeds, we fail to enjoy the day-by-day satisfaction of what gardening should be all about—raising healthy plants.

It's much the same with raising children. Our goal should be to cultivate strong, well-adjusted children who can remain so all

MARY, MARY, QUITE CONTRARY

Mary, Mary, quite contrary.
How does your garden grow?
Silver bells and cockle-shells,
And pretty maids all in a row.

Mother Goose Rhyme

41

their lives, rather than to concentrate on removing all misbehavior (weeds) from their lives. And, just as in gardening, parenting can be more satisfying if we concentrate less on removing the "weeds" and spend more time in "cultivating" happy, well-adjusted children. (When we do have to remove the "weeds," whether from the garden or our homes, we must be careful not to injure or weaken the "plant." Of course, some "weeds" must still be dealt with and Units Five and Six will offer more help there.)

SO WHY DOESN'T MY CHILD DO WHAT'S RIGHT?

Ever found yourself asking, "So why doesn't my child do what's right?" Sure you have. In fact, all parents find themselves asking this at some time or another. It's an important question and one whose answer points out something very important about human nature.

Because so many parents ask "Why isn't my child acting right?" it becomes apparent that most of us have an important misconception about human nature. Somehow we have come to believe that there is a strong force within each of us that drives us to do what is right. But as you recall from Unit Two, Mother Nature gave mankind the freedom of choice that includes the choice of deciding what is right and what is wrong. Instead of having instincts that force us to act in certain ways, we have intelligence and problem-solving abilities which allow us to decide for ourselves whether clothes should be worn, whether we should be honest with each other, or whether working is better than lying around. So there is no instinctual force inside little Billy pushing him to be good. That push to be good needs to come from parents in a way that the child learns it is more beneficial to do what is right than what is wrong.

We all have the freedom to choose the good or the bad. Neither just happens.

TIMELESS VALUES

We need to keep in mind that Mother Nature has given us almost free rein to decide what is good and what is bad, what is right and what is wrong. While belching is a sign of appreciation in some cultures, it is a sign of bad manners in others. One society chooses to specialize its work force into teachers, clothiers, cooks, maids, policemen, and such, while other societies choose a way of life where each family hunts for or grows its own food, makes its own clothes, and has no radio or television. Who is to say which is right, which is wrong?

Because mankind can learn to value almost anything, that does not mean everything is of equal value. Some actions and attributes that we can choose for ourselves are better than others. These include such things as honesty rather than dishonesty, health rather than sickness, wealth rather than poverty, kindness rather than cruelty, responsibility rather than irresponsibility. If mankind is to survive, generation after generation, it is apparent that we need to select certain actions and values over others. Mankind can continue to exist only if such things as dishonesty,

irresponsibility, and cruelty are committed by but a small portion of society. If everyone did such things consistently, society would soon collapse. Think what would happen if, for example, everything each person said was a lie. Truthfulness, on the other hand, has meaningful, timeless and eternal value.

In some cases the choices we have either involve putting in the time to learn a valuable skill, i.e., playing the piano, getting an education, or they focus on having fun now. Most of society's great accomplishments come from situations where people have learned to put off short-term pleasures for the more long-term and far-reaching rewards of life.

LASTING ACCOMPLISHMENT COMES FROM PUTTING OFF SHORT-TERM PLEASURES FOR LONG-TERM REWARDS.

Because the choices we make are important and guidance is needed so wrong choices with long-term negative consequences are less likely to be chosen, Mother Nature has given us the family plan, with the child apprenticing under the parents.

So, what does all this mean? Well, it means that children should not be expected to automatically develop positive actions. It means that parents can arrange conditions so children may learn to act positively. And it means parents **should** arrange conditions to help children learn what is right rather than leaving it to chance. So how does a parent most effectively do this?

Parents SHOULD arrange conditions to help children learn what is right rather than leave it to chance.

SO WHAT ARE POSITIVE THOUGHTS AND ACTIONS?

The place to start is deciding what are positive things your child should learn. And that shouldn't be too difficult. We could start with some common everyday things such as picking up clothes, making beds, and washing dishes, and then include what seems to be less specific like being honest, being a good worker, being responsible and so on. Table 4.1 gives two lists of positive actions most parents desire in their children. List A is more basic, while list B is more general. Keep in mind that things like those found in list B develop by doing things like those in list A.

Table 4.1 List of Positive Actions Parents Find Desirable for Children to Do	
A	B
dress correctly	be honest
keep clothes picked up	be patient
follow instructions	be good at saving money
be good at schoolwork	be a good worker
say "Thank you" and "Please"	be responsible
take out the trash	be friendly
wipe feet before entering home	act to please parents
wash dishes	be able to develop his/her capabilities
make own bed	be good at problem solving
care for own belongings	be helpful
	be courteous

Those listed in column *A* represent procedural learning—actions that can be learned fairly easily and quickly, especially if following a step-by-step "hands-on" experience. Those in column *B* deal more with developing attitudes—how a person thinks or feels about something. Such learning takes place over a longer period of time and is made up of many learning activities similar to those in column *A*. For instance, washing dishes could be a part of learning to be a good worker, learning to be responsible, learning to please parents, or learning to be helpful. Learning to say "Thank you" and "Please" are representations of courtesy.

Actions such as these are generally considered positive in most societies. In the day-to-day environment children encounter, there are natural situations which tend to foster the development of such actions. Children may develop most of them with parents having done little, if anything, out of their ordinary daily routine. For many children, however, the natural day-to-day forces are not enough to help the child pick up these tendencies. So let's look at how we can use the three main methods (presented in Unit Three) for **increasing** positive actions.

NATURAL DAY-TO-DAY FORCES ARE NOT ENOUGH TO HELP A CHILD ACQUIRE (OR DEVELOP) POSITIVE ACTIONS.

USING THE BIG THREE METHODS TO GET POSITIVE ACTIONS

Apply What They Like

In Unit Three it was said that one way to increase a certain action of a child was to **apply** something the child likes **when** the child performs the act. (In other words, give the child something he likes **when** he does what you want.) Give Audrey praise for picking up her toys. Let David use the car because he cleaned the garage.

Remove What They Dislike

A second way to increase positive actions is **remove** something the child dislikes **when** the child does what you want. (See the examples given in Unit Three.)

Situational Planning

A third way to increase positive actions is to **plan** the circumstances or situations in which a child is to act. Ask Jeffrey to take out the trash when he has nothing to do rather than during his favorite TV program. (Having a family rule where the TV is to remain off from six to eight o'clock often makes it easier to get children to do their school work and chores during that time.)

Increasing the Power of the Big Three Methods

In many situations where parents want to develop positive actions, using any one of the Big Three methods alone will be all the parent has to do. Getting a six-month-old child to smile often works by just prompting the infant with a smile and then **applying** positive hugs and squeals when the infant laughs. Getting three-year-old Audrey to pick up her toys can often be

GEORGE, WILL YOU PLEASE GO TO THE STORE FOR SOME MILK?

THE END

accomplished if her mother sternly tells her to pick them up, then, remaining stern, stands quietly until the last toy is put away, and then **removes** this hovering sternness and returns to her normal, happy self.

But what about that more difficult child? What about little Jeffrey, who seems to have a mind of his own and doesn't appear to be influenced by any of the three methods mentioned? Well, keep in mind that these methods **will** work on **any** child. These three methods are the basis of Mother Nature's plan for helping us learn to increase positive actions. The problem, however, that some parents run into is that any one of these three methods by itself may not be powerful enough.

Parents can increase the power of these methods by combining them. A parent can use all three methods together and be more effective at getting positive actions out of the child. Let's look at three situations and solutions.

"THE BIG THREE" WILL WORK ON ANY CHILD.

Parents can increase the power of "The Big Three" by combining them.

SITUATION 1: Little three-year-old Audrey won't go to her room and pick up all her toys when mother promises her a cookie for doing so. She continues playing out in the back yard and ignores her mother's requests. (The *application method* by itself is not working.)

Solution: Mother says, "Audrey, you must come in the house and you may not go back outside and play until the toys in your room are put away. And when they are put away, you may not only go back outside, but also I'll give you a glass of punch." In this case mother is using both the *application method* (giving punch) and the *removal method* (removing the opportunity to play outside until toys are picked up). If mother selects the correct consequences, using the two methods in combination will be more powerful than using just one method by itself.

SITUATION 2: Fourteen-year-old Daniel regularly fails to make his bed before school. In response to mother's attempts to get him to do it, he either ignores her or complains he does not have enough time in the morning.

Solution: Using the *situational planning method*, mother purchases an alarm clock for him and has it go off fifteen minutes earlier so he has more time, **plus** she uses the *application method* by saying "If you make your bed before you go to school, you may go to your friend's house for one hour after school," **plus** she includes the *removal method* by saying "By the way, you may eat breakfast **if** your bed is made." Using all three methods together makes getting Daniel's bed made much more likely than using just one of the three methods alone.

SITUATION 3: Ten-year-old Jason does not come home after school as instructed, does not do his homework, and does not clean his room or make his bed.

Solution: Mother wisely decides not to try to change all of Jason's misbehaviors at once. She first picks one thing he is not doing which she has the best chance of changing (coming home right after school). Using the *application method*, mother makes sure one of Jason's favorite snacks (ice cream or donuts) is there for him if he is home as requested. Using the *removal method*, mother also tells Jason "Your bedtime has been changed from ten to nine o'clock. I will remove that additional hour requirement each day that you get home right after school. Once mother has "coming home" occurring regularly, she then includes having the bed made as part of the arrangement, then a clean room and so on.

If parents select wisely the things their child likes and dislikes, the use of two or three of the methods in combination will be more effective than any single method. That is why it is so important that a parent make a list of a child's likes and dislikes.

IT IS VERY IMPORTANT TO KNOW THE LIKES AND DISLIKES OF YOUR CHILD.

GETTING CHILDREN TO DO WHAT THEY KNOW HOW, BUT WON'T

The secret to getting children to exhibit positive actions they know how to do but don't is to **give them a reason to do that positive act**. Make it so the child's mind sees that it is profitable for him to do it. Telling him he should do it is not enough. Words are often cheap. Parents and teachers often make threats they don't carry out. They also make many promises of what will happen, but it doesn't.

GIVE YOUR CHILD A REASON TO ACT POSITIVELY.

Most of those positive actions listed in Table 4.1 are those that will be profitable for a child when he or she becomes an adult. Saving money, developing good work habits, being courteous, and doing things to please others are actions that can be profitable as one becomes older. Unfortunately, when we were children, people often made allowances for us, so perhaps we ourselves did not develop strong habits of all these positive actions. Those around us made it more profitable for us **not to do** such things. Why save money if mom or dad will provide it when needed?

DON'T MAKE IT PROFITABLE FOR A CHILD TO NOT DO SOMETHING YOU REQUEST BE DONE.

USE AN *OUTLINE FOR ACTION*

Besides using the *application, removal,* and *situational planning* methods, there are other things parents can do when trying to develop positive actions in children. NAP has developed a special *Outline for Action* form parents can use. There are two kinds of forms, *A* and *B*, for developing positive actions. Form *A* is designed to help develop positive actions in situations where the child knows how to do what is wanted, but won't. Form *B* is designed to help develop positive actions in situations where the child does not know how to do so. While both forms consist of

five basic steps and are quite similar, they differ on one or two important points.

Examples of these two forms (plus four others which concentrate on *decreasing* misbehavior) can be found in Unit Seven. We suggest you learn how to use them and then make them a part of your parenting procedures, whether you are trying to increase good behavior or decrease misbehavior.

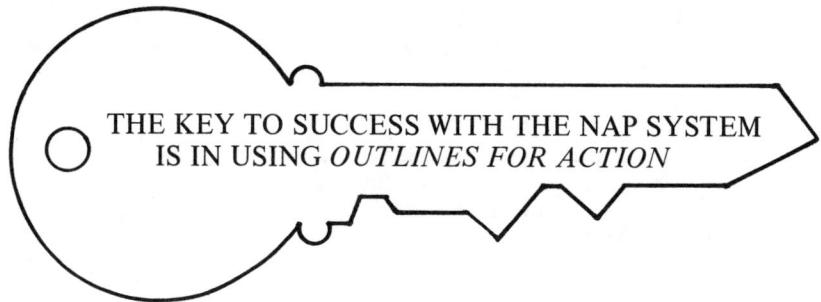

THE KEY TO SUCCESS WITH THE NAP SYSTEM IS IN USING *OUTLINES FOR ACTION*

THE KEY TO SUCCESS WITH THE NAP SYSTEM IS IN USING *OUTLINES FOR ACTION.*

OUTLINE FOR ACTION — FORM A
Getting Children to Do What They Can But Won't *

Step 1: Specifically define what action habit you want to strengthen.

This may sound like an obvious thing to do, but it is surprising how many parents fail to do so. Do you want your daughter to be honest? Well, specify exactly what actions in your daughter you want that would indicate honesty. Do you want your son to be courteous? Write down four or five specific actions that would represent courtesy. In other words, **specify** what you want. It is easier to develop actions in little Jeffery when you know exactly what you want.

BE SPECIFIC.

STEP 2: Determine what might be causing the action not to occur.

If Amy knows how to do something but does not do it, there is a reason. She may not clean her room because mom will eventually do it and save her the trouble. If she does not save money, it is most likely because her parents always come up with the money when she needs it. If she is discourteous, she has found that it has a better pay-off than being courteous. Usually it is because some alternative action pays off better. In this step parents should write down what the child is doing, instead of the positive action desired, and why. There is always a reason. When parents spot what that reason is, they are in a better position to get the desired positive action going.

STEP 3: Identify the most powerful rewards, penalties, and situational planning ideas for your child.

This step has already been discussed in some detail. Parents should select effective rewards and penalties that will encourage a particular child to exhibit positive actions, and also look over the situation to see what can be done to make it more likely that the child will act as desired. If various combinations of the Big Three (application, removal, and situational planning) do not seem to work, try some other combinations. There is always at least one combination that will work. Be persistent.

* (See Unit Seven for this form and further explanation.)

Step 4: Record specifically when, what behavior, what consequence given.

When the plan is implemented, be sure to keep track of when the rewards and penalties are given, and for what. Write down the date (and time, if it happens more than once a day), what behavior occured (either the positive act or a misbehavior), and whether the consequence was a reward or penalty. Keep this up until the positive act has occured 15 to 20 times. This is similar to the close observation of a newly-planted tree and should continue until the parent feels the positive action seems to be "taking root" in the child. It is a time when extra effort should be made and rewards given.

Repetition helps positive actions "take root" in the child.

STEP 5: Develop habit strength.

Mother Nature never intended each positive act of a child to be rewarded. Once a parent has intentionally rewarded a child's action 15 to 20 times, the parent should begin weaning the child from expecting the consistent rewarding that was necessary to help the positive habit begin to take root. The objective is to produce a situation where the natural consequences of everyday life or the internal satisfaction for doing it are enough to keep the child performing the act. The method for accomplishing this is called *value shifting* and is discussed in more detail later in this unit and in Unit Ten.

GET THE ACTION GOING

In conjunction with the Outline for Action, there are things the parent should consider for getting the action going. To accomplish this most effectively, do the following:

Be prepared to follow-up on what a child is to do. Don't start off half ready.

1. Set aside a specific time to work on the problem. Most efforts to develop positive actions in children fail because parents do not set aside a particular week or two-week period where they commit themselves to follow through with what needs to be done. Do not start off half ready. After a week or two the demands on you will decrease.

2. Use whatever consequence it takes to get the action going. Don't be too conservative. (Later on you can reduce the amount of consequence.)

3. For the first ten to twenty times the act occurs, give the consequence every time—and as immediately as possible.

4. To begin with, pick consequences that satisfy some of the more basic needs, i.e., food, material things, activities.

5. Give verbal praise with each consequence so your words of praise can become of more value to the child.

MAINTAIN AND STRENGTHEN POSITIVE ACTION

Once the desired action is occurring consistently (10–20 times) begin rewarding it intermittently. Mother Nature never intended a child's every action to be noticeably rewarded. In fact, habits become stronger when rewarded on a schedule where the payoff does not occur every time. After rewarding 10 to 20 occurrences of the action, you might spin a dial—one that points to the numbers one through six. (Use one from a child's table-game or make a simple one.) Each time the child acts properly, reward the act only when the dial points to any one of the three even numbers. Do this until the child has been rewarded five times in this way. Then reward the child only when the numbers three or six come up. After five such rewards have occurred, reward only when the number six comes up with the spin. (This reward schedule is somewhat similar to that which strengthens a gambler's habit of playing the slot machines.) This same process can strengthen a child's habits for positive action.

Give verbal praise every time the act occurs, but only include the material reward in the manner just prescribed. The visual chart can be done away with after the action has been rewarded about 25 times.

Mother Nature never intended our every action to be noticeably rewarded.

Verbal praise should be given every time.

Material rewards should be intermittant.

INTERNALIZE MOTIVES THROUGH VALUE SHIFTING

The ultimate goal is to have the positive act occur because the child gets a good feeling inside from doing it. As mentioned in Unit Two, man has an inborn hierarchy of needs which can be satisfied with a hierarchy of consequences which range from the basic consequences of food, to material things, to words of praise as consequences, and to internal feelings of satisfaction. Actions are most easily initiated by using material consequences such as money, food, or toys. Once the action is occurring consistently, you then work on getting that action to occur for the right reason—because the child feels good internally for just doing it.

This is most likely to be accomplished using *value shifting*. A possible sequence for value shifting could go as follows:

1. Reward each of the first five acts with some material object (food, money, whatever they like).

2. Reward the next ten acts with a material reward **plus** praise. (This will help make praise more rewarding in and of itself for the child.)

3. For the next 60 acts give praise every time, with a material reward on a random schedule as discussed earlier.

4. After verbal praise has been given 30 or so times, continue to give it (such as *"Hey, that is terrific, Johnny. I am proud of you."*) **plus** add comments such as *"Doesn't that make you feel good inside?"*

VALUE SHIFTING:

Getting the child to do something for the right reason.

HOW DO YOU FEEL ABOUT IT, SON?

49

5. Next, verbally respond to each act for about 15 times (plus give the intermittent material rewards) with comments like *"That is great, Mary. I feel good about you doing that. How do you feel?"* (Be sure to give hugs and signs of affection when the child answers such questions in a positive way, but respond passively to negative answers.)

Through the basic principle of association upon which value shifting is predicated, the rewarding feelings can come about by the praise being paired with material rewards. The answers to the question "How do you feel?" will take on more value by being paired with the words of praise . . . and so on.

IMPLEMENTATION CONSIDERATIONS

While some specific ideas and steps have been laid out here to help parents more effectively develop positive actions in their children, a few general considerations should be kept in mind.

DO NOT DEMEAN A CHILD FOR NOT DOING SOMETHING YOU WANT DONE.

1. Do not demean the child for **not doing** the positive action. Focus more on the occurrence of the positive act than on its failure to occur.

2. If the tendency for the positive action begins to fade, re-implement the program. Fill out the Outline for Action, make the chart, and start again.

3. Remember, do not try to implement an Outline for Action form until you can arrange for the time commitment necessary to be successful.

4. Keep in mind the child may try to talk you out of reducing the amount of material reward for doing the act. Diplomatically ignore such attempts by the child and they will fade.

5. Don't be overwhelmed about having to keep track of five of this, ten of that, and 60 of something else. It's not the exact number of times you are keeping track of, but rather that you and the child are doing something that counts. Use these instructions as general guidelines that will help you get started and move forward.

Some actions, such as playing the piano, eventually become their own reward.

Remember that most positive actions, i.e., piano playing, honesty, problem solving habits, courtesy, responsibility, are not easily learned in a short while. They take time. However, piano playing, problem solving, and the like typically become inherently rewarding once the child has perservered through those initial stages where the act itself does not produce feelings of positive satisfaction.

50

GETTING THEM TO DO IT
WHEN THEY DON'T KNOW HOW

Ever notice how a young child learns to speak or walk? Generally speaking, a child does not just start talking in a fluent way using all words. First comes the learning of a few sounds, then a simple "ma," then a "mama," then a second word, then a few more, and so on. For the development of most actions, Mother Nature works on the *Principle of Gradual Development:* **a portion is learned, then a larger portion is learned, and so on.**

Over the past few years psychologists have taken a close look at Mother Nature's *gradual development* approach and have identified some effective techniques for improving it. Just as Mother Nature provided surgical methods and medicines that doctors could learn to use to improve on her basic good health program, so has she provided psychological techniques that can be learned to make her gradual development learning approach more effective. Pigeons can be taught to play ping-pong. Chickens can be taught to dance. Bears can be taught to play basketball. Skiers can learn to do flips out on the slopes (something unheard of 30 years ago).

Many of the so-called positive actions parents want developed in children are not as easy to learn as they look. Parents want children to be courteous, show respect, and be gracious. But often we forget how difficult such skills can be to learn. Take the action of thanking someone for a gift. Have you, yourself, felt uncomfortable and awkward when trying to thank someone? We all have at some time.

Good actions such as being responsible, being courteous, being honest, saving money, and doing schoolwork are often not learned by children just because we expect them to. Such learning doesn't **just** happen. When confronted with the fact that our children do not seem to be picking them up automatically, we find ourselves confused as to exactly what can be done to help them learn.

There are two essential ingredients in developing a habit in a child: (1) The act must be made so it is within the capabilities of the child, and (2) a satisfying consequence must follow the act so the desire within the child to do that act increases. There are two basic ways acts may be arranged so they are initially within the capabilities of the child: (1) Start with a simpler form of the act, then increase its complexity, and (2) break the act down into a sequence (or **chain**) of four or five simpler acts.

SIMPLER FORM METHOD

The *simpler form method* is illustrated by the child learning to speak. Saying "mm," then "ma," the "mama," then "dada," and so on. Training a child to be patient by having him or her sit quietly for one minute, then five minutes, then 10 minutes, and

THE PRINCIPLE OF
GRADUAL DEVELOPMENT:

A portion is learned, then a larger portion is learned, and so on.

Good actions in children do not JUST happen.

The act must be within the capabilities of the child.

Satisfying consequences must follow the act so the child will keep doing it.

Many tasks can be broken down into a number of simpler steps.

BE SPECIFIC.

*(See Unit Seven for this form and further explanation.)

on up to an hour, can be accomplished using the *simple form method.* Requiring the child to learn by initially sitting quietly for 60 minutes will most likely fail. Asking a child to sit quietly for 60 minutes is normally more than he or she can do without training.

CHAIN METHOD

Just as a chain is composed of many links, so can many tasks be broken down into a number of separate parts (*sub*acts). Making a bed, setting a table, or tying a shoe are all tasks that involve a chain of actions. Regular chaining, often referred to as *forward chaining*, and a unique and revolutionary chaining variation, called *backward chaining*, are explained in detail in the unit following Unit Thirteen, entitled **Special Helps.**

With the basic idea of gradual development of an action using the simpler form and/or chaining methods, let's now look at the steps involved in using Form B.

Form B is designed to help parents develop a positive action that the child does not yet know how to do. It is surprising how often parents expect children to do things they have not learned to do. Does your child know how to tie his shoe, clean the bath-tub, iron a shirt, or make her bed? Has your child developed enough self-control to sit quietly for 15 minutes, refrain from asking repeatedly for what she wants, hold his temper, or complete a lengthy task?

OUTLINE FOR ACTION — FORM B
Getting a Child to Do What He Doesn't Know How*

STEP 1: Specifically define what action habit you want to strengthen.

This step is identical to that of Form A.

STEP 2: Determine what might be presently causing the action not to occur.

This step is a bit different from Form A in that the reason it is not happening is that the child doesn't know how to do it. Therefore the parent does not search for some "misbehavior" preventing its occurrence. Instead, questions should focus on the parents understanding exactly what the situation is.

STEP 3: Identify the most powerful rewards and situational planning ideas for your child.

This step is quite different from Form A. It has an expanded situational planning section in which the parent should break the to-be-learned action down into four or five easily learnable steps using the simpler form method or chaining method. (The Special Helps section explains chaining—backward and forward—in more detail.) Penalties are not given in developing this type of positive behavior; therefore no part of the form is needed to list them.

STEP 4: Record specifically when, what behavior, what consequence given.

This step is much like Step Four of Form A, except when recording the behavior being rewarded. The parent may first reward a smaller portion of the desired action, i.e., reward the child for washing one dish; later reward for two dishes, etc. This step continues until the child has fulfilled the complete desired action ten times.

STEP 5: Develop habit strength.

This step is essentially the same as Step 5 of Form A.

DON'T FORGET TO CONSEQUATE

Remember, when the child performs the act (or subact), provide some consequence that produces satisfaction for the child. Those consequences are so important in developing that internal desire within the child to do the act again in the future. Some special tips to consider when consequating are:

MAKE SURE REWARDS, PAYOFFS, OR POSITIVE CONSEQUENCES ARE:

Visibly available
Immediate
Something child likes
Special (not usually available)

• Have the payoff available rather than promising you will go buy it.

• Give the payoff immediately after the act.

• Make sure it is something your child likes.

• To really increase the power of the consequence, make it something that the child can **only** receive for doing that particular act.

SO, HOW ARE POSITIVE THOUGHTS AND ACTIONS DEVELOPED?

Positive actions can be developed much easier than most parents realize if an *Outline for Action* is used to: (1) define what the child is to do, (2) identify why it does not already occur, (3) select the proper rewards, penalties, and situational planning ideas, (4) keep a close record to help the action habit take root, and (5) work at increasing the habit strength.

DEVELOPING POSITIVE THOUGHTS AND ACTIONS IN CHILDREN
Exercise 4.1

1. List two positive acts you would like your child to do that the child "knows how to do" but doesn't do. Also write down why he/she doesn't do them.

Positive Action Wanted	Why I Think It Does Not Occur
Example:	
Hang up his clothes	*I pick them up for him.* *He has not been rewarded to do it.*
1. _____	_____
2. _____	_____

2. List two positive actions you would like your child to do that he/she "does not know how to do." Also explain how you could make it easier to teach the child to do them.

Positive Action Wanted	What I Could Do To Make It Easier To Do
Example:	
Make bed	*Bed must be low enough to reach* *Make it accessible from both sides* *Show step by step how to do it: Pull back* *top covers, move pillow out of way... etc.*
_____	_____
	_____
	_____
	_____
	_____
_____	_____
	_____
	_____

3. If parents want to teach a child to dress himself/herself, there are several situational planning method ideas they could use including:

   a. use pullover instead of button shirts
   b. use slip-on shoes instead of shoes with shoestrings
   c. put clothes in drawers child can reach
   d. use pants with elastic waist rather than belt

Now suppose you want to teach your child to hang up and/or put away his/her clothes. List four things you could do using the situational planning method to encourage this.

a. _____   b. _____

c. _____   d. _____

continued on next page

4. Explain the difference between the two types of *Outline for Action* forms:

>"Getting Children to Do What They Can, But Won't" (Form A)
>"Getting a Child to Do What He Doesn't Know How to Do" (Form B)

_____

_____

_____

_____

5. What are some DON'Ts for parents who want to develop positive actions in children?

_____

_____

_____

6. Pick an action you want to develop in your child and explain how you could develop it using the "simpler form method."

_____

_____

_____

7. Pick one positive action you want to develop in your child, then fill out the following portion of an *Outline for Action* form. (See p.47 and Unit Seven for help in answering this question.)

OUTLINE FOR ACTION — Form A
GETTING CHILDREN TO DO WHAT THEY CAN, BUT WON'T

I. Define what action is desired.

a. Basically define it (i.e., honesty, courtesy, etc.) _____

b. If needed, specifically define 4 or 5 actions that demonstrate the desired action:_____

_____

_____

II. Situational Analysis: Ask yourself questions about the overall situation.

Ask questions such as:

a. How old is the child? _____   b. Does the child know how to do it? _____

c. Could the action be taught in simpler steps? _____

d. Can brothers and sisters help teach? _____   e. Is the child physically capable of doing it?_____

f. Would child do it if there was a better way to check and make sure it would be done?_____

g. What are the child's likes and dislikes?_____

_____

h. Why doesn't the child do it now?_____ 55

QUESTIONS and ANSWERS

Q. In this unit you talked about not letting a boy have breakfast unless he made his bed. Isn't that putting pressure on the boy to make his bed. Won't he get mad and hate you as a parent for doing such things?

A. You bet it puts pressure on him to make his bed. He learns he has certain obligations in the family. Why should mother put herself out to make him breakfast, then have to make his bed and clean his room? Most parents have the mistaken idea that the more they wait on their children, the more children appreciate it. Frankly, families that expect their children to share family responsibilities have happier families. Do not apologize for having to take steps on occasions to get the child to do things. It is something every parent has to do at one time or another. Keep in mind that children **will** get mad at you for doing such things **if** getting mad **pays off**—if it causes mom and dad to feel bad and go back to giving breakfast anyway.

Q. In the section on value-shifting it says parents should use material rewards like food to get the child's actions going. Is this always true?

A. Frankly, when asked to work with little children, I prefer to use opportunities for activities and games as the reward to begin with. And nine times out of ten I will be successful. But if it does not work I will shift to using food and perhaps control when the child eats so I can make sure the food being offered is desirable. Use what it takes to get the action started. If a child will do it for a hug plus some affectionate words, then don't go back to using food.

Q. I have tried what you call value-shifting on my child, and he seems to try to get me to give him more money. He resists my attempts to verbally praise him and give him less money. What is wrong?

A. Nothing is wrong. That is a natural reaction. You would pester your boss to get more money if it would work, wouldn't you? Well, your son somehow senses his demands will work on you. Do they?

Let me add a useful tip. When you have him doing what you want and decide to fade out the giving of money, pick a second action to start rewarding. Children often accept the reduction of money more easily **if** there is another source for it. After four or five times of doing this, the child more easily accepts being weaned from the money.

Q. What if I start to wean my child from receiving money for tasks and the child begins to stop doing the action? What do I do then?

A. This can often happen when children find words of appreciation, hugs, etc. not rewarding enough **or** when (because of the Principle of Profit of Action) the action is not worth the time or effort. Once a child's action has been developed through rewards, penalties for it not occuring may be used to maintain it. Cities use penalties in the form of parking tickets to control illegal parking, because rewarding people for parking correctly is an impractical approach. Just be sure not to totally ignore a child's positive actions. Positive actions (like plants) die when people fail to nourish them.

Six Ways to Handle Misbehavior in Children

> This is the unit most parents cannot wait to read. It provides them with six "no-nonsense" methods for handling misbehavior in children of all ages. Try them. You'll like the results. Chances are they will help make parenting fun again. Raising children is always more fun and rewarding when parents see they can successfully handle their misbehaving youngsters.

"Six Ways to Handle Misbehavior in Children." Surely that title caught your attention when you first looked at the contents of this handbook. After all, what parent has a child that has not misbehaved. At some time or another every child misbehaves, and every parent searches for ways of dealing with that misbehavior.

Shouldn't Parents Put Up With Misbehaving Children?

But shouldn't parents expect children to misbehave? And shouldn't they accept that misbehavior in their children as a natural part of life which they can do little about? It is certainly true that misbehaving is a natural part of life, but parents should not consider it inevitable. They should attempt to influence the child's misbehavior, not just accept it. It is surprising, however, how many parents have come to feel there is nothing they should do about it.

"Children who misbehave are going through stages. They will grow out of it."

"Children misbehave because they are discouraged. Just be positive with them and the misbehavior will go away."

"Misbehaving children cannot control themselves. You need to be extra considerate of the misbehaving child."

"Misbehaving children result from too strict parenting. They are rebelling against authority."

What you have just read are four popular philosophies that

Parents should attempt to influence a child's misbehavior, not just accept it.

CHILDREN MISBEHAVE BECAUSE DOING SO PAYS OFF.

parents are told about misbehaving children. The NAP system disagrees with all four. **Children misbehave because doing so pays off.** And as long as misbehavior pays off for little Billy, little Billy will continue to misbehave.

Often times we parents watch children crying, biting, hitting, whining, pouting, fighting, or committing any of dozens of other anti-social actions. Because we consider such behaviors as somewhat abnormal, we conclude that children who do such things are psychologically disturbed. The fact is, however, that such actions pay off for the child. Such actions produce benefits for Andy, Toni, Andrea, and Todd. They get results, so they are used.

All through this handbook the point has been emphasized that children do things because of the consequences their actions produce. Children do things that produce pleasant consequences and avoid doing things that pay off negatively or do not pay off at all. Therefore, **the reason a child misbehaves can be determined by looking at what** *follows* **(not precedes) the misbehavior of the child.** And parents have the ability to influence the consequences children receive.

A child's misbehavior can be determined by looking at what FOLLOWS (not precedes) the misbehavior.

SIX METHODS FOR HANDLING MISBEHAVIOR

What the parent is going to read now are **six** of the most effective methods known to psychologists for handling misbehavior. They can be used on children of all ages, and their usefulness is limited only by a parent's ability to think up ways of fitting them into their particular problem situation with a child. The simplicity of these methods often makes parents wonder if they work. **They will work!** Mother Nature's plans are almost always beautifully simple, but **effective.** Through the years psychologists have found out tips for making them even more effective. This unit not only tells the parent how to implement these six methods, it also gives special tips and suggestions for their use. (*Manipulating Parents,* a paperback by Dr. Paul Robinson available through your local bookstore or Lion House Press, also includes additional examples and information about these six methods that the reader may find valuable.)

The essential key to handling misbehavior in children is to reduce the positive payoff for the act. This can be accomplished six different ways by:

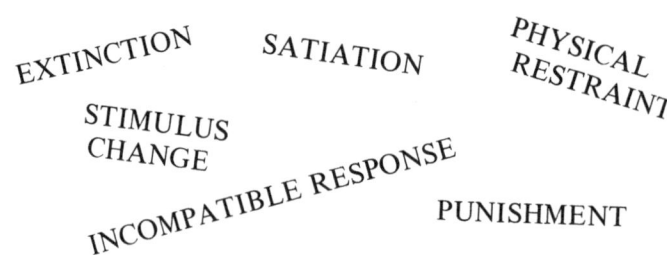

EXTINCTION   SATIATION   PHYSICAL RESTRAINT

STIMULUS CHANGE

INCOMPATIBLE RESPONSE   PUNISHMENT

EXTINCTION

Don't Make It Worth the Effort

When a child misbehaves, it is because such actions produce some positive satisfaction for him. A child screams in the shopping center until he gets the ice cream. The three-year-old continues to cry until mother picks her up. The twelve-year-old "shows off." The *extinction method* is based on the idea that misbehavior will go away if you remove the payoff that resulted from the misbehavior in the past. Hold out—don't give the child the ice cream. And after three or four tantrums at the shopping center, the child will quit. Ignore him. Don't respond to the crying child who is expecting such cries to get you to pick him up. **Remove the payoff for misbehaving and the misbehavior will stop.** This is the secret to using the extinction method effectively. A child's desire to misbehave will fade **when** five to ten repeats of that misbehavior fail to produce a payoff.

Keep the following points in mind when using the extinction method:

1. Extinction is one of the most effective methods for removing misbehavior, but it takes a little time and persistence.

2. The frequency (or intensity) of the misbehavior actually increases when you first implement the extinction method. When you begin ignoring the crying child, the cry will become more intense before it begins to gradually weaken and fade. This increase is a good sign. It tells you that what you are doing is having an effect on the child. Hold out!

3. Extinction will not work if you cannot control the payoff the child is receiving for misbehavior, i.e., a teacher decides to ignore the child who is clowning around in class, but the children in class respond to the antics.

4. Misbehaviors which have an inherent satisfying component—smoking, kicking, biting, an infant playing with food—are not as effectively handled through the extinction method as they can be with other methods. Ignoring such behaviors does not remove the child's satisfaction for doing them.

5. If you are not consistent in removing the payoff for the misbehavior (you respond to the child's tantrum only every third time or so) you are actually **strengthening** that misbehavior and making it more persistent.

Remove the payoff for misbehavior and the misbehavior will stop.

BE CONSISTENT.

INCONSISTENCY STRENGTHENS MISBEHAVIOR.

SATIATION
Make Them Sick and Tired of It

Many childhood misbehaviors do not depend on attention or outside rewards for satisfaction. They are satisfying in and of themselves. The eighteen-month-old child may enjoy seeing oatmeal splatter on the kitchen floor. The three-year-old may find satisfaction in biting his twelve-year-old sister who won't give him his way. A thirteen-year-old boy may sneak off to smoke a cigarette. A ten-year-old may swear because it makes him feel he's more "grown-up."

Swearing, biting, kicking, hitting, smoking, yelling, throwing mud pies are examples of misbehavior that may (not automatically will) be controlled through the *satiation method*. This method is based on the principle: **too much of almost anything is unpleasant.** And if you increase the unpleasantness of some activity, that activity will decline in frequency.

To get an idea of how parents might use the satiation method, several illustrations are given below:

TOO MUCH OF ALMOST ANYTHING IS UNPLEASANT.

Make sure misbehavior is repeated long enough to become unpleasant.

1. Johnny kicks. His parents make him kick a cement step repeatedly until it becomes apparent to them he is truly tired of kicking.

2. After biting a neighbor boy, Mary is required to bite down on a one inch diameter soft rubber ball 300 times in succession (or until the parent realizes the child is really tired of biting).

3. A ten-year-old who swears is told to repeatedly swear into a tape recorder for 15 minutes. Then that child is required to put earphones on and listen to those words one or two times through. (This may be done more than once.)

4. A child throwing rocks is required to throw until he is very tired of doing so.

5. A father whose son is just starting to smoke sits with his boy in the garage while the boy smokes two "cheap" cigars.

6. A child who yells and screams is required to yell and scream in a tape recorder for 15 minutes, then listen to it.

Some things parents need to remember about the satiation method are:

1. Make sure the misbehavior is repeated long enough to become unpleasant.

2. You can repeat the method more than once.

3. The child must believe the parent fully intends for him to do the task and will forcibly require it if necessary.

STIMULUS CHANGE
Mental Modification

Often times misbehavior in children can be removed by diverting their attention to something else. A crying five-year-old who is injured falling off his bike may stop crying if you point into the air and say, "Look at that bird in the tree!" Changing the subject in the conversation may reduce arguments. An unhappy child can often be made happy by someone sitting with him and discussing happy things. A school teacher may use pep talks (like athletic coaches) to stimulate an unachieving, prankish child to do schoolwork. Fighting between sisters to use the bathroom can often be circumvented by setting up a time schedule which specifies when certain people are to wash and fix their hair.

The *stimulus change* method for changing misbehavior is based on the principle that **actions are determined by the stimuli a child is focusing on. Change what a child is thinking about and you may change his actions.**

One summer afternoon I was busy in our fruit orchard with seven of our children. Two of the teenage foster girls staying with us were throwing not too subtle comments back and forth at each other. They had not been friendly for several days and things seemed to be getting worse. I decided to try the strategy of stimulus change. We were hooking up a sprinkler system. I had the two girls working together on one pipe fitting. I intentionally turned the system on before they were ready and they were drenched with water. I then ran over and yelled at them for being slow. I told them they would now have to finish the job by themselves, while the rest of us went into the house. Now they were mad, but not at each other. They were mad at me. Having joined together to verbally rebuff me, they let their differences dissipate. I later apologized—one more problem diffused.

The stimulus change method is often used (rightly or wrongly) in the home:

1. Sensing a rebuff for misbehavior, Johnny becomes sick to distract mom or dad.

2. Sensing an upcoming argument with a teenage daughter, mother says, *"Let's go shopping."* Later, when better prepared, mother addresses the argumentative issue.

3. Hearing two five-year-olds arguing and running to mother to settle the fight, the wise mother distracts the boys by using one of three techniques—praise, threat, curiosity:

    a. *"Hey, Johnny and Jimmy, your teacher told me something wonderful about you two—"*

    b. *"Hey, did you two clean your room? You go get your work done right now!"*

WAIT A MINUTE. LOOK AT THAT PRETTY LITTLE BIRD.

CHANGE WHAT A CHILD IS THINKING ABOUT AND YOU MAY CHANGE HIS ACTIONS.

TO DISTRACT A CHILD FROM MISBEHAVIOR:

- **PRAISE**
- **THREATEN**
- **CREATE CURIOSITY**

61

c. *"Boys! Look what I see. Two mosquitos are trying to get out the window. How many legs does a mosquito have? Look at that tube it has for a mouth—"*

4. Using a challenge, the parent says to an unruly child, *"Amy, I'll bet you can't sit quietly for five minutes— By golly, you sure can. That's great!"*

WHEN ISSUING A CHALLENGE, BE SINCERE.

When using stimulus change techinque:

1. Make sure your effort does not seem phony.

2. Keep in mind this method produces only temporary results, so combine it with other more permanent methods.

3. The effect is usually immediate; therefore, it is good for spur of the moment problems.

4. This method is good for dissipating misbehaviors (such as arguing) that arise repeatedly in all families.

PHYSICAL RESTRAINT

MISBEHAVIOR WILL NOT OCCUR IF IT CANNOT OCCUR.

Misbehavior will not occur if it cannot occur. This is the principle behind the *physical restraint* method:

1. If grandma puts the breakable knick-knacks away before the grandchildren arrive, they cannot break them.

2. A child sitting in a shopping cart cannot be running around.

3. A teenage girl not allowed around boys cannot get pregnant.

4. A boy in a fenced back yard cannot run into the street.

5. A child cannot drink drain cleaners if he cannot get the lid off.

6. A child cannot steal the bike that is locked up.

7. A child cannot start a fire if matches, etc. are not available.

Physical restraint does not teach a child to behave— it only restrains misbehavior.

Physical restraint is a common method for controlling misbehavior in our society. Some points to consider about its use are:

1. This method has immediate effects (not like extinction).

2. The effect is only temporary. It does not teach the child **not to do** an act. It only provides a temporary condition

where the child **cannot** do it.

3. This method often challenges children to try to overcome the restraint, i.e., climb the fence, find ways to meet boys, etc..

4. This method has value, but should be used with extinction, satiation, or punishment to produce permanent changes.

INCOMPATIBLE RESPONSE METHOD

Parents often find themselves in situations where children are doing what they shouldn't, yet the parents either cannot or will not stop it. The four-year-old runs around the doctor's office after mother repeatedly asks her to stop. The fourteen-year-old drives around in cars with older kids, and his parents cannot convince him not to. The five-year-old takes mother's pitcher outside with lemonade, yet mother does not like her kitchenware taken out of the kitchen.

No matter what a child is doing, it is almost always possible for him or her to do something else. With this in mind, the *incompatible response* method is based on the principle—**give a child a more desirous alternative and misbehavior will cease.** If a child is misbehaving, arrange conditions such that a desirable activity is available that pays off more handsomely than the misbehavior. Some examples are:

GIVE A CHILD A MORE DESIROUS ALTERNATIVE AND MISBEHAVIOR WILL CEASE.

1. If Johnny runs around the doctor's office you might say, *"Johnny, I have a piece of gum. You may have it and chew it as long as you sit quietly next to me and read."* (Make sure he does not get the gum **and** still get to run around.)

2. A fourteen-year-old skipping school gets money for modeling lessons as long as no tardies or sluffs occur at school.

3. The child taking mother's kitchenware to set up a lemonade stand is given something of his "own" to use, and then only as long as he doesn't use mother's things again.

The incompatible response method has several points to keep in mind:

1. It only works if the payoff for the new behavior you want is more desirable **to the child** than the payoff for old behavior. Be sure you make it worth it for the child.

2. Make sure the child does not get your payoff, i.e., gum in the doctor's office, **and** is allowed to misbehave, i.e., continue to run around the doctor's office. Most children will try to manipulate the situation to get both.

Don't allow a child to enjoy rewards of new, acceptable behavior and STILL maintain old behavior.

3. Watch out for the child who intentionally misbehaves so he will get a choice.

4. This approach often leads to a permanent change in behavior. (The fourteen-year-old works for money instead of hanging around street corners because earning money becomes a more positive part of his life.)

Bribery is the use of rewards and payoffs to help the GIVER, not the receiver.

5. Do not worry that you are bribing your child. **Bribery is the use of rewards and payoffs to help the** *giver,* **not the receiver.** If you give a child a cookie so **you** can have peace and quiet, you **are** bribing your child. If you give your child a cookie to help him learn to be quiet and patient, you have not bribed your child. Learning to do things for material goods in return is a natural and healthy part of life.

PUNISHMENT

UNPLEASANT CONSEQUENCES FOR INCORRECT ACTIONS ARE AS NATURAL AS PLEASANT CONSEQUENCES FOR CORRECT ACTIONS.

Few parenting issues hold more emotion than that of punishing children. Receiving unpleasant consequences for incorrect actions is just as natural and informative in life as receiving pleasant consequences for correct actions. The human mind is well equipped to deal with feelings of both pleasure and pain. Pain is no awesome, primitive stranger that the mind cannot cope with. If you sprain your ankle, how does your body convince you to stay off it? If you step down, you feel pain—and intense pain at that. Your body does not conjure up a painless, positive approach such as making you think "My goodness, I think I would like to hop around on one foot for a week or two." (This is something the mind has the ability to do.) Instead, the body simply applies pain if you unwisely try to use the ankle. Yet you do not become neurotic and emotionally unbalanced from experiencing such consequences. You do not come to hate your body for doing that. Your body provides so much positiveness to you that you accept its painful reprimand in stride. Such is also true with punishing a child.

Mother Nature's ultimate creation in terms of intelligence, curiosity, and problem solving is mankind. Unlike lower life forms, mankind is not limited by instincts to act in only ways that provide for survival of the species. Man has the ability to intellectually rise to unknown heights. He is given the ability not only to do right, but also to make mistakes, and learn from those mistakes. The experince of adversity through punishment can be as effective a learning tool as positive consequences. According to most psychological research, punishment is an excellent method for getting rid of undesirable behaviors.

There are two basic kinds of punishment: *positive* and *negative.* Positive punishment causes unpleasantness to the child by **applying** something. Negative punishment causes unpleasantness to the child by **removing** something. Examples of the two kinds of punishment are:

Positive Punishment

1. *Apply* spanking
2. *Apply* verbal chastisement
3. *Apply* uncomfortable feeling

Negative Punishment

1. *Remove* privileges—phone, car, staying up late, going to friend's house, having friends over
2. *Remove* items—stereo, radio, .22 caliber rifle, clothes, toys, favorite blanket, allowance
3. *Remove* environment—have to sit on chair, stay in room, stand in corner

Positive punishment causes unpleasantness by applying something undesirable.

Negative punishment causes unpleasantness by removing something desirable.

Either by **applying** aversive things (spanking, verbal reproof, etc.) or **removing** desirable privileges, items, or environments, parents can provide consequences which make misbehaving undesirable to the child. Some points to keep in mind when using punishment are:

1. The secret to effective punishment is that the consequence for misbehaving is unpleasant to the child.

2. Children differ as to what is the most effective form of punishment. Spanking may work best with one child, while sitting on a chair is more unpleasant for another.

3. Be sure your child's weekly dish of punishments and rewards balances out to nine pleasant consequences for good actions to every one punishment for misbehaving.

4. Punishment only tells the child what not to do.

PUNISHMENT ONLY TELLS A CHILD WHAT NOT TO DO.

5. Negative punishments can be as effective as positive punishments. The key is not whether it is negative or positive, but the degree of unpleasantness the misbehavior produces.

SO, WHAT ARE THE SIX METHODS?

The key to using the six methods presented in this unit is **do not let misbehavior pay off.** Using *extinction*, parents remove the possible pay-off that a child normally receives for misbehaving. With *satiation* the desire to misbehave is reduced by making the child sick and tired of the misbehavior. *Stimulus change* works on the principle that if you can get a child's mind off the desire to misbehave, misbehavior will stop. The *incompatible response* method is based on giving the child a more pleasing alternative. The *physical restraint* method says: "If they can not do it, they will not do it." *Punishment* is an effective method that provides unpleasant consequences for misbehaving. Some methods work better than others. Unit Six tells which methods work best with which misbehaviors.

SIX WAYS TO HANDLE MISBEHAVIOR
Exercise 5.1

1. Pick two misbehaviors you exhibited as a child that your parents were successful in treating. Identify what the misbehaviors were and state which method they used to eliminate them.

       Misbehavior   **Method**

   Example: *Called my sister*   *Satiation: had to repeat them*
             bad names   *infront of the mirror for one hour.*

   a. _____   _____

      _____   _____

   b. _____   _____

      _____   _____

2. Suppose your three-year-old throws tantrums. You ignore him but he continues to throw them. Explain why that might happen.

   _____

   _____

   _____

   _____

3. Give an example where your parents used the stimulus change method on you. Explain how you would use this method on your child's misbehavior.

   _____

   _____

   _____

   _____

4. Write down a misbehavior in your child that you could use the satiation method on. Explain how you would do it.

   _____

   _____

   _____

   _____

5. Pick one misbehavior in a child of a friend or neighbor. Explain what the misbehavior is and how you think the child's parent should handle it.

   _____

   _____

   _____

QUESTIONS and ANSWERS

Q. I'm trying to wean my child from breast-feeding. Amy is quite cantankerous and makes the rest of the family upset when I try, so I quit. Is there anything I can do to solve this problem?

A. When weaning an infant by trying to ignore her tantrums, you are using the extinction method. If weaning can be done during a time when the rest of the family has gone somewhere (such as camping) for the first few days, it often helps. Family members often unknowingly reward the infant's actions with their attention. Use distractions (stimulus change) when weaning. And, when you decide to wean the child, **do it.** Doing it halfway strengthens the infant's efforts to fight being weaned the next time mother tries it.

Q. Can you really cure a child from smoking by having him smoke a lot of cigarettes at one time?

A. Smoking is a difficult habit for a child or adult to break. Satiation is not a guaranteed cure for smoking. One of the more successful methods for getting people to stop smoking is a *rapid smoking* technique based on the principle of satiation. In regard to teenagers, the weaker the smoking habit, the more effective the satiation method is. Being a good model in the home is one of the best helps for keeping children from smoking.

Q. My son is sixteen and quite large. He gets physical when I try to stop him from misbehaving, so I can <u>not</u> stop him. What can I do?

A. The first rule of discipline is: *Do not threaten to do something you can <u>not</u> do.* Those children will invariably test you and if you cannot back up your words, you have real problems. At NAP Parenting Workshops we encourage parents to form small support groups of four or five couples. Whenever a teenager tries to overpower his/her parents, the others are called in as support. The purpose is obviously not to overpower the child, but to have the child realize he/she can <u>not</u> do whatever is wanted. Acting together, the parents stand firm, but show positive support to that teenager when he/she learns to respect the presiding authority of parents in conflict situations. Such support groups have been very effective. In such groups the parents also share suggestions and give each other feedback on how they are doing.

Q. What about showing love to your child when disciplining him/her. My wife explains why she is going to punish the children before she spanks them. Does doing that help?

A. Suppose a big football player came to your door and said, "Dr. Robinson sent me here to beat you up because you said bad things about his NAP Handbook. But I like you, so before I hit you, let me tell you how much I like you." Would his words help you? Of course not. You will just try to say or do something to avoid being hit. The same is true for children. Trying to love while disciplining dilutes the intensity of the punishment. Punish the child. Get it over with. Then an hour or two later (perhaps the next morning) sit down and say, "You know, I felt bad having to discipline you. Let's talk about what happened so, hopefully, it won't happen again."

continued on next page 67

Questions and Answers continued—

Q. Doesn't pain cause neurosis in children? I was told that spanking hurts children psychologically.

A. The idea that spanking causes neurotic anxiety in children was proposed in the 30's and 40's by Sigmund Freud. Many people have repeated the claim that applying pain to a child causes emotional instability. However, these claims are **not** supported by psychological research in the area of physical punishment. (References are included in the **Special Helps** unit at the end of this handbook.) In terms of everyday logic, does feeling pain from spraining your ankle cause you to be emotionally unbalanced? Did slamming your finger in the car door damage your psychological well-being? Are boys and girls who engage in contact sports more emotionally disturbed? Pain is a natural (though obviously unpleasant) part of life. Children can learn from pain if it is wisely administered.

Four Types of Misbehavior: What to Do About Them

> While children can misbehave in hundreds of different ways, there are four basic reasons for misbehaving. This unit helps parents determine why their child is misbehaving; then it provides tips on what they can do to get rid of the misbehavior. It ends by showing parents which of the six methods for controlling misbehavior (discussed in Unit Five) can most effectively be used on the four types of misbehavior.

What child-rearing problems are you trying to deal with in your home—lying, stealing, sibling rivalry, pouting, tantrums? Figure 6.1 lists many of the childhood problems parents are trying to cope with.

MISBEHAVIORS

crying	talking back	swearing	fear of bugs
tantrums	stealing	arguing	fear of water
fear of darkness	not minding	teasing	fear of losing a friend
pouting	fear of dogs	showing off	failure to follow instructions
unkempt room	bad dreams	interrupting	biting
forgetfulness	fear of school	toilet training	kicking
bedwetting	hyperactivity	shyness	playing with food

Figure 6.1

Every family is plagued by a number of these problems, for each child in every family expresses several of these. Taken individually, these problems can confuse even the most dedicated parents who are trying to raise their children properly. However, these problems share some common patterns and characteristics. Identifying those shared characteristics has helped child-care professionals better deal with family problems. In this unit childhood misbehaviors are categorized and identified with certain childhood traits so parents can better deal with these misbehaviors.

There was a little girl
who had a little curl
Right in the middle
of her forehead;
When she was good,
she was very, very good,
And when she was bad
she was horrid.

Mother Goose Rhyme

69

TYPES OF MISBEHAVIOR

There are four basic types of problems into which almost any childhood misbehavior can be catalogued. These four types include:

GOAL-GETTING
REACTION-SEEKING
INDOLENCE
FEARS

Figure 6.2 (below) gives a brief description of the four types of misbehavior.

THE FOUR GENERAL TYPES OF MISBEHAVIORS	
GOAL-GETTING Many actions of children are motivated by the payoff (consequences) they receive from doing them. Children simply do many things because of the results those actions produce or the **goal** they are after.	**REACTION-SEEKING** Man is Mother Nature's most sociable creation. Social interaction is a central part of our personality fabric. Children often perform actions because of the reaction it produces in others. Reaction-seeking often includes dimensions of goal-getting.
INDOLENCE Man's mind works on an effort/payoff cost-efficiency basis. In many cases **not doing** is more cost-efficient than **doing**. Indolent actions of children are designed to reduce the effort they have to put out, while still producing desired payoffs. With indolence the child often gets what is wanted with no effort, or he learns how to avoid putting out effort which has no immediate or specific benefit to him. Indolent children are very effective at using time and effort to their advantage.	**FEARS** Our fear system is basically a positive system, designed to alert us to danger and motivate us to action. Because man is a problem-solver, Mother Nature allows new fears to be developed through association and positive strokes—physical pain and psychological pain. Our fear system is quite automatic and can incorrectly develop fears of non-dangerous objects. The key to fear removal is confrontation (non-payoff).

Figure 6.2

Figure 6.3 (next page) takes the misbehaviors listed in Figure 6.1 and orders them in terms of the type of misbehavior category they fit into.

GOAL-GETTING

Goal-getting misbehaviors are those whose payoffs are in achieving a particular goal.

One of the most common reasons a child misbehaves is because it **pays off** by resulting in achieving a particular **goal**. A child may steal because it results in the goal of having money. A toddler's goal may be getting an older sister to leave him alone—so he bites her when she tries to tease him. A five-year-old may

EXAMPLES OF MISBEHAVIORS ACCORDING TO TYPE

Goal-Getting	Reaction-Seeking		Indolence	Fears
Biting	Crying	Interrupter	Unmade bed	Darkness
Kicking	Tantrums	Talking back	Unkempt room	Thunder
Playing with food	Pouting	Arguing	Unkempt clothes	Water
Lying	Complaining	Teasing	Failure to follow	Dogs
Taking toys	Sibling rivalry	Toilet training	instructions	Bees
Stealing	Shyness	Swearing	Forgetful	Snakes
Talking back	Will not go to school	Lying	Bedwetting	Loss of friend
Won't mind	Loss of friend	Stealing	Learned helplessness	School
Interrupts	Showing off	Bad dreams	Not my fault	Bad dreams
Crying	Because I'm adopted	Fear of school	Toilet training	
Tantrums	Because I'm foster	Hyperactivity	Lying	
Sibling rivalry			Arguing	
Arguing				
Pouting				
Hyperactivity				
Sexual behavior				

Figure 6.3 The misbehaviors listed in Figure 6.1 arranged into the type of misbehavior category they fit into.

cry so mother will buy him some ice cream. A teenager may pout so dad will let her go to her friend's house.

Unit Two of this handbook focused on the fact that a child's actions are motivated by desires which have developed to produce certain satisfactions in one's life. A person's actions are guided by his or her desire to reach certain goals. These goals may be material (such as obtaining a radio, money, food), activity oriented (go to the movies, play on the swing), or socially oriented (be left alone, be the leader of a group). Goals may be long term (get through college) or short term (get sister to let me have my way).

A list of childhood misbehaviors that would be considered *goal-getting* actions is shown below:

Goal-Getting Misbehaviors

pouting	*biting*	*inconsiderateness*
kicking	*lying*	*taking toys*
hyperactivity	*stealing*	*sibling rivalry*
sexual activity	*tantrums*	*playing with food*
interrupting	*crying*	*talking back*
	arguing	

Sometimes children's misbehavior is not due to any deep-seated psychological turmoil. Sometimes the child misbehaves simply because such misbehavior results in the child reaching some personal goal.

"If I cry, I can get what I want."

"If I tell mom she likes my sister best, she will let me have my way."

"If I pout, Dad and Mom will let me go to Mary's house."

"If I kick my older sister, she will leave me alone."

All of these indicate a child's intent to reach a certain goal that will provide some satisfaction for the child. It will result in the child gaining something he wants. In some cases the child may not be conscious of the motives for his actions. Whether it is consciously or unconsciously motivated, however, the solution to decreasing goal-getting actions in a child is the same. **Goal-getting misbehaviors will stop when they fail to provide adequate payoff for the child.**

GOAL-GETTING MISBEHAVIORS WILL STOP WHEN THEY FAIL TO PROVIDE ADEQUATE PAYOFF FOR THE CHILD.

Remember, a child's mind works by the *Profit of Action* principle. The mind weighs all the pluses and minuses of any potential act. If the mind determines the child has more to gain than lose by a certain act, that act will occur. If the child has more than one course of action possible, the mind will select the alternative that results in the most profit for the least effort.

The key to handling goal-getting misbehavior is to reduce the overall desire for the act.

The *key* to handling goal-getting misbehavior is to **reduce the overall desire for the act.** This can be done by using one of three different methods:

1. **Reduce the profit for the act.** Parents can reduce the profit a child receives by one of two alternatives. One option is to remove the desired payoff—don't give in or respond to arguing, pouting, or tantrums. Parents can eliminate many forms of goal-getting misbehavior by not making it profitable for the child by giving in. This option is what Unit Five called *extinction*.

    A second alternative way of reducing the profit or joy a child receives from misbehaving is to make him repeat the act until he no longer likes to do it. Making Johnny throw rocks until he is sick and tired of doing so, making Lori, who likes to kick other children, kick a cement step until she really dislikes kicking, making Richard throw spit-wads until he is tired of it, or making a novice smoker smoke several cigars are all examples of decreasing a child's desire to misbehave by *satiating* the activities.

REDUCE THE PROFIT FOR THE ACT BY:

• **EXTINCTION**
• **SATIATION**

2. **Increase the penalty of the act.** Some forms of misbehavior cannot be ignored because the misbehavior includes its own inherent payoff. Biting results in an immediate effect or reaction. Stealing results in a desired goal. Sexual activity can be rewarding in and of itself. Playing with food can be enjoyable.

    Society has learned that many people's desires to misbehave can be changed by increasing the penalty for the act. Parking tickets must be paid by those who misbehave with improper parking. Fines are levied on overdue library books. Penalties in the form of sitting on a chair, spankings, loss of privileges can reduce goal-getting misbehavior when administered properly. *Punishment* is the method discussed in Unit Five that parents can use to increase the penalty for what is usually in and of itself a rewarding misbehavior. Keep in mind that punishment is not limited to physcial methods such as spankings. Forms of punishment include *time-out* procedures (sitting child on a chair), and *response-cost* procedures (taking away money or privileges).

PUNISHMENT IS NOT LIMITED TO PHYSCIAL METHODS.

3. **Increase desirable options.** A third way to reduce goal getting misbehavior is to provide more desirable alternatives. The misbehavior in many children can be reduced by making positive options available. A boy on a scouting trip cannot be on a street corner getting into trouble. Some children steal because earning money to buy items in not an alternative they see as realistic. Sometimes children throw tantrums to get what they want because other approaches are ignored by parents. Parents can eliminate some forms of misbehavior by being receptive to other modes of action. This method is obviously inappropriate where the child's act has no positive alternative. There are three main methods (discussed in Unit Five) that parents can use to increase the desirablility of alternative actions. These three methods are the *incompatible response,* the *stimulus change*, and the *physical restraint* methods.

REACTION-SEEKING

The human race is definitely composed of individuals who have a strong desire for social interaction. Interpersonal relationships form the basis for our being. Few things in life can provide the internal satisfaction and emotional feelings that a second human being can. It is no wonder, then, that one of the main types of problems parents have with children centers around those actions of the child that focus on getting a reaction from another person, usually a parent.

It should be apparent that a child's desires for parental attention are healthy and are generally satisfied in a positive way by most children most of the time. There are times, however, when children use undesirable methods for gaining parental attention. They can learn socially unacceptable methods for seeking such attention. Throwing tantrums, lying, stealing, arguing, pouting, and swearing are but a few of the undesirable reaction-seeking strategies (listed in Figure 6.3) that children develop to interact with mom and dad.

Reaction-seeking is a type of misbehavior that is an extension of *goal-getting* misbehavior. Reaction-seeking obviously leads to some goal the child has. But this type of misbehavior also includes the important dimension of attempting to satisify a child's desire for social contact.

Few things in life can provide the internal satisfaction and emotional feelings that a second human being can.

Children believe a response from mom or dad for bad behavior is better than no response at all.

**REACTION-SEEKING
ACTIONS ARE MASKED
ATTEMPTS FOR ATTENTION.**

*Speak roughly to your little boy,
And beat him when he sneezes:
He only does it to annoy,
Because he knows it teases.*

Lewis Carroll
Alice's Adventures in Wonderland

**Too often parents
try to solve the problem
by pouring words on it.**

There are several characteristics of reaction-seeking misbehaviors that parents should be aware of if they are to successfully deal with such problems. **First,** both parents and children seldom realize the real dynamics of what is going on in reaction-seeking situations. Usually reaction-seeking actions are masked attempts for attention. Often the child is driven by desires for social contact that he or she is not consciously aware of. These desires often result in the child acting in some unpleasant way because unpleasant, socially unacceptable acts are often more successful at producing a reaction than are socially acceptable ones.

A child may learn that such unacceptable actions are "wrong," yet they are also "right" because they **work.** Caught in the confusion where a so-called "wrong" act is "right" because it works, the mind searches for a logical explanation. This search for a good reason is often magnified by parental demands for reasons with queries such as *"For heaven's sake, Johnny, why did you make such a fuss?"* The real answer, *"To gain your attention,"* is soon found to be unacceptable as parents respond negatively to such comments. So a child might respond:

"Because you are unfair."
"Because you give my sister more attention."
"Because you don't really love me."
"Because you never listen to me."
"Because I can't control myself."
"Because I don't think very well."

These verbal statements given by children in such situations are usually false, but they will produce a reaction because most parents are particularly sensitive to such comments. And it is difficult to prove such comments are totally false. Such comments cause parents to back away from dealing with tantrums, interruptions, sibling rivalry, swearing, and the like as they should be dealt with. So, such comments work for the child. Therefore, not too surprisingly, the child uses them the next time also. And because these comments work, the child often begins to believe them. (*"If dad and mom react to them, there must be some truth in them."*)

A **second** characteristic of reaction-seeking problem situations is that parental words are seldom the successful salve for healing the problem, yet we parents repeatedly find ourselves trying to solve the problem by pouring words on it. Our children's comments in these situations affect us, so we automatically counter with words. Our words are forms of attention and automatically feed the problem.

A **third** characteristic is that reaction-seeking children often seem to have a "thick skin." Our words seem to do little to change their actions, so we conclude they don't listen. To us it appears as if our words fail to penetrate the child. In actuality our words of condemnation are received as positive attention in the child's mind.

A **fourth** characteristic is that the problem often *snowballs.* To illustrate, think of the pregnant young mother. Desiring to lie down because of morning sickness, she fails to interact with the two-year-old unless he is misbehaving. The more the child misbehaves the more the mother only attends to him when he misbehaves. The boy's proper behavior goes unattended. Reaction-seeking misbehavior increases as reduction of parental attention to positive actions occurs. **Reaction-seeking misbehavior often begets more misbehavior.**

REACTION-SEEKING BEHAVIOR OFTEN BEGETS MORE MISBEHAVIOR.

A **fifth** characteristic of reaction-seeking problems is that it indicates that the parents are of value to the child. You, as the parent, mean something to your child. You provide some needed satisfaction. In other types of situations (goal-getting, indolence) the parent is searching for some payoff powerful enough that it can be used to change the child's actions. With reaction-seeking problems you don't need to search very far—**your attention is the powerful payoff.** You simply have to redistribute your attention to your child's positive actions.

A parent's attention is a powerful payoff for good or bad behavior.

While the payoff for reaction-seeking is parental attention, there are a number of conditions which can cause a child to initiate such misbehavior. **First,** your attention may result in goal-getting. Your daughter, by pouting, may cause you to give in and let her go to her friend's house to play. **Second,** it may satisfy a child's desire for social contact—mother stops to talk and console the pouting child. **Third,** the child may feel afraid and anxious. Creating a scene may remove fears of being alone or of harassment from others—it brings mother or dad into the child's present social arena. **Fourth,** a child may be trying to identify with something bigger than himself—something like a family. Identification with groups and causes becomes a driving force in most of us. Demanding attention, even in socially unacceptable ways, may help a child satisfy that need for identification. However, no matter what the cause for reaction-seeking misbehavior in children, the remedy is basically the same. It requires the parent to do several things. It is like a multi-ingredient medicinal capsule, which contains a combination of medications necessary to treat the complete problem.

Treatment for Reaction-Seeking Misbehaviors

There are three basic dimensions to consider when dealing with reaction-seeking problems: (1) the six methods for reducing misbehavior, (2) the specific kind of reaction-seeking being exhibited by the child, and (3) the unique sensitivities of the child.

The unique sensitivities— likes and dislikes—of each child must be considered.

Specific reaction-seeking acts are more effectively dealt with by using some of the six methods than others. Each child is sensitive to particular payoffs—be they penalties or rewards. Children also differ in their sensitivity to the six different

methods for reducing misbehaviors. By taking a serious look at these three dimensions, most parents can put together the right combination of conditions to deal with their particular reaction-seeking situation. While a thorough coverage of how to handle reaction-seeking misbehaviors is available on tape *(How to Handle Reaction-Seeking in Children)*, a few tips are presnted here. (The last page of this Handbook has information on how to obtain this and other tapes.)

As earlier mentioned, the basic treatment strategy for reaction-seeking misbehavior involves a multi-ingredient remedy: (1) employ methods to specifically reduce the particular misbehavior the child exhibits, (2) identify and strengthen alternative, socially acceptable ways the child may gain your attention, and (3) develop a stronger and more satisfying relationship with your child.

To accomplish the **first** part, conditions should be arranged to employ one (or more) of the six methods to reduce misbehavior. (Use an Outline for Action form to analyze the situation and implement its remedy.)

Be sure a child's positive actions gain your attention.

To accomplish the **second**, use the methods discussed in Unit Four for developing positive actions. Keep in mind most children act up because proper modes of action don't work. If you want a child to deal in a positive way with you, **be sure such positive actions gain your attention.**

The **third** part is accomplished by giving *resultant love* and *unconditional love* to your child. Resultant love is the expression of appreciation—either verbal or material—a parent gives a child as a result of the child's positive actions. Unconditional love is the expression of affection—either verbal, physical, or material—a parent gives irrespective of the positive or negative actions of the child. Unconditional love helps raise the value of the child in **his** own eyes, plus it helps him identify with the positive values he sees in you, the parent who is giving the love. Resultant love not only strengthens the child's self-worth and identity through feelings of success, but also directs the child toward strengthening those positive actions which resulted in the expressions of love. No matter what the cause for the reaction-seeking—goal-getting, desire for social contact, anxiety, or need for identity—resultant love and unconditional love are a good remedy.

UNCONDITIONAL LOVE:

loving a child no matter what the child does

RESULTANT LOVE:

expressing appreciation for positive actions.

INDOLENCE

While *indolence* is a seldom used word in our society, it represents a childhood problem every parent must deal with. Webster defines indolence as an "inclination toward inactivity" and an "aversion to exertion." For parents, those words refer to a child who fails to do such things as make his bed, do the dishes, follow instructions, remember, or be ready on time. The indolent

child is often categorized as lazy, slothful, wasteful, not efficient, and not very bright. Such is **not** the case. Indolent children may appear lazy and slothful, but there is "method in their madness." Indolent children are generally more efficient and bright than they are given credit for.

It was earlier pointed out that a child's mind works on the *Principle of Least Effort.* A child's mind evaluates all aspects of any situation where effort is required and decides how something can be accomplished with the least effort. Given two alternatives, the mind will select the choice requiring the least effort for the biggest payoff. While every child's mind does this, the indolent child is much more effective at making these decisions. The child who does not make his bed finds out that mother makes it anyway, so why not save the effort. The forgetful child always has a parent close by continually reminding and making allowances so the child seldom feels any consequences for his forgetful habit. So why remember?

Contrary to popular thought, indolent children are not typically mentally slow. They are brighter than the average child. Their minds more effectively weigh the pluses and minuses of effort-requiring situations. They know best the weaknesses of their parents. They know best what tactics are effective for getting their parents to accept their laziness and lack of follow-through. They learn to ignore parental requests. They say they will do the task later, yet get away with not doing it at all. They argue and complain until mother and dad conclude it is easier to do it themselves.

INDOLENT CHILDREN ARE BRIGHTER THAN THE AVERAGE CHILD.

Causes of Indolence

What causes indolence in children? Why do they fail to do chores, follow instructions, be on time, and remember? The family environment they find themselves in **allows** such inaction to be more profitable than doing the opposite. Generally speaking, the child's mind has come to conclude that the advantage of not doing certain things outweighs the advantages of doing them. There is more profit and less effort in not doing than doing. Lack of action is a viable alternative in the child's world. We parents often make it so.

Often the family environment allows indolence to be more profitable.

Tips for Treatment

Many parents attempt to deal with the indolent child only to find the solution is not as easy as first thought. Treatment for indolence is more successful when parents realize indolence is deceptively more complex that it first appears. To treat indolence three things must be remembered: (1) indolence involves the failure of a child to do something, (2) the indolent child has developed an efficient misbehavior for getting out of doing what is wanted, and (3) a "good behavior" has to be developed.

INDOLENCE IS MORE COMPLEX THAN IT FIRST APPEARS.

To successfully handle indolence, the parent should fill out an *Outline for Action* form designed for indolence problems. (See Unit Seven.) A tape entitled *How to Handle Indolence in Children* tells step by step how this should be done. (See the last page of this Handbook for information on ordering this and other tapes.) Basically, the solution involves selecting from among the six ways to handle misbehavior (refer either back to Unit Five or look at Figure 6.4 of this unit) in order to best deal with the misbehavior the child is using to avoid doing the task, plus implementing effective incentives and penalties for doing what the parent feels the child should be doing.

Treatment for indolence is like treating reaction-seeking in that the parent should: (1) focus on the positive rather than the negative actions of the child and (2) use incentives and penalties. Do not demean the child. Unlike reaction-seeking, treatment of indolence should include the use of feedback charts. For indolence, parents should post charts which visually show the times the child **did do** what was requested. Visually accentuating the accomplishments of a child greatly reduces indolence.

Visually accentuating the accomplishments of a child (by using charts) greatly reduces indolence.

*Tommy's tears
and Mary's fears
Will make them old
before their years.*

Mother Goose Rhyme

NINETY-NINE PERCENT OF THE THINGS WE FEAR WE LEARN TO FEAR.

FEARS

Mother Nature endowed mankind with a system which is designed to help us better survive and deal with dangerous situations in our lives. That system is based on the emotion of *fear.* Typically, fear springs forth from the emotional cauldron in our minds when there is potential harm around. This emotion of fear arouses us and stimulates us to act in ways that will take us out of harms's way.

While the fear system is basically a good and beneficial part of our makeup, it is not a perfect system. Like a somewhat unreliable fire alarm, nondangerous conditions in our lives may trigger the feeling of fear within us and cause us discomfort when it is not really needed. A child bitten by a dog may come to fear all dogs, even those he need not be afraid of. A child involved in a car accident may fear all cars. A youngster may develop a fear of school or darkness or swimming or losing a friend or any of thousands of other things that may not hurt him. Unrealistic fears are childhood problems most parents face at one time or another.

What Causes Fear?

We have come a long way in understanding how to handle fears because we know now what causes fear. A child is born with few fears. A child is born with a fear for falling or lack of support. A child is born with the tendency to be afraid of loud sounds. Pain will automatically produce fear in a child. Children **are not** born with a fear of darkness, bees, school, bad dreams, or almost any other thing. Ninety-nine percent of the things we fear, we fear because we learn to fear them. A child is painfully bitten by a dog. In the future the sight of a dog will elicit fear in the child. The sight of the dog is *paired* with the pain received from the bite. So by being paired with something that previously produced fear, the otherwise non-fear provoking sight of a dog now elicits fear.

In the child's mind the thought of mother leaving can produce fear because past experiences without mother were unpleasant and perhaps painful. Losing a friend may not result in a physical pain, but the possibility of losing a friend or loved one can be just as frightening to a child as being physically bitten by a dog. The fear elicited by the sight of a dog is the exact same kind of fear felt when fearing the loss of a loved one. Both can be real to the child and both can be painful.

Children can develop fears for objects, people, or activities because those things were *paired* (either physically or through the mind) with something the mind perceives as painful. The fear is then transferred from the one to the other. In psychological laboratories researchers frequently cause a fear of light to develop in animals by pairing the presentation of that light with the presentation of an electric shock. Fears can also develop by rewarding a child when he says he is afraid. Showing signs of affection to children expressing a fear can feed that fear and make it grow. Fears, then, can develop through the process of *association* (pairing) or through *consequation* (rewarding fearful feelings).

Tips for Treatment

The key to getting rid of fears is *confrontation*. A person must confront the fearful situation. When a person develops a fear for some object or situation, that fear is like a charged flashlight battery whose only means of discharging is to dissipate the energy by letting it escape through the activation of the light. As the light burns, so the energy level of the battery drains until it no longer provokes or creates illumination. When a person confronts a fear object, that internal fear battery discharges and continues to drain until the ability to induce the fear is gone. If a boy, fearful of dogs, is repeatedly confronted with dogs without being bitten, the fear will fade. If, however, a second dog bites him, that will recharge the boy's fear battery for dogs.

So the key to eliminating fears is to confront the fear object without pain or displeasure resulting from doing so. There are three basic ways fears can be confronted.

Subliminal approach. With the subliminal approach the fear object is presented at low intensity, and gradually increased. With a boy afraid of dogs, a dog may first be placed 100 feet from the boy, then 75 feet away, then 50, then 25, then 20, 15, 10, 9, 8, 7, 6, 5, 4, 3, 2, 1. By gradually doing this over a period of time, the boy is confronting the fear object in small doses. This method of confrontation allows the fear battery to drain slowly

MISS MUFFET

Little Miss Muffet
Sat on a tuffet,
Eating of curds and whey;
There came a big spider,
And sat down beside her,
And frightened Miss Muffet away.

Mother Goose Rhyme

Fears can be strengthened when a child is rewarded with affection when being afraid.

The key to getting rid of fears is **CONFRONTATION.**

with little apparent discomfort. If the child does start reacting to the dog, move it back and continue bringing it closer, but at a slower rate. As long as reactions to the fear object are not inadvertently rewarded during the process, the fear **will** fade.

Superthreshold approach. A young child afraid of dogs can lose that fear by being placed directly in amongst non-biting dogs until the child quits responding with the fear. Such an approach can work, but it requires the child to confront the fear at full force which will automatically create a strong unpleasant feeling in the child (something the subliminal approach need not do). If this approach is used, it must be continued until the child totally quits exhibiting fear. Trying this approach half-way can magnify the fear.

Confronting a fear at FULL force can eliminate it, but trying this approach half-way can magnify it.

Incompatible Response approach. A third method for confronting fears entails reducing the unpleasantness of the situation by increasing the positive value. If a child is afraid to put his head under water, throw quarters and dimes in the pool and tell him the money is his **if** he will dive down and get it. The money in the pool increases the positiveness for the child to put his head under water the same way sugar flavoring makes medicine more palatable. (A mother who goes with the fearful kindergartner on his first day of school is making the going to school event more pleasurable.) As the boy dives for the money he is confronting a fearful underwater experience. And that fear will dissipate as the number of dives increases.

FIGURING OUT WHICH TYPE OF MISBEHAVIOR FITS YOUR CHILD

Now that the four types of misbehavior have been explained, can you figure out which category your child's misbehavior fits into? Don't be surprised if you begin to realize that your child's misbehaviors fit into more than one category. That is typical. Most children have misbehaviors that fit in two or three categories—sometimes all four. Reaching goals, seeking attention, trying to save effort, and developing fears are things that are a part of everyone's life. It should not be surprising then if a child does some or all of them. Once a parent determines why a child is misbehaving, then that parent can more effectively handle the situation.

MANY BEHAVIORS FIT IN TWO OR THREE CATEGORIES.

Some of the forms of misbehavior are easy to categorize. Unmade beds and unkempt rooms generally mean indolence. Showing-off usually implies reaction-seeking, and a frightened looking child near dogs generally means fear. But some forms of misbehavior—lying, arguing, crying, interrupting—could be indications of goal-getting, reaction seeking, or indolence. How does a parent tell?

When a misbehavior could indicate one of two or three possible types of misbehavior, there are often questions that can be asked to help pinpoint which type of misbehavior that action represents. Table 6.1 lists four misbehaviors that could be occurring for two or three reasons. By asking the kinds of questions shown in the boxes, a parent could get an idea as to why that misbehavior is occurring. Then the parent would be able to more effectively deal with that misbehavior.

MISBEHAVIOR	POSSIBLE QUESTIONS PARENTS MIGHT ASK TO DETERMINE WHAT TYPE OF MISBEHAVIOR IS INVOLVED			
	GOAL-GETTING	REACTION-SEEKING	INDOLENCE	FEARS
LYING	Does it keep the child from getting punished for doing something wrong? Does it result in the child receiving something?	Does it involve telling tall-tales?	Does it result in keeping the child from exerting effort?	
ARGUING AND TALKING BACK	Does it result in the child not getting punished? Does it help the child get his or her way? Does it result in the child obtaining something?	Does it happen repeatedly and for relatively long lengths of time? Does it occur mainly when "opinions" are involved?	Does it keep the child from having to exert effort?	
CRYING	Does it result in the child not getting punished? Does it result in the child getting his or her way? Does it result in the child obtaining something?	Does it result in attention from others?	Does it result in the child getting out of exerting effort?	Was it precipitated by some object? Does the child seem afraid?
HYPER-ACTIVITY	Does it result in the child getting to do more things? Does it result in the child receiving something?	Does the child talk a lot?		

Table 6.1

Notice how similar many of the questions are. If some misbehavior helps keep the child from exerting effort, then most likely indolence is the problem. If the child produces attention with his misbehavior, then reaction-seeking is the problem the parent must deal with. If the misbehavior gets a child something or keeps him from being punished, then it is used to reach a goal for that child.

Different misbehaviors require different treatments, so do not expect one cure for all. Some parents feel love in the home is all that is needed. Not so! Just as specific medicines help love heal the physically sick child so will specific treatments help love in the home change misbehavior in children.

Love in the home is not **ALL** that is needed to correct misbehavior.

Figure 6.4 summarizes some tips parents should consider when treating the four types of misbehavior.

TIPS FOR HANDLING MISBEHAVIOR	
GOAL-GETTING • Remember that children do things that are profitable and avoid doing things that are unprofitable. As long as kicking, screaming, pouting, talking back, etc. are profitable, the child will misbehave. • The main focus for treatment is to *decrease* the misbehavior using any of the six methods to: (1) reduce the profit of the misbehavior, (2) increase the penalty for the misbehavior, (3) provide a desirable alternative to the misbehavior. • Be consistent and follow through. • Develop a plan of action. (Use an Outline for Action)	**REACTION-SEEKING** • Treatment involves three basic things: (1) *decrease* the unacceptable way of getting attention using some of the six methods, (2) *increase* acceptable attention-getting behaviors with a plan for action, (3) strengthen the relationship with the child through unconditional love and sharing pleasurable experiences. • *Do not* use feedback charts or demean the child for misbehavior. • Develop a plan of action. (Use an Outline for Action)
INDOLENCE • Keep in mind that indolence is more difficult to treat than it looks. • There are two basic things to be done: (1) to *decrease* the misbehavior tactic the child used to avoid the task you should use some of the six methods for treating misbehavior, (2) *increase* the desired action through proper management of incentives and penalties. • Be sure to use feedback charts and watch out for relapses. • Focus verbal comments on the positive actions and avoid talking about the failure to do tasks. • Do not demean the child. • Develop a plan of action. (Use an Outline for Action)	**FEARS** • Remember that fears are generally good. • The key to getting rid of undesirable fears is to *confront* the fear. This can be done using 1 of 3 methods: (1) *subliminal method*—increase the strength of the feared object gradually, (2) *superthreshold method*—confront the fear at full intensity, (3) *incompatible response method*—add positive elements to the unpleasant, fearful situation. • Fears can also develop when parents reward children for acting fearful. Be careful not to "feed" the fear by rewarding it with supportive comments and actions. • Develop a plan of action. (Use an Outline for Action)

Figure 6.4

MATCHING TYPES OF MISBEHAVIORS WITH THE SIX METHODS FOR CONTROLLING MISBEHAVIOR

In Unit Five, six methods for handling misbehavior were explained. Now that misbehavior has been categorized into four basic types, let's look and see if certain methods for controlling it work better on the four different types of misbehavior. Table 6.2 matches up the **six** methods for handling misbehavior to the **four** types of misbehavior.

From Table 6.2 it is easy to see that not all six methods for handling misbehavior are equally suitable to be used on all four types of misbehavior. It is also important to keep in mind that each of the four types of misbehavior includes specific problem behaviors that may be more sensitive to certain methods. For example, goal-getting behaviors such as talking back, interrupt-

METHOD FOR CONTROLLING MISBEHAVIOR	TYPE OF MISBEHAVIOR			
	Goal-Getting	Reaction-Seeking	Indolence	Fears
Extinction	* * *	* * *	*	* * *
Physical Restraint	*	*		
Satiation	* *	* *	*	*
Incompatible Response	* *	* * *	* *	* * *
Stimulus Change	* *	*	* *	*
Punishment	* * *	* *	* *	

Table 6.2
A look at which method of handling misbehavior works best with the four types of misbehavior. The number of asterisks indicates the effectiveness level of each method. (***very good, **good, *can work)

ing, crying, arguing, pouting, and tantrums most likely can be reduced with the method of extinction (ignoring) because such acts are rewarded by parental attention. On the other hand, the activities of sexual behavior, smoking, playing with food, stealing, kicking, and biting are inherently rewarding in and of themselves, so they won't go away if mother and dad just try to ignore them. Satiation can be effective for smoking, kicking, and biting, while being counter-productive in reducing overeating and sexual activity.

Another particularly important dimension that must be considered, when deciding which method to use, is the past experiences and environment of a child. One child may have been raised in a home environment where the child has learned to be very sensitive to mother's feelings. In such a case the child may be particularly sensitive to the extinction technique where mother's ignoring is easily sensed by the child. On the other hand, another child, raised in a large, noisy family, may be little affected by mother's ignoring him. In large families extinction is more difficult to use successfully because the acting-out child may be rewarded by brother's and sister's attention when mother and dad are attempting to ignore those behaviors.

Stimulus change techniques work better on children with short attention spans who are distracted easily while extinction works better on the quieter child who continues to dwell on situations. The incompatible response technique works well in families where parents are consistent in what they say and do not give in to haggling.

A child's home environment will determine the success of a method for controlling misbehavior.

What works in one home may not work in another.

83

SO, WHICH OF THE FOUR TYPES OF MISBEHAVIOR ARE YOU DEALING WITH?

By being able to place a child's misbehavior into one of the four categories, parents can gain insights on how to better handle a particular situation. Identifying misbehavior as either goal-getting, reaction-seeking, indolence, and/or fears can tell a parent much more about a child and his/her misbehavior than the fact that he/she is lying, throwing tantrums, or such. Using an *Outline for Action* will help you analyze the problem and plan a means for handling it. Additional information and examples of *Outlines for Action* for each of the four types of misbehavior are found in Unit Seven, which follows.

UNIT SIX: FOUR MAIN TYPES OF MISBEHAVIORS
Exercise 6.1

1. Every child at some time in life exhibits misbehaviors which could fit into more than one of the four categories. Pick two misbehaviors your child exhibits, point out which category it fits into, and explain how you know.

Misbehavior	Category	How You Know
Example:		
Doesn't clean room	indolence	Because it involves something that should be done that is not. It does not occur to get attention.

continued on next page

Exercise 6.1, continued.

2. The unit explains *three* ways of handling goal-getting misbehaviors in children. List the three and tell which of the six methods for controlling misbehavior mentioned in Unit Five are examples of those three ways.

**Way of Handling
Goal-getting Misbehavior**

**Which of the Six Methods
for Controlling Misbehavior**

_____   _____   _____

_____   _____   _____

_____   _____   _____

_____   _____   _____

_____

3. Explain why indolence is such a difficult problem to handle.

_____

_____

_____

_____

4. Suppose a child is lying. How could a parent determine whether the lies are due to indolence, reaction-seeking, or goal-getting?

_____

_____

_____

_____

5. List two or three things this unit mentioned about handling misbehavior that you feel will help you as a parent better deal with your child in the future.

_____

_____

_____

_____

QUESTIONS and ANSWERS

Q. I seem to be having a difficult time trying to figure out whether my child is lying because of reaction-seeking, indolence, or goal-getting. Do other parents have the same problem? What happens if I categorize it wrongly and try the wrong remedy?

A. Yes, other parents have the same problem. However, the more you think in these terms, the easier it becomes to spot what category a child's misbehavior fits into. Sometimes parents are so close to the problem that friends and relatives can see the situation more clearly than they can. Ask personal friends and close relatives to help in the matter. Explain the four categories to them and tell them which misbehaviors you are concerned with. Then ask for their opinion.

If you use the wrong remedy (and we all do at some time or other), adjust and try again. Thank heaven our system of life allows us to make mistakes without typically causing irreparable damage. Using the wrong approach seldom produces negative effects. It is much more likely to simply be ineffective. So shift to the correct remedy and do not worry too much about it.

Q. I find it difficult to determine exactly what to do to my child. I can see indolence is the problem, but I feel uneasy when I try to figure out exactly what consequences to use. Any comment?

A. You are not unusual. Most parents want to know exactly what they should use on their children. In parenting workshops we used to give parents lists of possible consequences. We found that such lists did not help.

Outlines for Action:
The Key to Behavior Change

Most parents wish something were available that would help them go step by step through the procedures of developing positive actions or removing misbehaviors in children. Well, that is exactly what this unit does. It provides six *Outline for Action* forms. Four of them specialize in handling the four types of misbehaviors discussed in Unit Six. Two of them are for developing positive actions, as discussed in Unit Four.

HERE'S WHERE THE ACTION IS!

After reading Units Two through Six a parent should have a pretty good idea not only why children act the way they do, but also what can be done to develop positive actions or get rid of misbehavior in children. This unit introduces the reader to six different *Outline for Action* forms that can be used to help change a child's actions. Two of the Outline for Action forms (A and B) are designed to help develop positive actions in children, while four of the forms (C, D, E, and F) are designed to deal with misbehavior in children.

This unit contains material that can help you put into action what you have read in the NAP Handbook. However, we suggest you continue reading and studying the remainder of the material which follows this unit; then return to these colored pages for help in handling the particular parenting problem you have.

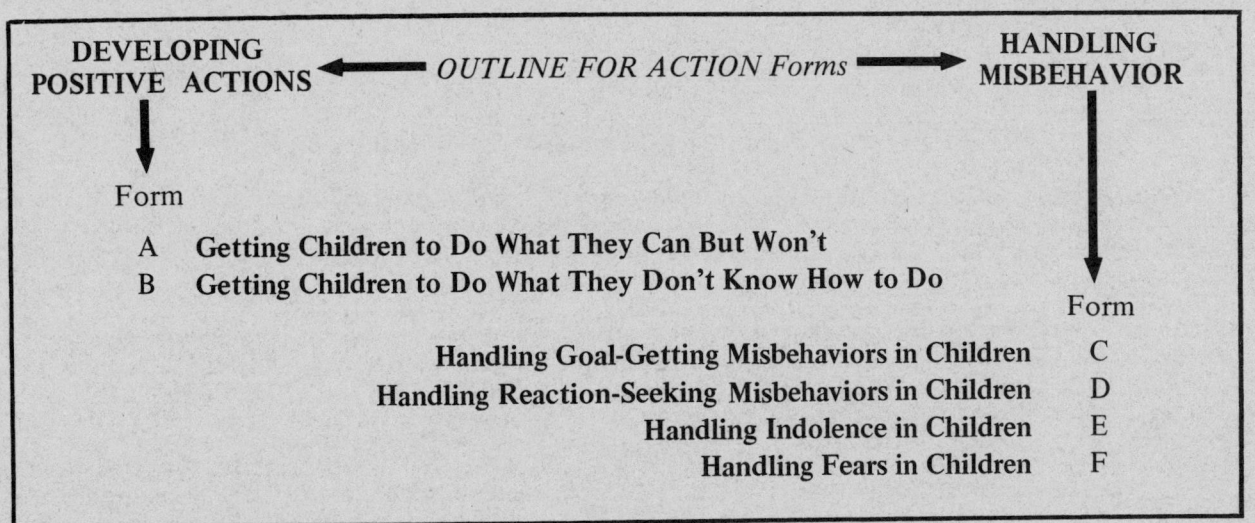

DEVELOPING POSITIVE ACTIONS ←—— *OUTLINE FOR ACTION Forms* ——→ HANDLING MISBEHAVIOR

Form

A Getting Children to Do What They Can But Won't
B Getting Children to Do What They Don't Know How to Do

Form

Handling Goal-Getting Misbehaviors in Children C
Handling Reaction-Seeking Misbehaviors in Children D
Handling Indolence in Children E
Handling Fears in Children F

DEVELOPING POSITIVE ACTIONS

FORM A — GETTING CHILDREN TO DO WHAT THEY CAN BUT WON'T (pages 89-92)

Outline for Action—Form A focuses on getting a child to do something positive that he knows how to do but won't. This was discussed in some detail in Unit Four, where it was stated that there are five basic steps involved in filling out Form A.

Step 1: This step has two parts. First, write down the basic action you wish the child to do, such as honesty, courtesy, etc. Second, be more precise and list specific acts of the child that will help the more basic act (honesty, courtesy) develop. This second part is particularly important if parents desire to develop such things as honesty, kindness, courtesy, responsibility, dependability, and patience in a child.

Step 2: Analyze the situation by asking yourself many questions. How old is the child? What can the child do? How many children in the family? Can brothers or sisters help get the child to do it? Be sure to ask why the child does not do it now. There is always a reason a child does not do what he knows how to do (i.e., alternatives are more rewarding).

Step 3: Identify the most powerful rewards, penalties, and situational planning ideas for this situation.

Step 4: Plant the Habit. In this step the parent rewards the child every time he/she does it. Both material and verbal rewards should be used together. In this step the parent rewards 10-20 times in a row to help the habit start "to take root." Be sure to record what you did.

Step 5: Wean the use of rewards. In this step the parent begins to wean the child away from being rewarded every time. For five times the child could be rewarded every other time, then five material rewards given every third or fourth time. Then five material rewards could be randomly given for a total of five times for a whole week. Verbal praise could be given more often than the material reward. On the chart a filled-in circle (●) indicates the positive action occurred. A filled in circle with an angled line in it (◕) indicates the action occurred and verbal praise was given. A filled circle with an X in it (⊗) indicates both a material reward and verbal praise was given. Remember that intermittently rewarding a habit after it has been "planted" helps strengthen that habit.

FORM B — GETTING CHILDREN TO DO SOMETHING WHEN THEY DON'T KNOW HOW (pages 93-96)

Outline for Action—Form B focuses on getting a child to express some positive action that he/she does not know how to do, but is physically capable of doing.

Step 1: Define what you want the child to do (the same as STEP 1 for Form A).

Step 2: Situational Analysis: Analyze the situation by asking yourself all the questions that may relate to the situation. The Form B EXAMPLE includes a special group of questions that relate to the specific problem of making a bed. This is the step where parents become detectives and think about all the WHYs, WHENs and HOWs. Form B differs from Form A in that you don't have to ask what the child is doing instead, because he/she does not even know how to do what is wanted.

Step 3: Identify powerful rewards and situational planning ideas. This step is different from STEP 3 in Form A because penalties are not needed; yet more space is required to explain how to go about developing the behavior. In this step parents should break the task down into steps. Have the child do a portion of the task, then more . . . and so on until the child can do it all.

Step 4: Record the data. This step is different from STEP 4 on Form A. When developing a behavior the parent specifies exactly what the child did, and what reward was given. The EXAMPLE FORM for Form B illustrates with the task of teaching a child to make a bed. STEP 4 continues until the child has done the complete task 10 times.

Step 5: This step is the same as STEP 5 in Form A. Once the habit has begun to take hold, the parent begins weaning the child from being rewarded every time he/she completes the task. This weaning process is what strengthens the newly-developing habit.

OUTLINE FOR ACTION — Form A

GETTING CHILDREN TO DO WHAT THEY CAN, BUT WON'T

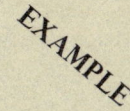

I. Define what action is desired.

a. Basically define it (i.e., honesty, courtesy, etc.) _Have Cody be helpful._

b. If needed, specifically define 4 or 5 actions that demonstrate the desired action: _Do chores when asked._ _Help someone bring in things from the car when the child sees others doing it. Help unpack the car when family returns from trip. Help clear table after dinner._

II. Situational Analysis: Ask yourself questions about the overall situation.

Ask questions such as:

a. How old is the child? _six_   b. Does the child know how to do it? _yes_

c. Could the action be taught in simpler steps? _Sort of, can pick easy, helpful tasks first._

d. Can brothers and sisters help teach? _not necessary_   e. Is the child physically capable of doing it? _yes_

f. Would child do it if there was a better way to check and make sure it would be done? _no_

g. What are the child's likes and dislikes? _Likes money, praise, ice cream, toys, affection; dislikes sitting on chair, being spanked, not watching TV._

h. Why doesn't the child do it now? _Our family situation does not reward a child for being helpful. Helping takes effort, but seldom do we show appreciation to each other for helping._

III. Identify powerful rewards, penalties, and situational planning ideas.

a. Rewards: _Give Cody 10 cents when he helps and thank him. Let him stay up 15 minutes later for each time he helps._

b. Penalties: _Must leave TV room if he fails to help someone going through the room who needs help, or must go to bed early if he fails to help unload the car after a trip, or must sit on chair for 10 minutes._

c. Situational Planning Ideas: _Intentionally arrange conditions where help is needed. Let Cody see other family members being helpful. Initially reward him every time he helps, but later slowly wean him from getting rewards for helping._

d. Plan Development: Lay out a step-by-step plan of what you intend to do to get child to do what you want.

1. Tell Cody exactly what is expected of him and what rewards and penalties are in store.

2. I'll pick a definite time to start so I can watch what I am doing–this Thursday.

3. Reward him each time he does it for the first 10-15 times. Then fade out giving rewards (5-10 every other time, 5 times every third time, 5 payoffs randomly during the week). Give penalty every time he fails to help.

Continued on reverse side

89

VI. Plant the Habit Chart. Write down the date, what behavior, and the consequence (reward or penalty) given. (Continue this for 10-20 times to firmly extablish the action.)

Date	What behavior	What consequence given
Sept 3	helped unload car	15 minutes later bedtime and said thanks
3	took dishes to sink	said thanks and gave 10 cents
4	opened door for mother	said thanks
4	turned off lights in rooms	said thanks and 15 minutes later bedtime
4	took dishes to sink	said thanks and praised him
5	answered door for mother	said thanks and praised him plus 10 cents
5	brought newspaper to dad	said thanks and gave 10 cents
5	took dinner dishes to sink	said thanks and gave 10 cents
6	helped unload car after trip	said thanks and praised
6	took dishes to sink	said thanks
6	cleaned TV room	said thanks and gave 25 cents
7	helped brother find shoe	said thanks
8	helped mom find earring	said thanks plus 10 cents
8	closed door for mom	said thanks and praised
8	took dishes to sink	said thanks and gave hug
8	rocked baby	said thanks, gave 10 cents
8	helped mom pick up trash	said thanks, gave 10 cents
9	helped set table	gave hug
9	helped mom clean backyard	said thanks, gave 25 cents, got to stay up 15 minutes
10	brought dad the newspaper	said thanks, gave 10 cents

V. Weaning Chart. Switching to intermittent rewards actually strengthens the habit as it reduces the frequency of the material reward given. On the chart fill in a circle each time the child does what is required. Add a diagonal line (/) when you give verbal praise and a cross (X) when verbal praise plus a reward (money, food) is given. (If action seems to decline in frequency, re-institute the whole program.)

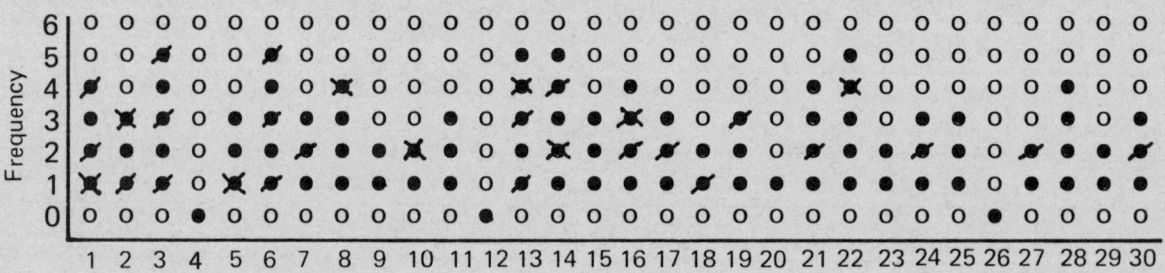

The numbers 0-6 show how many occurrences during a day (week).

Each of the 30 columns can represent a day or a week. Circle which you are using.

OUTLINE FOR ACTION — Form A

GETTING CHILDREN TO DO WHAT THEY CAN, BUT WON'T

I. **Define what action is desired.**

   a. Basically define it (i.e., honesty, courtesy, etc.) _____

   b. If needed, specifically define 4 or 5 actions that demonstrate the desired action:_____

_____

_____

II. **Situational Analysis: Ask yourself questions about the overall situation.**

   Ask questions such as:

   a. How old is the child? _____   b. Does the child know how to do it? _____

   c. Could the action be taught in simpler steps? _____

   d. Can brothers and sisters help teach? _____   e. Is the child physically capable of doing it?_____

   f. Would child do it if there was a better way to check and make sure it would be done?_____

   g. What are the child's likes and dislikes?_____

_____

   h. Why doesn't the child do it now?_____

_____

_____

III. **Identify powerful rewards, penalties, and situational planning ideas.**

   a. Rewards: _____

_____

   b. Penalties: _____

_____

   c. Situational Planning Ideas:_____

_____

   d. Plan Development: Lay out a step-by-step plan of what you intend to do to get child to do what you want.

_____

_____

_____

_____

Continued on reverse side

UNIT SEVEN

Form A (Getting Children to Do What They Can, But Won't), page 2.

VI. Plant the Habit Chart. Write down the date, what behavior, and the consequence (reward or penalty) given. (Continue this for 10-20 times to firmly extablish the action.)

Date	What behavior	What consequence given

V. Weaning Chart. Switching to intermittent rewards actually strengthens the habit as it reduces the frequency of the material reward given. On the chart fill in a circle each time the child does what is required. Add a diagonal line (/) when you give verbal praise and a cross (X) when verbal praise plus a reward (money, food) is given. (If action seems to decline in frequency, re-institute the whole program.)

Frequency

6 | o o o o o o o o o o o o o o o o o o o o o o o o o o o o o o
5 | o o o o o o o o o o o o o o o o o o o o o o o o o o o o o o
4 | o o o o o o o o o o o o o o o o o o o o o o o o o o o o o o
3 | o o o o o o o o o o o o o o o o o o o o o o o o o o o o o o
2 | o o o o o o o o o o o o o o o o o o o o o o o o o o o o o o
1 | o o o o o o o o o o o o o o o o o o o o o o o o o o o o o o
0 | o o o o o o o o o o o o o o o o o o o o o o o o o o o o o o

1 2 3 4 5 6 7 8 9 10 11 12 13 14 15 16 17 18 19 20 21 22 23 24 25 26 27 28 29 30

Day   Week   starting _____

The numbers 0-6 show how many occurrences during a day (week).

Each of the 30 columns can represent a day or a week. Circle which you are using.

OUTLINE FOR ACTION — Form B

GETTING A CHILD TO DO SOMETHING WHEN HE/SHE DOESN'T KNOW HOW

EXAMPLE

I. Define what action is desired.

a. Basically define it (i.e., clean his room, mow the lawn, etc.) *Teach David to make his bed.*

b. If needed, specifically define 4 or 5 actions that demonstrate the desired action: *Not needed.*

It is specific enough.

II. Situational Analysis: Ask yourself questions about the overall situation.

Ask questions such as:

a. How old is the child? *8 yrs. old*   b. Does the child know how to do it? *No*

c. Could the action be taught in simpler steps? *Yes*

d. Can brothers and sisters help teach? *possible*   e. Is the child physically capable of doing it? *Yes*

f. What are the child's likes and dislikes? *Likes to play at Danny's house, likes treats, likes money;*

dislikes missing a meal, sitting on chair, losing allowances, spankings.

g. Other questions asked in this section should be quite specific to the problem being dealt with.
If parents wanted to teach a child to make his bed, they could ask questions like:

Does he know how to make his bed?   Is there a good time to do it?
How does he avoid making his bed?   Is a better check-up system needed?
Does bed get made by others?   Why haven't promptings and rewards worked before?
What has been tried to get action to occur? Can it be put as part of a routine?
Does the child know what is expected?   Is it a bunk bed?

III. Identify powerful rewards and situational planning ideas.

a. Rewards: *Give 25 cents when he makes it.*

b. Situational Planning Ideas: *Use proper size blankets and sheets that tuck in easily, if a bunk bed put him*

on bottom so it is easier. Move bed away from wall so he can get around it easily.

c. Describe the steps to develop the action: *Break tasks into 7 steps:*

1. pull blankets, bedspread and top sheet to foot of bed.   2. bring top sheet to top of mattress and smooth

out wrinkles, plus tuck it in bottom.   3. bring blankets to one hand's width from top of mattress; smooth

and tuck. 4. fold top sheet back over blankets.   5. put pillow on bed.   6. pull bedspread over blankets

and pillow. 7. tuck bedspread under pillow and smooth equally over the bed.   The seven steps should be

done first with David helping mother as she explains each step.   Next, the seven steps are done with mother

explaining the first 5 steps and David explaining the last two.   Keep requiring more of David until he does it

by himself.

Continued on reverse side

Form B (Getting a Child to Do Something When He Doesn't Know How), page 2.

EXAMPLE

IV. Plant the Habit Chart. In this step the action is being developed by rewarding the child to do more and more of the action alone.

Date	What behavior	What reward given
Feb. 2	Mother and David do it with mom explaining.	*25 cents plus said thanks*
3	Mother and David do it, mom explains.	*25 cents plus said thanks*
4	Mother and David do it. Mother explained 1st 5 steps. David last 2	*25 cents plus said thanks*
5	Mom and David did it. David explained all steps.	*Thanks plus go to friend's home*
6	Mom and David did it. David explained all steps.	*Thanks plus 25 cents*
7	Mom and David did 1st 5 steps. David did last 2 alone.	*Thanks plus 25 cents*
8	David did last 3 steps alone.	*Thanks plus go to friend's home*
9	*David - last 4 steps*	*Thanks plus 25 cents*
10	*David - last 5 steps*	*Thanks plus 25 cents*
11	*David - all alone*	*Thanks plus 25 cents and treat*
12	*David - all alone*	*Thanks plus 25 cents*
13	*David - all alone*	*Thanks plus 25 cents*
14	*David - all alone*	*Thanks plus 25 cents*
15	*David - all alone*	*Thanks plus 25 cents*
16	*David - all alone*	*Thanks plus 25 cents*
17	*David - all alone*	*Thanks plus 25 cents*
18	*David - all alone*	*Thanks plus 25 cents*
19	*David - all alone*	*Thanks plus 25 cents*
20	*David - all alone*	*Thanks plus 25 cents*

V. Weaning Chart. Switching to intermittent rewards actually strengthens the habit as it reduces the frequency of the material reward given. On the chart fill in a circle each time the child does what is required. Add a diagonal (/) when you give verbal praise and a cross (X) when verbal praise plus a reward (money, food) is given. (If action seems to decline in frequency, re-institute the whole program.)

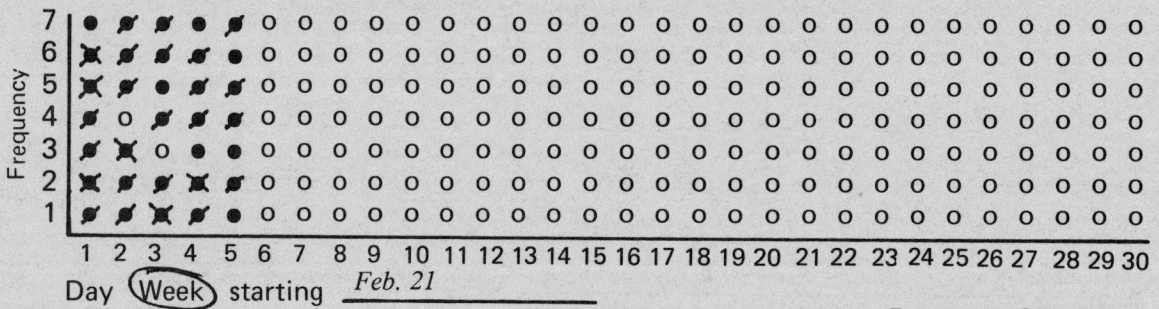

Day (Week) starting _____Feb. 21_____

The numbers 0-6 show how many occurrences during a day (week).

Each of the 30 columns can represent a day or a week. Circle which you are using.

OUTLINE FOR ACTION — Form B
GETTING A CHILD TO DO SOMETHING WHEN HE/SHE DOESN'T KNOW HOW

I. Define what action is desired.

    a. Basically define it (i.e., clean his room, mow the lawn, etc.) _____

    b. If needed, specifically define 4 or 5 actions that demonstrate the desired action: _____

_____

_____

II. Situational Analysis: Ask yourself questions about the overall situation.

    Ask questions such as:

    a. How old is the child? _____   b. Does the child know how to do it? _____

    c. Could the action be taught in simpler steps? _____

    d. Can brothers and sisters help teach? _____   e. Is the child physically capable of doing it? _____

    f. What are the child's likes and dislikes? _____

_____

    In the space below you should write down specific questions and answers that pertain to the particular problem you are dealing with:

_____

_____

_____

III. Identify powerful rewards and situational planning ideas.

    a. Rewards: _____

_____

    b. Situational Planning Ideas: _____

_____

    c. Describe the steps to develop the action: _____

_____

_____

_____

_____

_____

_____

Continued on reverse side

Form B (Getting a Child to Do Something When He Doesn't Know How), page 2.

IV. Plant the Habit Chart. In this step the action is being developed by rewarding the child to do more and more of the action alone.

Date	What behavior	What reward given

V. Weaning Chart. Switching to intermittent rewards actually strengthens the habit as it reduces the frequency of the material reward given. On the chart fill in a circle each time the child does what is required. Add a diagonal (/) when you give verbal praise and a cross (X) when verbal praise plus a reward (money, food) is given. (If action seems to decline in frequency, re-institute the whole program.)

Frequency 7 6 5 4 3 2 1

1 2 3 4 5 6 7 8 9 10 11 12 13 14 15 16 17 18 19 20 21 22 23 24 25 26 27 28 29 30

Day Week starting _____

The numbers 0-6 show how many occurrences during a day (week).

Each of the 30 columns can represent a day or a week. Circle which you are using.

HANDLING MISBEHAVIOR

FORM C — HANDLING GOAL-GETTING MISBEHAVIORS IN CHILDREN (pages 101-106)

Unit Six discusses **goal-getting** as one of the four basic types of misbehavior in children that parents must deal with. *Outline for Action — Form C* is designed to help parents handle goal-getting misbehaviors. To be effective in this process, parents need to do two things: (1) review the DO's and DON'T's of goal-getting listed below, and (2) fill out an *Outline for Action — Form C.* (See pages 101-106.)

I. Review DO's and DON'T's of Goal-Getting

1. Remember this type of misbehavior occurs because it pays off.
2. Don't let goal-getting pay off and it will stop.
3. Don't automatically assume misbehavior is due to deep psychological turmoil.
4. The three main ways of stopping goal-getting are:
   a. Reduce the profit of the act (extinction, satiation).
   b. Increase the penalty of the act (punishment).
   c. Increase desirable options to the act (incompatible response, stimulus change, physical restraint).
5. Use some combination of all three ways where possible.

II. Fill out an Outline for Action — Form C (see pages 105-106)

Step 1: Define specifically what misbehavior needs to be changed.

Step 2: List which of the six methods will be used to decrease the misbehavior. Keep in mind that three things can be done. (See number four above.)

Step 3: Set out the plan. List what penalties will be used, what rewards for alternative behaviors may be used, and state things you will do to implement the plan effectively.

Step 4: Implement the program and keep track of how frequently the misbehavior occurs over the next two weeks.

Step 5: Keep in mind certain things about goal-getting.

Things to remember about getting rid of goal-getting misbehaviors.

1. Pick a time to work on the problem.

2. Make sure the consequences occur every time the misbehavior occurs.

3. Provide a positive alternative where possible.

4. If one thing does not work, try something else.

HANDLING MISBEHAVIOR

FORM D — HANDLING REACTION-SEEKING MISBEHAVIORS IN CHILDREN (pages 107-112)

Unit Six discusses **reaction-seeking** as one of the four basic types of misbehavior in children that parents must deal with. *Outline for Action — Form D* is designed to help parent handle reaction-seeking misbehaviors. To be effective in this process, parents need to do two things: (1) review the DO's and DON'T's of reaction-seeking listed below, and (2) fill out an *Outline for Action — Form D*. (See pages 107-112.)

I. Review DO's and DON'T's of Reaction-Seeking

1. Parents and child seldom realize the real dynamics of their reaction-seeking situations. (Don't keep asking the child **why** he/she did it.)
2. Don't pour words on the situation. (Don't talk about the misbehavior.)
3. Be careful not to **feed** reaction-seeking misbehavior with words and attention.
4. Remember that reaction-seeking indicates the parents are of value to the child. (Therefore redirect the giving of attention to positive actions.)
5. Do select one of the six methods in Unit Five to reduce the reaction-seeking misbehavior. (Table 6.2 on page 70 in Unit Six can also offer some good ideas about which method to use.)
6. Select a positive action of the child to give attention OR arrange a good time when the reaction-seeking misbehavior is acceptable (i.e., teacher says, "Johnny, if you quit standing around my desk during class and sit in your seat, then after school you may come to my desk and we will talk about whatever you want.").
7. Do not use a visible feedback chart showing how much less the child is reaction-seeking. Keep such information to yourself.

II. Fill out an Outline for Action — Form D (see pages 111-112)

Step 1: Focus on getting rid of the misbehavior.

Step 2: Focus on providing an acceptable alternative for receiving attention.

Step 3: Emphasize the giving of unconditional love and resultant love.

TIPS FOR HANDLING REACTION-SEEKING

Provide controlled times when acceptable reaction-seeking behavior may take place.

Give child attention when you and he/she are doing other things together (doing chores, such as dishes, washing the car, etc.)

Let child know that he/she has some scheduled time with you each day.

HANDLING MISBEHAVIOR

FORM E — HANDLING INDOLENCE IN CHILDREN (pages 113-114)

Keep in mind three things when dealing with indolence: (1) the child fails to do what is desired (and may be doing some undesirable alternative), (2) the child has developed an efficient tactic to avoid parental attempts to get the child to act, and (3) some positive action needs to be strengthened. With these things in mind, the parent should then do the following three things:

1. Be aware of the DO's and DON'T's for handling indolence.

2. Fill out an *Outline for Action — Form E* to remove the tactics the child used to avoid doing what is wanted.

3. Fill out an *Outline for Action* form that focuses on developing some positive action.

I. Review the DO's and DON'T's of indolence.

1. Indolence is a much more difficult problem to handle than it looks.
2. Indolent children are sharp and know the weakness of their parents.
3. Indolent children develop tactics to avoid doing what mom or dad request.
4. Indolent children evaluate rewards and penalties for action better than the average child.
5. Indolence can be changed!
6. Do not demean an indolent child by attacking the child's self-worth. (Focus on actions rather than personalities.)
7. Use encouragement and reward more on what you want the child to DO rather than griping about the child failing to do something.
8. Make a chart to hang on the child's bedroom door which shows each time he/she does what is wanted.
9. Watch out! Indolence is a type of misbehavior that often returns because it is easier.
10. Listen to the tape on *Handling Indolence*. (Information on the source of this and other tapes is found on the last page of this handbook.)

II. Stop Indolent tactics.

Fill out an *Outline for Action — Form E* to stop the tactics the child used to get out of doing things.

III. Develop a positive Action

Strengthen the desired action by filling out an *Outline for Action — Form A* (if the child knows how but does not do what is expected) or *Form B* (the child needs to be taught how to do it).

HANDLING MISBEHAVIOR

FORM F — HANDLING FEARS IN CHILDREN (pages 115-118)

There are five basic steps involved in using *Outline for Action—Form F* for handling fears:

STEP ONE: Looking for a Cause

There are basically two kinds of fear situations that a child may encounter: (1) the child has a fear of something that **could** actually harm him/her (being bitten by a dog, being hit by someone, falling from a high place), or (2) the child has a fear of something that most likely **could not** actually harm him/her (darkness, being without mother, going to school, afraid of a picture, scary movie, putting head under water, mirrors, loss of a friend). If the fearful situation more than likely could not harm the child, the basic plan is to have the child repeatedly confront the situation. (See Unit Six for such methods as subliminal approach, superthreshold approach, incompatible response, extinction.)

If the fear-provoking condition could harm the child, then other things need to be included, such as:

1. Teaching the child to better handle the object such as how to approach growling dogs, how to walk carefully in high places.
2. Teaching the child more about the fear object (i.e., how far a snake can lunge when striking, what spiders and bees can really do).
3. Sometimes you may have the person experience the situation. (A child afraid of being hit may be required to box.)

The types of questions that should be asked in looking for the causes are:

1. Was there a specific precipitating incident? (bitten by dog, fall off horse)
2. Is the fear still provoked by what started it? (i.e., boy initially hit in face by other boy is now afraid when just being threatened).
3. Is the fear fed by people giving attention to the child when he/she talks about it. (If so, this is most likely a fear situation that should be dealt with as if the child cannot actually be harmed.)
4. Is the fear due to something that **could** or **could not** harm the child?

STEP TWO: Situational Analysis

One of the secrets behind the success of professionals dealing with childhood fears is that they critically analyze the situation more than parents do. Parents could better handle fears if they took the time to act like a detective and closely scrutinized the situation. Too often we think the fear situation is simpler (or more complex) than it really is. In this step parents could ask themselves all sorts of questions to get a better grasp of what the situation really is.

STEP THREE: Options for Fear Removal

Unit Six talked about three basic ways fears could be handled (subliminal approach, superthreshold approach, incompatible response approach). A fourth approach (extinction) is included here for situations where the fear may be due to people giving the child attention for acting afraid. This happens mostly with fears that cannot really hurt the child.

STEP FOUR: Planning Options for Fear Removal

In this step the parents should elaborate on exactly how they plan to deal with the fear. This should include information about how they will have the child confront the fear, and what they and the child did in the actual confrontation situations.

STEP FIVE: Recording What's Happening

We suggest you keep a journal or record of what the child did and what happened. In terms of what the child did, try to record how strong the reaction of the child was. Does it seem to be working? If not look closely at what you are doing. **Be sure you are not feeding the fear.**

OUTLINE FOR ACTION — Form C

HANDLING GOAL-GETTING MISBEHAVIOR

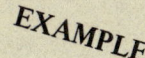
EXAMPLE

I. Define specifically what the misbehavior is. *Johnny repeatedly asks for things after being told "No".*

_____

_____

II. List at least three alternative ways of handling the misbehavior with the six methods presented in Unit Five. Put a star (★) by the one(s) you want to try first.

a. Extinction: *★Make sure you do not respond at all to Johnny after saying "no" the first time.*

b. Physical Restraint: *Tape his mouth shut for 15 minutes after I say "no." (This is obviously not a good strategy.)*

c. Satiation: *Have him repeatedly ask and say "no" (Again, not a good strategy.)*

d. Incompatible Response: *★If Johnny does not ask while rubber band is on he will get an additional surprise.*

e. Stimulus Change: *★Once I say "no" I quickly think up a task for Johnny to go do that gets his mind off the request.*

f. Punishment: *★Once I say "no" I place a thick rubber band on his wrist and say "Johnny, if you ask again while this rubber band is on your wrist I will pull the rubber band and flick your wrist."*

III. Look specifically at the Big Three Methods for decreasing misbehaviors.

a. Penalties: *Flicked by rubber band when Johnny continues to ask.*

b. Rewards: *If Johnny goes 10-15 minutes without asking, comment on how good Johnny has been for not asking again, AND give him a reward (i.e., cookie, 10 cents).*

c. Situational Planning Ideas. (State things you can do to develop a more optimum situation for getting the penalties and rewards to work.)

I will tell other family members about what I am doing. I will tell Johnny, "Johnny, I want to help you break the habit of repeatedly asking after people tell you "no." From now on everytime you ask (and I say No) I will place this rubber band on your wrist for a length of time that could be short or long. If you ask again while you have the rubber band on, I will flick your wrist with the rubber band. On some occasions, if you are able to not ask again while you have the rubber band on, I will give you a small surprise."

Continued on reverse side

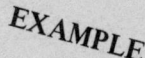

d. Extra things to help. (Write special things here you can do to help make your program work better.)

1. I will start by placing the rubber band on for just a few minutes then gradually increase the time up to an hour.

2. If I spot Johnny intentionally asking just so he can get the rubber band and an opportunity to win a surprise, I will not give the surprise.

3. I will use extinction plus punishment plus try to reward positive alternatives.

IV. **Misbehavior Chart.** Record the frequency of the misbehavior. (Don't show this to the child.) A filled in circle represents an occurrence of the misbehavior.

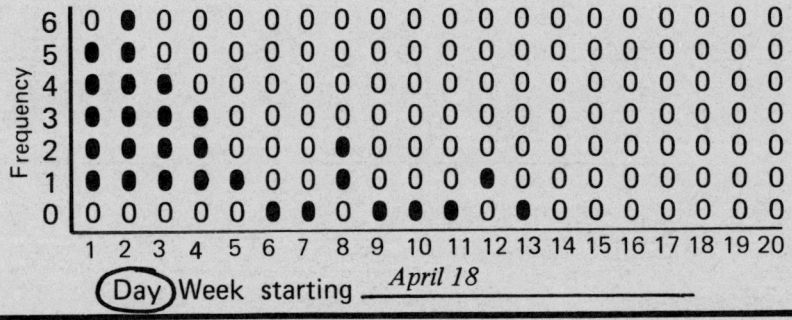

The numbers 0-6 show how many occurrences during a day (week).

Each of the 20 columns can represent a day or a week. Circle which you are using.

(Day) Week starting _April 18_

Things to remember about getting rid of goal-getting misbehaviors.

1. Pick a time to work on the problem.

2. Make sure the consequences occur every time the misbehavior occurs.

3. Provide a positive alternative where possible.

4. If one thing does not work, try something else.

DO's and DON'T's of Goal-Getting

1. Remember this type of misbehavior occurs because it pays off.
2. Don't let goal-getting pay off and it will stop.
3. Don't automatically assume misbehavior is due to deep psychological turmoil.
4. The three main ways of stopping goal-getting are:
   a. Reduce the profit of the act (extinction, satiation).
   b. Increase the penalty of the act. (punishment).
   c. Increase desirable options to the act (incompatible response, stimulus change, physcial restraint).
5. Use some combination of all three ways where possible.

OUTLINE FOR ACTION — Form C

HANDLING GOAL-GETTING MISBEHAVIOR

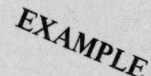

I. Define specifically what the misbehavior is. *Kim runs through the house.*

II. List at least three alternative ways of handling the misbehavior with the six methods presented in Unit Five. Put a star (★) by the one(s) you want to try first.

a. Extinction: _____

b. Physical Restraint: _____

c. Satiation: *When caught running, have Kim repeat running through the house over and over until she is really tired of it.*

d. Incompatible Response: *★Give Kim $1.00 if she can go one week without running in the house.*

e. Stimulus Change: _____

f. Punishment: *★When caught running, Kim has to sit quietly on a chair for 10 minutes. OR when caught running, she must pay 25 cents or 50 cents to the family bank.*

III. Look specifically at the Big Three Methods for decreasing misbehaviors.

a. Penalties: *Every time Kim is caught running in the house, she will sit quietly on a chair for 10 minutes.*

b. Rewards: *If Kim goes one week without running in the house, she gets an extra dollar with her allowance.*

c. Situational Planning Ideas. (State things you can do to develop a more optimum situation for getting the penalties and rewards to work.)

I will start tomorrow implementing the plan. I will inform the family about the plan so they may help.

I will tell Kim about the new rules by saying, "Kim I want to help you break the habit of running through the house. Every time you run in the house you will be required to sit quietly on a chair for 10 minutes. If you go a whole week without running in the house you will get an extra dollar with your allowance."

Continued on reverse side

103

Form C (Handling Goal-Getting Misbehavior), page 2.

d. Extra things to help. (Write special things here you can do to help make your program work better.)

After Kim goes 3 weeks in a row, I will remove the $1.00 pay off and just use the chair sitting penalty.

I will use the incompatible response method, plus punishment.

_____

_____

_____

_____

_____

_____

_____

_____

_____

_____

IV. **Misbehavior Chart.** Record the frequency of the misbehavior. (Don't show this to the child.) A filled in circle represents an occurrence of the misbehavior.

```
  6 │ O O O O O O O O O O O O O O O O O O O O
  5 │ O O O O O O O O O O O O O O O O O O O O
F 4 │ O O O O O O O O O O O O O O O O O O O O
r 3 │ O O O O O O O O O O O O O O O O O O O O
e 2 │ ● O O O O O O O O O O O O O O O O O O O
q 1 │ ● O O O ● O O O O O O O O O O O O O O O
  0 │ O ● ● ● O ● ● ● ● ● ● ● ● O O O O O O O
    └─────────────────────────────────────────
      1 2 3 4 5 6 7 8 9 10 11 12 13 14 15 16 17 18 19 20
```

(Day) Week starting *July 23*

The numbers 0-6 show how many occurrences during a day (week).

Each of the 20 columns can represent a day or a week. Circle which you are using.

Things to remember about getting rid of goal-getting misbehaviors.

1. Pick a time to work on the problem.

2. Make sure the consequences occur every time the misbehavior occurs.

3. Provide a positive alternative where possible.

4. If one thing does not work, try something else.

DO's and DON'T's of Goal-Getting

1. Remember this type of misbehavior occurs because it pays off.
2. Don't let goal-getting pay off and it will stop.
3. Don't automatically assume misbehavior is due to deep psychological turmoil.
4. The three main ways of stopping goal-getting are:
   a. Reduce the profit of the act (extinction, satiation).
   b. Increase the penalty of the act. (punishment).
   c. Increase desirable options to the act (incompatible response, stimulus change, physcial restraint).
5. Use some combination of all three ways where possible.

OUTLINE FOR ACTION — Form C

HANDLING GOAL-GETTING MISBEHAVIOR

I. Define specifically what the misbehavior is. _____
_____
_____

II. List at least three alternative ways of handling the misbehavior with the six methods presented in Unit Five. Put a star (★) by the one(s) you want to try first.

   a. Extinction: _____
_____

   b. Physical Restraint: _____
_____

   c. Satiation: _____
_____

   d. Incompatible Response: _____
_____

   e. Stimulus Change: _____
_____

   f. Punishment: _____
_____

III. Look specifically at the Big Three Methods for decreasing misbehaviors.

   a. Penalties: _____
_____

   b. Rewards: _____
_____

   c. Situational Planning Ideas. (State things you can do to develop a more optimum situation for getting the penalties and rewards to work.)

_____
_____
_____
_____
_____
_____

Continued on reverse side   105

Form C (Handling Goal-Getting Misbehavior), page 2.

d. Extra things to help. (Write special things here you can do to help make your program work better.)

_____

_____

_____

_____

_____

_____

_____

_____

_____

_____

_____

IV. **Misbehavior Chart.** Record the frequency of the misbehavior. (Don't show this to the child.) A filled in circle represents an occurrence of the misbehavior.

```
    6 │ O O O O O O O O O O O O O O O O O O O O
    5 │ O O O O O O O O O O O O O O O O O O O O
 ᵧ  4 │ O O O O O O O O O O O O O O O O O O O O
 c
 e  3 │ O O O O O O O O O O O O O O O O O O O O
 u
 q  2 │ O O O O O O O O O O O O O O O O O O O O
 e
 r  1 │ O O O O O O O O O O O O O O O O O O O O
 F
    0 │ O O O O O O O O O O O O O O O O O O O O
      └──────────────────────────────────────
        1 2 3 4 5 6 7 8 9 10 11 12 13 14 15 16 17 18 19 20
```

The numbers 0-6 show how many occurrences during a day (week).

Each of the 20 columns can represent a day or a week. Circle which you are using.

Day Week starting _____

Things to remember about getting rid of goal-getting misbehaviors.

1. Pick a time to work on the problem.

2. Make sure the consequences occur every time the misbehavior occurs.

3. Provide a positive alternative where possible.

4. If one thing does not work, try something else.

DO's and DON'T's of Goal-Getting

1. Remember this type of misbehavior occurs because it pays off.
2. Don't let goal-getting pay off and it will stop.
3. Don't automatically assume misbehavior is due to deep psychological turmoil.
4. The three main ways of stopping goal-getting are:
   a. Reduce the profit of the act (extinction, satiation).
   b. Increase the penalty of the act. (punishment).
   c. Increase desirable options to the act (incompatible response, stimulus change, physcial restraint).
5. Use some combination of all three ways where possible.

OUTLINE FOR ACTION — Form D

HANDLING REACTION-SEEKING MISBEHAVIOR

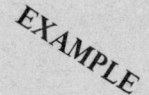
EXAMPLE

I. Focus on getting rid of misbehavior.

a. Define specifically what misbehavior the child exhibits: *Amy pouts and goes to her room.*

b. List at least three things you can do to stop the misbehavior using the six methods presented in Unit Five: extinction, physical restraint, satiation, stimulus change, incompatible response, punishment.

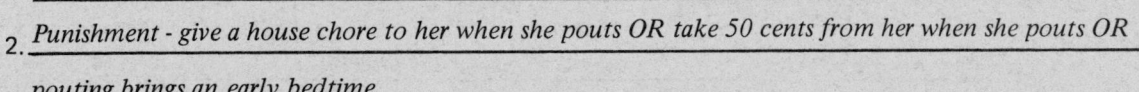

1. *Extinction - act like you don't care if she pouts.*

2. *Punishment - give a house chore to her when she pouts OR take 50 cents from her when she pouts OR pouting brings an early bedtime.*

3. *Incompatible Response - give Amy the choice of a special activity when she goes a week without pouting.*

c. Fill out an Outline for Action for goal-getting, if necessary.

d. **Misbehavior Chart.** Record the frequency of the misbehavior. (Don't show this to the child.) A filled in circle represents an occurrence of the misbehavior.

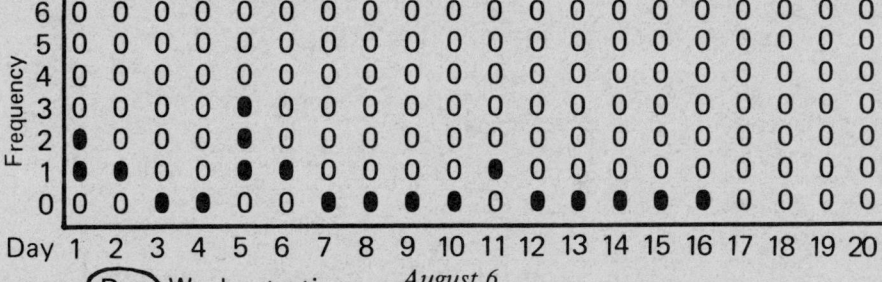

Frequency	1	2	3	4	5	6	7	8	9	10	11	12	13	14	15	16	17	18	19	20
6	O	O	O	O	O	O	O	O	O	O	O	O	O	O	O	O	O	O	O	O
5	O	O	O	O	O	O	O	O	O	O	O	O	O	O	O	O	O	O	O	O
4	O	O	O	O	O	O	O	O	O	O	O	O	O	O	O	O	O	O	O	O
3	O	O	O	O	●	O	O	O	O	O	O	O	O	O	O	O	O	O	O	O
2	●	O	O	O	●	O	O	O	O	O	O	O	O	O	O	O	O	O	O	O
1	●	●	O	O	●	●	O	O	O	O	●	O	O	O	O	O	O	O	O	O
0	O	O	●	●	O	O	●	●	●	●	O	●	●	●	●	●	O	O	O	O

Day 1 2 3 4 5 6 7 8 9 10 11 12 13 14 15 16 17 18 19 20

(Day) Week starting: *August 6*

The numbers 0-6 show how many occurrences during a day (week).

Each of the 20 columns can represent a day or a week. Circle which you are using.

II. Focus on providing positive alternative to receive attention.

a. Define acceptable behavior for getting attention. *When Amy talks about some positive topic (i.e. clothes, doing things, ask questions) I will plan to take 10 minutes to talk positively with her. I will talk about fun things with her while we do the dishes.*

b. Specify how often (hopefully daily) you will give attention. *I will do this at least once a day.*

c. Positive Attention Chart. Record how often each day you give positive attention to your child.

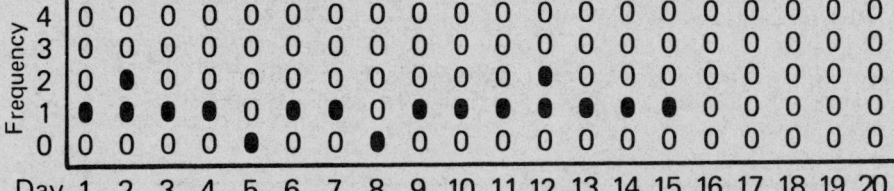

Frequency	1	2	3	4	5	6	7	8	9	10	11	12	13	14	15	16	17	18	19	20
4	O	O	O	O	O	O	O	O	O	O	O	O	O	O	O	O	O	O	O	O
3	O	O	O	O	O	O	O	O	O	O	O	O	O	O	O	O	O	O	O	O
2	O	●	O	O	O	O	O	O	O	O	O	O	●	O	O	O	O	O	O	O
1	●	●	●	●	O	●	●	●	●	●	●	●	O	●	O	O	O	O	O	O
0	O	O	O	O	●	O	O	O	●	O	O	O	O	O	O	O	O	O	O	O

Day 1 2 3 4 5 6 7 8 9 10 11 12 13 14 15 16 17 18 19 20

Continued on reverse side

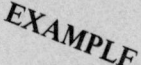

III. Emphasize the giving of *unconditional love* **and** *resultant love*. **A child needing attention can get along IF he/she is given experiences building up their self-worth.** (Unit 10 gives some useful suggestions.)

    a. Define three expressions of unconditional love you can give your child each day or week.

I will give Amy a smile and wink as we drive to the store.

I will find some quick thing today to laugh and talk about with Amy while we do house chores.

I will leave a note on Amy's pillow saying "Thanks for being you."

    b. Define three expressions of resultant love you can give your child each day.

I will praise Amy when she washes the dishes without being asked.

I will thank Amy for doing all her house chores this week and give her extra money.

I will thank Amy when I see her do something nice for someone else.

    d. Fill out a RUN Chart. (See page 164.)

TIPS FOR HANDLING REACTION-SEEKING

Keep in mind that one of the main keys to handling reaction-seeking is for parents to pay attention to their child. Some tips for doing this are:

1. Some reaction-seeking misbehaviors can be controlled by providing acceptable times for it to occur—

    a. a child pestering a teacher is given time to talk after school IF he does not pester during class.

    b. a boy who gets into mom's flour bin is allowed to play with an old can of flour on certain days.

2. Sometimes parents can give their child more attention without using more time than they have now—

    a. talk about positive things with a daughter while doing the dishes.

    b. plan family activities while father and son wash the car.

    c. talk to children while driving to the store, school, etc.

    d. talk during mealtime.

3. Children will exhibit less reaction-seeking misbehavior if they know there will be times each day that they can interact with the parents.

4. Children will not automatically quit reaction-seeking if parents give more attention. Besides giving attention, parents need to use methods to reduce the reaction-seeking misbehaviors.

OUTLINE FOR ACTION — Form D

HANDLING REACTION-SEEKING MISBEHAVIOR

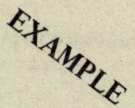

I. Focus on getting rid of misbehavior.

a. Define specifically what misbehavior the child exhibits: _Andy keeps pestering me with questions and interrupting me while I am talking._

b. List at least three things you can do to stop the misbehavior using the six methods presented in Unit Five: extinction, physical restraint, satiation, stimulus change, incompatible response, punishment.

1. _Punishment - spank him when he interrupts; OR set him on a chair for 5 minutes when he interrupts._

2. _Extinction - try to ignore his pestering and interruptions (this most likely won't work by itself)._

3. _Incompatible Response - tell him we will spend time with him at end of day IF he has not pestered you during the day._

c. Fill out an Outline for Action for goal-getting, if necessary.

d. **Misbehavior Chart.** Record the frequency of the misbehavior. (Don't show this to the child.) A filled in circle represents an occurrence of the misbehavior.

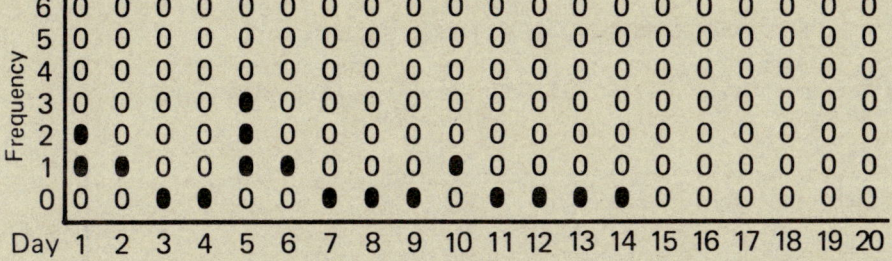

The numbers 0-6 show how many occurrences during a day (week).

Each of the 20 columns can represent a day or a week. Circle which you are using.

Day 1 2 3 4 5 6 7 8 9 10 11 12 13 14 15 16 17 18 19 20

Day Week starting: _Jan. 14_

II. Focus on providing positive alternative to receive attention.

a. Define acceptable behavior for getting attention. _I will let Andy help me set the table for lunch and talk with him then. I will talk about fun things with Andy while we drive to the store, AND when we go to pick up the older kids at school._

b. Specify how often (hopefully daily) you will give attention. _I plan to do it at least twice a day._

c. Positive Attention Chart. Record how often each day you give positive attention to your child.

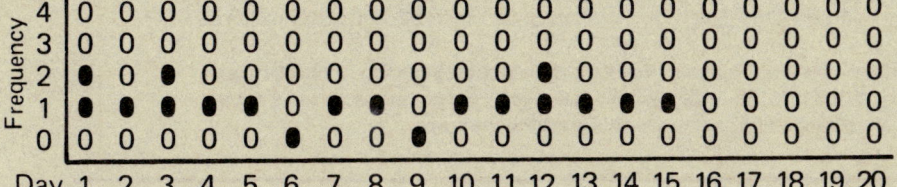

Continued on reverse side

Day 1 2 3 4 5 6 7 8 9 10 11 12 13 14 15 16 17 18 19 20

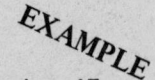

III. Emphasize the giving of *unconditional love* **and** *resultant love.* **A child needing attention can get along IF he/she is given experiences building up their self-worth.** (Unit 10 gives some useful suggestions.)

    a. Define three expressions of unconditional love you can give your child each day or week.

> *I'll put my arm on Andy's shoulder as we walk each week.*

> *I'll send Andy a card to be received in the mail.*

> *I'll give him a smile and wink at the dinner table.*

    b. Define three expressions of resultant love you can give your child each day.

> *I'll tell Andy thanks when he picks up his toys.*

> *I'll tell Andy thanks when he brings me my newspaper.*

> *I'll hug Andy and tell him how nice his room looks after he cleans it.*

    d. Fill out a RUN Chart. (See page 164.)

TIPS FOR HANDLING REACTION-SEEKING

Keep in mind that one of the main keys to handling reaction-seeking is for parents to pay attention to their child. Some tips for doing this are:

1. Some reaction-seeking misbehaviors can be controlled by providing acceptable times for it to occur—

   a. a child pestering a teacher is given time to talk after school IF he does not pester during class.

   b. a boy who gets into mom's flour bin is allowed to play with an old can of flour on certain days.

2. Sometimes parents can give their child more attention without using more time than they have now—

   a. talk about positive things with a daughter while doing the dishes.

   b. plan family activities while father and son wash the car.

   c. talk to children while driving to the store, school, etc.

   d. talk during mealtime.

3. Children will exhibit less reaction-seeking misbehavior if they know there will be times each day that they can interact with the parents.

4. Children will not automatically quit reaction-seeking if parents give more attention. Besides giving attention, parents need to use methods to reduce the reaction-seeking misbehaviors.

OUTLINE FOR ACTION — Form D

HANDLING REACTION-SEEKING MISBEHAVIOR

I. Focus on getting rid of misbehavior.

a. Define specifically what misbehavior the child exhibits: _____

_____

b. List at least three things you can do to stop the misbehavior using the six methods presented in Unit Five: extinction, physical restraint, satiation, stimulus change, incompatible response, punishment.

1. _____

_____

2. _____

_____

3. _____

_____

c. Fill out an Outline for Action for goal-getting, if necessary.

d. **Misbehavior Chart.** Record the frequency of the misbehavior. (Don't show this to the child.) A filled in circle represents an occurrence of the misbehavior.

Frequency

6	O O O O O O O O O O O O O O O O O O O O
5	O O O O O O O O O O O O O O O O O O O O
4	O O O O O O O O O O O O O O O O O O O O
3	O O O O O O O O O O O O O O O O O O O O
2	O O O O O O O O O O O O O O O O O O O O
1	O O O O O O O O O O O O O O O O O O O O
0	O O O O O O O O O O O O O O O O O O O O

Day 1 2 3 4 5 6 7 8 9 10 11 12 13 14 15 16 17 18 19 20

The numbers 0-6 show how many occurrences during a day (week).

Each of the 20 columns can represent a day or a week. Circle which you are using.

Day   Week   starting: _____

II. Focus on providing positive alternative to receive attention.

a. Define acceptable behavior for getting attention. _____

_____

_____

b. Specify how often (hopefully daily) you will give attention. _____

_____

c. Positive Attention Chart. Record how often each day you give positive attention to your child.

Frequency

4	O O O O O O O O O O O O O O O O O O O O
3	O O O O O O O O O O O O O O O O O O O O
2	O O O O O O O O O O O O O O O O O O O O
1	O O O O O O O O O O O O O O O O O O O O
0	O O O O O O O O O O O O O O O O O O O O

Day 1 2 3 4 5 6 7 8 9 10 11 12 13 14 15 16 17 18 19 20

Continued on reverse side

111

III. **Emphasize the giving of** *unconditional love* **and** *resultant love*. **A child needing attention can get along IF he/she is given experiences building up their self-worth.** (Unit 10 gives some useful suggestions.)

a. Define three expressions of unconditional love you can give your child each day or week.

_____

_____

_____

b. Define three expressions of resultant love you can give your child each day.

_____

_____

_____

d. Fill out a RUN Chart. (See page 164.)

TIPS FOR HANDLING REACTION-SEEKING

Keep in mind that one of the main keys to handling reaction-seeking is for parents to pay attention to their child. Some tips for doing this are:

1. Some reaction-seeking misbehaviors can be controlled by providing acceptable times for it to occur—

   a. a child pestering a teacher is given time to talk after school IF he does not pester during class.

   b. a boy who gets into mom's flour bin is allowed to play with an old can of flour on certain days.

2. Sometimes parents can give their child more attention without using more time than they have now—

   a. talk about positive things with a daughter while doing the dishes.

   b. plan family activities while father and son wash the car.

   c. talk to children while driving to the store, school, etc.

   d. talk during mealtime.

3. Children will exhibit less reaction-seeking misbehavior if they know there will be times each day that they can interact with the parents.

4. Children will not automatically quit reaction-seeking if parents give more attention. Besides giving attention, parents need to use methods to reduce the reaction-seeking misbehaviors.

OUTLINE FOR ACTION – Form E

HANDLING INDOLENCE

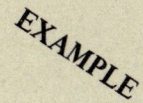

I. **Define the problem.** Answer the following three questions.

a. Specifically define what the child should do. _Shawn needs to study his school work_

b. Write down what he/she does instead. _plays sports and watches TV_

c. What tactics does he/she use to avoid the task? _says he will do it later, OR claims it is already done_

II. **Look at what is controlling the child's tendencies NOT TO DO what you want done.**

REWARDS (positive results for NOT DOING)	PENALTIES (reasons child may feel bad for NOT DOING)
gets to play sports instead of study	Mother may get mad when school work is not done
gets to enjoy TV instead of study	

III. **Explain how you, the parent, can rearrange the rewards and penalties so the tactics won't work for the child.**

REWARDS	PENALTIES
playing sports and watching TV allowed when	failure to study results in loss of playing and TV
studying is completed	privileges for two days plus one hour earlier bedtime

IV. **Develop a Positive Action.**

This step in handling indolence involves strengthening the desired action. To do this, fill out an Outline for Action Form A or B. If the child knows what is expected but does not do it, use Form A. If the child needs to be taught how to do it, use Form B.

113

OUTLINE FOR ACTION — Form E

HANDLING INDOLENCE

I. **Define the problem.** Answer the following three questions.

  a. Specifically define what the child should do. _____

  _____

  b. Write down what he/she does instead. _____

  _____

  c. What tactics does he/she use to avoid the task? _____

  _____

II. **Look at what is controlling the child's tendencies NOT TO DO what you want done.**

REWARDS (positive results for NOT DOING)	**PENALTIES** (reasons child may feel bad for NOT DOING)
_____	_____
_____	_____
_____	_____
_____	_____

III. **Explain how you, the parent, can rearrange the rewards and penalties so the tactics won't work for the child.**

REWARDS	**PENALTIES**
_____	_____
_____	_____
_____	_____
_____	_____

IV. **Develop a Positive Action.**

  This step in handling indolence involves strengthening the desired action. To do this, fill out an Outline for Action Form A or B. If the child knows what is expected but does not do it, use Form A. If the child needs to be taught how to do it, use Form B.

OUTLINE FOR ACTION - Form F

HANDLING FEARS

I. Look for the cause.

1. Was there a precipitating incident? Explain. *Child is afraid of lightning and thunder.*

2. Is fear still induced by what precipitated it? *Yes*

3. Is fear fed by positive strokes (attention)? *some*

4. Is fear due to something that could harm the child? *No*

II. Situational Analysis. Describe situation in which fear occurs. Ask questions like:

1. Is there a specific object or activity that brings on the fear? If so, what? *Yes - the sound of thunder.*

2. How often does it occur? *Whenever thunder storms occur.*

3. Where does it occur? *Danny expresses the fear wherever he is when it thunders.*

4. Does it occur mostly with a particular person? *No*

5. Will the child talk about the fear? *Yes*

6. Has the fear been discussed with the child? What was said? *Yes.*
   Danny was told it really cannot hurt him.

7. Other things the parent notices. *The child cries when he hears the thunder. Danny seems less afraid if mom or dad is present.*

III. Which method for removing fears shall you use? *The incompatible response approach.*

IV. Explain the specific things you will and did do to handle the fear.

I will purchase a special candy Danny really loves (perhaps a special cream filled chocolate). I will place the chocolates on the mantle of the fireplace and tell Danny it is "thunder candy". He can only have a piece when it thunders.

Continued on reverse side

Form F (Handling Fears), page 2.

EXAMPLE

V. Make journal entries showing your and your child's actions.

	WHAT DID YOU DO?	WHAT DID THE CHILD DO?
1st time	*Yelled "Hey, let's get the thunder candy."*	*He was afraid, but really wanted the candy.*
	3 times it thundered 3 pieces were eaten	*I did not hug him when he showed fear.*
2nd time	*Did the same as above*	*showed fear, but wanted the candy*
3rd time	*looked at Danny and smiled*	*Yelled "Let's get the thunder candy" and ate it.*
4th time	*looked at Danny and smiled*	*Yelled "Let's get the thunder candy" then ate it.*

Comments: *I made sure I picked a type of candy Danny really loved; and I made sure it was kept visible above the fireplace, PLUS I made sure he could not get the candy at any other time.*

SPECIAL TIPS FOR DEALING WITH FEARS
☆ Do not demean or chastize the child for the fear.
☆ Act in a non-emotional matter-of-fact manner in a supportive way.
☆ Do not approach the fear as indicating a deep seated emotional problem, but more as an ineffective learned emotional response.
☆ Keep in mind the role of fear in a person's life is good.
☆ Remember that fears can be related to physical or mental anguish.

TIPS TO REMEMBER ABOUT FEARS IN GENERAL
● Confrontation is the key to reducing fears.
● The fear system in humans is designed to not only signal when there is some sort of danger, but it also motivates us to do something to solve the problem.
● While Mother Nature instills in lower animals exactly what to do in fearful situations, man is given superior problem-solving capabilities to handle fears more effectively on an individual basis.
● Fears develop through processes of association. Man can learn to fear objects and situations **and** learn not to fear them.
● Fears can be developed in children by parents unintentionally rewarding fear reactions (e.g., fear of dark, fear of school).

● The mind can magnify a fear all out of realistic proportion.
● Fears do not typically fade over time. They need to be confronted.
● The mind often deals with fears by creating diversions, distortion, or repressions.
● Fear is a form a pain.
● Fear can be specific to a certain object or generalized to a whole situation.
● Psychological fears can be as painful (if not more) as fears related to physical pain.
● Fears such as those relating to the dark or going to school have no real physical pain dimension to them and can be treated with all three methods of confrontation. (However, the subliminal and the incompatible response approaches are most strongly recommended.)
● Stimulus change (mental modification) techniques can be effectively used on many fears in conjunction with the three confronting techniques.
● Fears of getting hurt can be effectively dealt with using the subliminal confrontation approach with positive strokes for good coping by the child.
● The extinction procedure for removing fears involves making sure a child's fear reactions are no longer rewarding. (The effectiveness of this extinction approach can be increased by intentionally giving positive strokes to a child who copes well with previously fear-provoking situations.)

OUTLINE FOR ACTION - Form F

HANDLING FEARS

I. Look for the cause.

1. Was there a precipitating incident? Explain._____

2. Is fear still induced by what precipitated it?_____

3. Is fear fed by positive strokes (attention)?_____

4. Is fear due to something that could harm the child? _____

II. Situational Analysis. Describe situation in which fear occurs. Ask questions like:

1. Is there a specific object or activity that brings on the fear? If so, what?_____

2. How often does it occur? _____

3. Where does it occur?_____

4. Does it occur mostly with a particular person?_____

5. Will the child talk about the fear?_____

6. Has the fear been discussed with the child? What was said? _____

_____

7. Other things the parent notices. _____

_____

_____

III. Which method for removing fears shall you use? _____

_____

_____

IV. Explain the specific things you will and did do to handle the fear.

_____

_____

_____

_____

_____

_____

_____

_____

Continued on reverse side

Form F (Handling Fears), page 2.

V. Make journal entries showing your and your child's actions.

	WHAT DID YOU DO?	WHAT DID THE CHILD DO?
1st time	_____	_____
	_____	_____
2nd time	_____	_____
	_____	_____
3rd time	_____	_____
	_____	_____
4th time	_____	_____
	_____	_____
Comments:	_____	_____

SPECIAL TIPS FOR DEALING WITH FEARS

☆ Do not demean or chastize the child for the fear.
☆ Act in a non-emotional matter-of-fact manner in a supportive way.
☆ Do not approach the fear as indicating a deep seated emotional problem, but more as an ineffective learned emotional response.
☆ Keep in mind the role of fear in a person's life is good.
☆ Remember that fears can be related to physical or mental anguish.

TIPS TO REMEMBER ABOUT FEARS IN GENERAL

● Confrontation is the key to reducing fears.
● The fear system in humans is designed to not only signal when there is some sort of danger, but it also motivates us to do something to solve the problem.
● While Mother Nature instills in lower animals exactly what to do in fearful situations, man is given superior problem-solving capabilities to handle fears more effectively on an individual basis.
● Fears develop through processes of association. Man can learn to fear objects and situations **and** learn not to fear them.
● Fears can be developed in children by parents unintentionally rewarding fear reactions (e.g., fear of dark, fear of school).

● The mind can magnify a fear all out of realistic proportion.
● Fears do not typically fade over time. They need to be confronted.
● The mind often deals with fears by creating diversions, distortion, or repressions.
● Fear is a form a pain.
● Fear can be specific to a certain object or generalized to a whole situation.
● Psychological fears can be as painful (if not more) as fears related to physical pain.
● Fears such as those relating to the dark or going to school have no real physical pain dimension to them and can be treated with all three methods of confrontation. (However, the subliminal and the incompatible response approaches are most strongly recommended.)
● Stimulus change (mental modification) techniques can be effectively used on many fears in conjunction with the three confronting techniques.
● Fears of getting hurt can be effectively dealt with using the subliminal confrontation approach with positive strokes for good coping by the child.
● The extinction procedure for removing fears involves making sure a child's fear reactions are no longer rewarding. (The effectiveness of this extinction approach can be increased by intentionally giving positive strokes to a child who copes well with previously fear-provoking situations.)

Communication:
Using the Power of Language

Good communication is important in everything we do. Effective communication happens when we *listen*. Four types of listening—silent, supportive, promptive, and reflective—are explained. What special way can you tell a child you *care?* Does how you say something affect what you say? This unit answers these and other questions.

OH! IS THAT WHAT YOU MEANT?

Communicating—sending messages or conveying ideas from one person to another—is perhaps the single most important activity we engage in in our role as neighbors, employees/employers, and especially as parents. Perhaps, because it's something we do from birth's first breath, day in, day out, to life's last moment, we fail to realize its importance. Communication is a part of **everything** we do. Even while sleeping we communicate. An infant unconsciously kicks the covers off. Is it too warm? Later, it draws arms and legs close together. Is it now too cold? Mother assumes the baby is communicating that it is cold and covers it up. The baby has sent some messages; mother has received some.

To understand this message sending procedure, let's consider the four major elements of the communication process. Then we can become more aware of ways to improve parent/ child communication—so important to the growth and development of both. The four are: the *sender*, the *message*, the *means by which the message is sent* (mode), and the *receiver*. If there is a problem, weakness, or interference (static) in any one or more of these four, miscommunication takes place.

Using the example of the sleeping baby, let's look at each of the four. The baby, of course, was the sender, the mother was the receiver. The means (mode) by which the baby sent its message was its body—first kicking, then drawing its arms and legs close together. And the message? Just what was it? Was the baby too hot or did it kick because it was experiencing a certain stage of sleep, a body restlessness? And later, was it too cold or

**COMMUNICATION
IS A PART OF MOST
EVERYTHING WE DO.**

THE COMMUNICATION PROCESS:

  THE SENDER
  THE RECEIVER
  THE MESSAGE
  THE MEANS OR MODE

did it pull arms and legs inward, unconsciously, for the secure feeling a fetal position offers? A message, however unclear, was sent and a message, however incorrectly interpreted, was received.

Three important things to learn from this example are (1) we are communicating—either sending or receiving messages—constantly throughout our lives, often without realizing we are doing so, (2) we do not have to speak or write—we send and receive messages in many different ways, and (3) a breakdown or misfunctioning of any of the four elements leads to poor communication, effecting any results that might follow.

Although there are many ways to send and receive messages and convey ideas, they are sent primarily by speaking and writing and are received by listening and reading. In a parent/child relationship, it is obvious that speaking and listening are most often used. There are a variety of ways we can "speak" and "listen" as we shall see later.

Who speaks and who listens? Granted, while parent and child are both either speaking, then listening, and listening, then speaking, it is the **parent as a listener** who is the key to successful communication.

IT IS THE **PARENT AS A LISTENER** WHO IS THE KEY TO SUCCESSFUL COMMUNICATION.

LISTENING TO YOUR CHILD: Four basic skills

In order for a child to believe that his message is being understood, he must know that it is being received—listened to. There are four basic listening skills a parent should be aware of in order to keep communication lines open. They are:

1. Silent listening
2. Supportive listening
3. Promptive listening
4. Reflective listening

Silent Listening

One of the first things we do, or should consider doing, when our child starts speaking to us is to listen silently. As a non-verbal form of communication, it is a silent response that tells him his message is being received. And only if it is received does he know it has a chance of being understood. (Another type of listening, considered shortly, will show him he is understood.) Initially, however, it is important only that he knows you are listening.

How do we respond silently? By using facial expressions and gestures—commonly referred to as *body language*. Here are a few examples:

ALLRIGHT, SON, WAY TO GO!

A nod ("I see.")
Eye contact ("I am here.")
A grin or smile ("That's okay. It's fine. It's great.")
Raised eyebrows ("Oh, you don't say.")
A pat on the back ("I'm with you.")
A "thumbs-up" ("Right on!")

The words in parenthesis suggest what the silent gestures might mean.

Silent listening does two things: (1) it says the parent is tuned in, ready to listen, and (2) it establishes a climate for continued message sending. (The following unit will present other ways for establishing or setting up a good atmosphere for communication, especially where non-compliant behavior has introduced a lot of static or interference.)

The parent as a silent listener may not have an immediate solution to the child's problem or initially even know very much about what the child is speaking. The parent is simply sending silent signals that act as a catalyst to the child's continued speaking. Here's an example:

Alan and his dad are walking along, on their way to a basketball game. They've just been talking about a few school related subjects. Their "conversation" continues:

Alan: *Ya know, dad—*
Dad: (looks down at son and smiles—eye contact)
Alan: *I've been wondering what I'd do for my science report.*
Dad: (puzzled look suggests "Tell me more.")
Alan: *First, I thought I'd do something on rocket development in the 40's. Then I thought something about computers would be better. You know, because they are everywhere nowadays.* (looks up at his dad)
Dad: (nods in agreement)
Alan: *But then everybody'll want to do a report on them. I wondered about holography, but it's too hard to explain to people.*
Dad: (again, a nod in agreement; he doesn't even know what holography is)
Alan: *I've been thinking about lasers, but I'm not sure what aspect to write about. I—I know!*
Dad: (returns Alan's enlightened glance)
Alan: *I'll do it on lasers used in video-discs. Yeh!*
Dad: (as they both arrive at the ticket window at the high school gym, he gives Alan a "thumbs-up" sign meaning "Great idea!" He then turns to window.) *Two in section C, please.*
Alan: *Gee, thanks, Dad. Video-discs. That's a great idea!*

As you can see, this method is especially useful where the child has the means of solving his own problem without parental suggestions or verbal help. Just being able to get it out in the open can help him. Often, hearing ourselves vocalize a problem triggers a solution, while constantly thinking and worrying about it provide no adequate results. Occasionally more involved forms of communication are not possible, because of time limitations. Silent listening can be effective in the car, in an elevator, or any time the sender and receiver can be together for only a short time.

Supportive Listening

This method not only says "I'm listening" but also stimulates the continued dialogue between parent and child. Some silent listening might have preceded it. And, like silent listening, it may be all that is needed for the child to solve his own problems. Supportive listening says in words what silent listening says through body language. The following might help with this type of listening:

SUPPORTIVE LISTENING ENCOURAGES A CONTINUED DIALOGUE.

SUPPORTIVE LISTENING COMMENTS

Really?	**That's right**
Is that right?	**Oh?**
Definitely.	**I agree.**
I see what you mean.	**Oh, I understand.**
You did?	**Of course.**
I see your point.	**Yes, that's great.**
Hmmm.	**You're kidding.**
Right.	**You bet.**
That's nice.	**That's too bad.**
I see.	**Oh, my.**
Oh, no.	**That's happened to me, too.**
I get it.	**Great!**

Let's see how the Silent Listening dialogue between Alan and dad might sound using Supportive Listening:

Alan: *Ya know, Dad—*
Dad: *Yes?*
Alan: *I've been wondering what I'd do for my science report.*
Dad: *Oh?*
Alan: *First, I thought I'd do something on rocket development in the 40's. Then I thought something about computers would be better. You know, because they are everywhere nowadays.* (looks up at his dad)
Dad: *You're right about that.*
Alan: *But then everybody'll want to do a report on them. I wondered about holography, but it's too hard to explain to people.*
Dad: *I guess you're right.*
Alan: *I've been thinking about lasers, but I'm not sure what aspect to write about. I—I know!*
Dad: *You'll what?*
Alan: *I'll do it on lasers used in video-discs. Yeh!*
Dad: *Great idea!* (turns to ticket seller) *Two in section C, please.*
Alan: *Gee, thanks, Dad. Video-discs. That's a great idea!*

In either case, Alan's dad did something that said, "I hear what you're saying." It was sufficient to allow Alan to think out loud, which helped him arrive at a solution.

Promptive Listening

Little Johnny comes home from school, silent and frowning. You can see something is troubling him. He has sent a silent message to you and you have received it. But it is incomplete and in order to help him you must know more. But he continues his dark silence. How can you acknowledge his non-verbal message plus urge him to open up, to tell what's troubling him?

Promptive Listening is effective here because it encourages him to speak without being criticized for his gloomy silence or anything else about it. It says, "I hear you and I want to understand." Only after you get the communication flowing will you be in a position to really show you understand.

In a sense this situation is the reverse of silent listening in that the "speaker" (Johnny) is silent and the "listener" (parent) speaks. Here are some helps for this type of listening:

PROMPTIVE LISTENING SAYS, "I HEAR YOU AND I WANT TO UNDERSTAND."

PROMPTIVE LISTENING COMMENTS

Wanna talk?
Let's go have a soda.
What happened next?
Why is that?
What's the matter?
Need a listening ear?
How'd your day go?
Need a friend?
What's *your* answer?

Can I help you with anything?
Would you like to go for a walk?
How does that make you feel?
How did school go today?
You look hurt. What happened?
Do you want to talk about something?
What do you think about what
    happened to Jeff? and
What could he do about it?

The list seems endless and is limited only by one's imagination and perception. Using promptive listening and some of the suggested comments from the above list, let's return to Johnny, silent and frowning.

Mom:	*Hi, Johnny. Is it that time already?* (notices his frown) *Say, you seem sad. Would you like to tell me about it?*
Johnny:	*Ah, it was nothin'.*
Mom:	*Are you sure? Come on into the kitchen and I'll get you some cookies and milk and you can tell me about it.* (gives Johnny cookies and glass of milk) *There, now do you suppose you could tell me about it. Okay?*
Johnny:	*Well, it was Robert. He—* (hesitates)
Mom:	*Oh, is that the boy who sits next to you?*
Johnny:	*Yes.*
Mom:	*And, what about Robert?*
Johnny:	*He dropped some papers in the aisle between our desks and—* (hesitates again)
Mom:	*—and then what happened?*
Johnny:	*Well, I grabbed for one, you know, to pick it up and then— and—*
Mom:	*—and?*

—AND THEN WHAT HAPPENED, SON?

WELL...

123

Johnny:	*He grabbed the other edge and it tore.*
Mom:	*What happened next?*
Johnny:	*Miss Rollins must've heard the paper tear, I guess and—*
Mom:	*—and what did she do?*
Johnny:	*She scolded us both for fighting over a piece of paper and made us stay after school.*
Mom:	*Do you think she was right?*
Johnny:	*No. We weren't fightin' or anything.*
Mom:	*Did you tell Miss Rollins what had happened?*
Johnny:	*No. 'Cause we didn't think she'd believe us.*
Mom:	*That might have helped. You see, sometimes a person doesn't know the whole story about something and—*

Johnny's mother has now found out what was bothering him and can continue talking to him, helping him understand and learn from his experience.

Reflective Listening

When we look in a mirror, several things happen. Our image is reflected back to us. We see ourselves as we are and as we think we are. It reflects back our physical reality or self. But also it triggers responses within us such as positive or negative attitudes about our appearance, our height or facial features (things we can't easily change) or our clothing or hair style (which can be modified or adjusted).

MIRROR MIRROR STANDING TALL...

Parents act like mirrors in reflecting back to the child (through any of the various communication methods) attitudes or impressions about him, his appearance, or his actions. Some parents are like broken mirrors, however, reflecting back to the child ideas and opinions about him that give him a distorted image or concept of himself.

It is the parental mirror that needs to be fixed if the child is to be helped. One of the best ways is through *Reflective Listening.*

Reflective listening means that the parent sends back the child's message to him—but in special ways. Repeating a child's message back to him almost word for word—this is called *parroting*—says that you are hearing what he is saying, but not necessarily understanding what he is meaning. A slightly better approach is *paraphrasing*—using your words to tell him what you heard him say. It gives him a chance to say, "That's not what I said." It still does not suggest understanding, but it moves the dialogue in that direction.

There are times when parroting and paraphrasing are sufficient. For example, if someone gave you directions on how to find a certain address, you could parrot back or paraphrase what you heard him say, so you would be able to reach your destination without having to ask someone else later. Here we are dealing with a process—understanding directions. No feelings or attitudes are involved.

But, when we realize that more than understanding of instructions or directions is involved, we should see that *reflective listening* is warranted.

When we listen reflectively, we should use words that show we understand the child's feelings. For example: Mary comes into the house with a forlorn look on her face and says to her mother, "Debbie is moving to the other side of the state in two weeks." Is she doing something besides relaying information? You bet. For mother to paraphrase, "Oh, Debbie is moving across state in a few weeks?" doesn't help. It isn't enough. Instead, saying, "Mary, I can see you're very upset that your best friend is moving so far away" acknowledges not only information but also feelings. Mary's mother has now placed herself in a position to help Mary handle her disappointment. (She might suggest writing letters regularly, controlled telephone calls, and perhaps summer visits.)

REFLECTIVE LISTENING SHOWS THAT WE RECOGNIZE AND UNDERSTAND A CHILD'S FEELINGS.

Effective reflective listening should include the following: *reference to the child, identification of the feeling and its intensity,* and *the reason for the feeling.* Let's look at mother's response to Mary:

Reference to the child *(c)* — *Mary*

Intensity of the feeling *(i)* — I can see that you are *very*

Identification of feeling *(f)* — *upset*

Reason for the feeling *(r)* — that *your friend is moving.*

Here are a few others:

(c) *(i)* *(f)*
"*John,* I can see you are *extremely upset* with Robert *(r)* because *you thought he was unfair.*

(c) *(i)* *(f)* *(r)*
"*Julie,* you're *terribly excited* about *staying overnight at Nancy's,* aren't you?"

As the above example shows, reflective listening doesn't have to be used in problem-based situations only. Sometimes a child has something to share and words alone don't convey the whole message. In this case, Julie knows that mother, because of her response, understands her enthusiasm. It has been said that **sharing doubles a pleasure and halves a problem.**

Reflective listening, as you can see, is a means of helping a child sort out his or her feelings, and for parent and child to understand the real reasons for them.

Sharing doubles a pleasure and halves a problem.

125

I-MESSAGES

While reflective listening let's the child know that you know how **he** feels about a situation, it doesn't tell him how **you** feel about his behavior or his problems. Sending *I-Messages* can show him you not only understand but also that you **care**. They are intended to focus on you, not the child. So much parental conversation is laced with "you."

*"**You** go to **your** room."*
*"If **you** don't stop, **you**'ll get a spanking."*
*"Don't (**you**) be impolite."*
*"Why don't **you** make **your** bed."*
*"**You**'re being awfully careless."*
*"It's not like **you** to act that way."*
*"**You**'re naughty."*
*"**You** always bother me when I want to rest."*
*"Who taught **you** to say that?"*

"You" messages, directed so specifically toward the child, tend to be critical of him. They suggest that he, not his behavior, is the problem.

Using I-Messages, we are able to tell him how we feel about his behavior, rather than being judgemental of him. An I-Message usually consists of three parts:

1. **Reference to child's behavior**
2. **How the I-Message sender feels about it**
3. **Why the I-Message sender feels that way**

Here is an example, using 1, 2, and 3 above:

"When you don't come right home from school (1), I get very worried (2), because I think something might have happened to you (3)."

When a child receives a "you" message, he usually hears something negative about himself. For example, if you are tired and don't want to be bothered and you say, "Please stop bothering me," the child thinks "I'm bad," However, if you say,"I'm too tired right now," he thinks only "Dad's tired." He still may not have received the attention he wanted but at least nothing was said to promote a negative image of himself.

Remember then, while reflective listening lets the child know you understand **his** feelings, using I-Messages helps him understand **yours**.

I-Messages may not always work in changing a child's behavior. But they are important because they tell the child something about you (the parent) rather than point out something bad about him.

> **"I"-messages not only show that you understand, but also that you care.**

> **"You"-messages tend to be critical of the child.**

Voice Tone

Because I-Messages are expressing how *we feel,* we need to make sure that the tone of our voice agrees with these messages. In fact, if voice tone is not matching or supporting the understanding any of our words are meant to convey, then we're sending conflicting messages and our child can't help but be confused. Our voice can convey anger, impatience, fear, or frustration or it can express interest, happiness, enthusiasm, or concern.

The same words, with different tones or gestures (body language), can send opposite messages. For example, let's take the short message:

"Well, I like you, too."

If Patty whispers this softly in Dave's ear, she is most likely responding to an endearing remark he's just made. But, if she puts voiced exclamation marks after "Well" and "too" when speaking to Barbara, she's most likely responding to a negative comment or action from Barbara. Shaking your fist and shouting angrily at your dog, "Hey! You're a nice dog!" doesn't get his tail wagging. These are, of course, exaggerated examples, but hopefully they show that mixed signals do not help your child or any other member of your family move forward and grow in a positive direction.

LET'S PUT IT ALL TOGETHER

Let's contrast two different dialogues talking about the same subject—buying a car—and see how the four main types of listening skills, plus I-Messages and voice tone can make a difference.

DIALOGUE ONE

Tom: *Dad—*
Dad: (Busy with paper, doesn't look up)
Tom: *—uh, Dad. Chris and I saw this car that—*
Dad: (grunts a response) *Mmm-m?* (continues reading)
Tom: *—that'd be a great buy—a real steal and—*
Dad: *What'd you say?*
Tom: *I found a car I'd—*
Dad: *You've got to be kidding! You can't afford a car. You're too young to own one. You're—*
Tom: *But, Dad—*
Dad: *Don't 'but' me. I don't want to hear another word. Besides, can't you see I'm busy.* (returns angrily to his newspaper)

Both Tom and his dad are frustrated. Almost all of dad's comments are "you" messages. Now consider the following version.

MAKE SURE THE TONE OF YOUR VOICE MATCHES THE MEANING OF YOUR WORDS.

DIALOGUE TWO

	Tom: *Dad—*
silent listening ❱	**Dad:** (glances up from newspaper)
	Tom: *—uh, Dad. Chris and I— uhh—*
supportive listening ❱	**Dad:** *Yes, son?*
	Tom: *Chris and I were looking in the paper and saw this car that was advertised and—*
promptive listening ❱	**Dad:** *—and you want to buy it. Am I right?*
	Tom: *Yeh.*
promptive listening ❱	**Dad:** *Tell me about it.*
	Tom: (describes the car)
reflective listening ❱	**Dad:** *Tom, I can see you'd be very happy if you had this car.*
	Tom: (grins) *Yeh, Dad.*
	Dad: *I want to make sure you'd be happy with it. Let's see what it would actually cost you.* (Dad points out monthly payments, interest costs, insurance, operation, and repair expenses)
	Tom: *Gee, $195 a month?*
paraphrasing ❱	**Dad:** *Yes, at least $195.*
	Tom: *I could work on Saturdays.*
I-message ❱	**Dad:** *I'd be a bit concerned about your working so much extra because it might interfere with your basketball practices, especially on Saturdays. I know you were hoping for that sports scholarship next year.*
	Tom: *You're right. I hadn't thought about that.*
silent listening reflective listening ❱	**Dad:** (puts arm around Tom's shoulder) *Son, I know you really had your heart set on getting a car now. I'd feel better if you waited until next summer. Then you'd have time to earn more money and basketball would be over. Let's talk about it again later, okay?*
	Tom: *Yeh, Dad. Thanks.*

In neither example did Tom get what he originally wanted—a car. But in the second example he got something perhaps more important at the time—a listening ear from an understanding father. He knows his dad gave him a fair hearing and that his dad is interested in him.

All forms of communication—especially listening—used with understanding and open-mindedness can solve many behavioral problems and set a positive tone to parent/child relationships. Perhaps even more important, developing good listening skills and communication patterns early in a parent/child relationship will prevent many potential behavioral problems from developing in the first place.

Surely, if we were to wear the hearing-aid of understanding and follow the advice of an elderly lady as to her success in life: "I always taste my words, before I let them pass between my teeth" we would establish an atmosphere of love and harmony in our home.

The next unit presents other ways of establishing a positive climate of communication in the home.

SUMMARY OF BASIC COMMUNICATION TECHNIQUES			
TECHNIQUE	WHAT DOES IT SAY?	EXAMPLES OF MESSAGES	WHEN TO USE
SILENT LISTENING	I hear you.	Eye contact Wink Pat on back Positive shrug	Limited time. Child can solve own problem.
SUPPORTIVE LISTENING	I hear you.	Yes. That's too bad. Is that so? Hmm-m.	Limited time. Child can solve own problem.
PROMPTIVE LISTENING	I hear you. I'm trying to understand.	Why is that? What happened next? How'd your day go? What's your answer?	To draw out reluctant speaker. Encourage without criticizing.
REFLECTIVE LISTENING	I understand how you feel.	I can see that you are very upset that you can't go to the dance.	To show you are interested and you're trying to understand.
Parroting	I want to make sure I know what you are saying.	(Repeat message back word for word.)	To make sure you know what they mean or say.
Paraphrasing	(same as parroting)	(Repeat message back in your own words.)	(same as parroting)
I-MESSAGES	I want you to know how I feel about you and why.	I worry when you climb up the tree because the branches are slippery and you might fall.	To show your feelings about their behavior. Use instead of showing criticism of them.

COMMUNICATION—USING THE POWER OF LANGUAGE
Exercise 8.1
UNDERSTANDING LISTENING SKILLS

SILENT LISTENING   See how much you can say without using words.

1. Stand in front of a mirror. Pretend someone is talking to you. Answer using only facial expressions and gestures. (For example, how would you express, "Is that so?" silently?)

2. Pair off with another person. Let that person do the talking. See how long you can sustain the conversation by using silent language only.

3. Pair off with another person. As you "speak" using facial expressions and body language, have the person repeat, using words, your silent language.

SUPPORTIVE LISTENING   In part 3 above you were a part of a supportive listening experience (your partner's comments should have been similar to what you would say in supportive listening.)

4. Without turning back to page 102, write as many supportive listening comments as you can in three (3) minutes. Compare your answers. How many new ones do you have?

PROMPTIVE LISTENING

5. Draw a circle around the following comments that are a part of promptive listening.

   That's right. Need a friend? How does that make you feel? What happened next? Right. I get it.

   How come? How'd your day go? That's too bad. I see. What's the matter? Of course. Can I help you?

   Need someone to listen? You seem excited; would you share it with me? Why the sad face? Great!

   (NOTE: What do most Promptive Listening Comments have in common?*)

6. Pair off with another person. That person starts off with a comment such as: "I went shopping yesterday." The only replies you may make are Promptive Listening Comments. See how long you can keep the conversation going. (Remember, a PLC is nothing more than a well-phrased question.)

REFLECTIVE LISTENING

   Debbie comes home and says to you, "Amy told me she didn't want to sleep over Friday night." (She's frowning.)

7. Parrot back her statement.

8. Now, paraphrase it.

9. Now, using reflective listening, write down what Debbie was probably trying to say. (See page 105 for help, if necessary.)

10. Having used reflective listening in part nine, what might you do to find out more about the Debbie/Amy problem?

I—MESSAGES

   Change the following "you"-messages to "I"-messages. (See page 106, if necessary, for the three parts of an "I"-message.)

11. "You never make your bed."

12. "Why don't you ever do what I say?"

13. "You sure were out late last night."

VOICE TONE

   Read the following short sentences and change their meaning using different tones of voice. (Support your words with facial expressions and/or body language, if you wish; consider using "voiced" punctuation, such as a question mark or exclamation point, to help you.)

14. Would you come here   Right now   You little devil
    I'm sorry you can't go   I said no   Aren't you nice

PUT IT ALL TOGETHER

15. Take a piece of paper and cover up the words in the column to the left of Dialogue Two on page 108. Now see how many listening and communication skills you can identify.

* Promptive listening comments are usually questions.

COMMUNICATION—USING THE POWER OF LANGUAGE

Exercise 8.2

ANALYZE YOUR LISTENING AND COMMUNICATION PATTERNS

Sometimes self-analysis is difficult, because when we are conscious of observing ourselves, our behavior changes somewhat from what it normally is. So, for this exercise, it would be best to have someone help you—someone who understands the listening and communication skills of this unit.

Have your helper/observer make note of how you use the following:

1. Silent listening
2. Supportive listening
3. Promptive listening
4. Parroting and paraphrasing
5. Reflective listening
6. I—Messages
7. Voice tone

SOME SUGGESTIONS:

1. At first, observer/helper might concentrate only on one of the seven at a time, until he or she can handle more, without getting confused.

2. Helper might pick one-half hour blocks for observing each of the seven. Of course, choose times when sufficient conversation is taking place.

3. Helper should not alert you **when** he or she is observing **which** type.

4. If a helper is not available, use a tape recorder. Naturally, this will not help you "observe" silent listening.

5. If neither a helper nor a tape recorder is available, try observing yourself, using, as best you can, suggestions one and two above.

6. Trade turns with your helper, if you have one. You be the observer. (This will help you also be more alert to your own communication patterns.)

A FAMILY EXERCISE IN OBSERVING COMMUNICATION PATTERNS:

TV programs are full of excellent examples of good and poor communication. Parents (and children old enough to understand any of the seven areas listed above) can watch a program together and see how many of the seven can be found in one program. (At first you may want to concentrate on only one or two areas and then expand your observation to others.)

After you have studied Unit Nine and become familiar with some patterns of miscommunication, you could use this TV exercise in identifying the various patterns of miscommunication.

This exercise can make TV viewing a more valuable family experience than it usually is.

131

QUESTIONS and ANSWERS

Q. Is it possible to use too much reflective listening with your child? My child often gets upset when I use reflective listening.

A. Yes. Anything can be overdone. Keep in mind the more reflective listening you do the better you will become at it. However, reflective listening is useful to the degree it helps the parent and child resolve problem situations.

Q. It seems to me that it could be quite boring if everyone sat around using reflective listening. Is it really necessary?

A. All families who are successfully communicating are not necessarily using reflective listening. Some families are comfortable in arguing with each other. Other families are quiet and seldom talk things out. A person who goes into a ghetto and tries reflective listening with a teenage gang may find himself in trouble fast because such tactics may not be considered acceptable. Life is full of sub-groups with different ways of communicating acceptably. Reflective listening is more suitable and acceptable in middle-class environments. But it is a basically sound and psychologically appealing means of listening that most of us could benefit from using.

Q. The unit argues "you" messages are bad. Is that always the case? My husband uses them on our teenager and their father/son relationship is good.

A. "You" messages may be interpreted by some as attacking their self-worth, but they are not always interpreted that way. It is just that I-Messages are less likely to be interpreted as being critical of the child. I-Messages tend to focus more on the act of the child rather than on the character of the child. Some children are used to dad griping at them, but through repeated experiences have come to realize that grumpy dad really loves them, and that what he says is not really what he means. It is best, however, for children to hear us say what we mean. I-Messages are good ways of expressing to our child what we mean and why.

Q. I've tried some of the listening techniques on my son and it doesn't seem to have helped. He still reacts negatively to what I do or say. So, what do I do now?

A. Remember, it has probably taken months and even years to create the relationship you find yourself in with your son. So, it can't be corrected overnight. Be patient. Persist in using positive listening techniques. You may not always agree with your child's views on certain matters, but let him know you respect his right to have them.

Communication: Developing a Good Climate

Can you change methods of miscommunication if you don't know you're using them? Not likely. This unit points out a number of misconceptions about and problems in the communication process: the *message*—where do words get their meaning?; the *receiver*—jumping to conclusions, making generalizations, frozen evaluations, labeling; the *sender*—the "know-it-all," the "I'm right and you're wrong" approach; the *method* of communication—proper timing and proper place. Many other tips for improving communication finish out this unit.

CLIMATE OF COMMUNICATION — CLOUDY OR BRIGHT?

The kind of communication in the home has a direct relationship on the misbehavior and non-compliance of children. As a general rule, it might be said:

communication = compliance
miscommunication = misbehavior

Two major purposes of this unit are to help parents (1) establish a positive atmosphere and climate for communication and (2) improve the behavior of non-compliant or misbehaving children through improved communication. Previous units have discussed misbehavior as a problem children should overcome. This unit will focus on miscommunication as a problem which the parent must make the greatest effort to solve. This does not mean that the child has to do nothing. Some children have well-developed skills in some types of miscommunication. However, it is the parents or other adults who unknowingly use and teach their children to use poor communication. Certainly, both parent and child must work together in correcting any problem, regardless of who was more the cause of its development, but it should be the responsibility of the parent to lead out, assist, and preside over any remedies for miscommunication.

Some of the most common forms of miscommunication will be considered here. Each one will consist of (1) a description or explanation of the problem, (2) an example, and (3) what might be done to correct it. Sometimes, an awareness of a problem is sufficient to initiate a correction of it.

PARENTS SHOULD LEAD OUT IN ESTABLISHING GOOD COMMUNICATION PATTERNS.

One of the best times and places to start: reading and talking to a child at bedtime.

Miscommunication takes so many forms and many are so interrelated that considering one separately from another becomes somewhat confusing and repetitious. To facilitate their explanation they are arranged into four groups:

1. misconceptions about the value of words (the message)
2. misconceptions parents have about the child (message receiver)
3. misconceptions parents have about themselves (message sender)
4. misconceptions about the environment of communication (atmosphere, time, and place)

MISCONCEPTIONS ABOUT THE VALUE OF WORDS (The Message)

Words have power—the power to build or to destroy, to strengthen or to weaken, to promote happiness or bring sadness. The positive power and value of words is increased when we understand just what words really do and learn some things they don't do.

The positve power of words is increased when we understand what they do and don't do.

Talking Past Each Other

Miscommunication can take place when parents think the words they use carry the same meaning to the child. As a result, the message sent is not always the one received. Consider the following example:

It's the day before Easter. Eight-year-old Julie calls out to her mother, who is going next door for a few minutes, "Mom, can I fix some Easter eggs?" "Okay," replies her mother, "put two dozen eggs in a large pan and cook them for at least 15 minutes."

Julie finds an extra large pan, fills it full of cold water, adds the eggs, and turns the burner on to medium. (Mother has told her before never to turn the burner on high when she is by herself.) Exactly 15 minutes later she removes the pan from the stove and spoons the eggs out to cool.

While she's getting the dyes ready, her brother, Chris, comes in and teases her. "I bet you didn't cook these long enough." "I did so," she replies. "Exactly 15 minutes—just like Mom said."

"Wanna see how hard my head is?" replies Chris as he grabs an egg. He hits it against his head and raw egg runs down his hair.

In the miscommunication which took place between Julie and her mother their understandings of the word *cook* were different. Mother's meant *to boil*; Julie's meant *put it on a burner*.

The above example represents just one type of talking past each other. (Another is where different words having the same meaning are used. In England you look under the *bonnet* (hood) of your car, open the *boot* (trunk) to get out a *tyre* (tire); then

PAIRS OR PEARS

Twelve pairs hanging high,
Twelve knights riding by,
Each night took a pear,
Yet left a dozen there.

Mother Goose Rhyme

you check the *petrol* (gasoline) before you go up the *lift* (elevator) that takes you to your *flat* (apartment).

A solution: The first step is to realize that **words do not have meaning—people do.** Words are merely vehicles for carrying meanings and ideas people send to each other.

Julie's mother failed to realize the word *cook* did not carry her meaning *boil.* Hopefully she learned next time to question her own messages to her daughter by asking: *Does she really know what I mean? Did she hear me in the first place? Does she know how to do what I ask?*

WORDS DO NOT HAVE MEANING— PEOPLE DO.

Deliberately Talking Past Each Other

Better than their parents, children often understand more about words as vehicles for communicating information and deliberately use them to manipulate messages. They use words to get their parents to hear and believe what their parents want to hear and believe. *"But, everybody's going."* (Translation: Jill and Nancy are going.) *"I came in second."* (Everyone else tied for first place.) *I lost five dollars . . ."* (. . . playing poker).

Not telling all the facts or withholding information is a form of talking past each other.

Rephrasing (paraphrasing), asking questions, and requesting feedback are all aids to lessening this problem.

Talking vs. Doing

Which is more important—the map or the territory it represents? Our evaluation of a person or the person himself? Talking about doing something or doing it?

Do we let attitudes, inferences, theories, feelings, imaginings—all in the form of talk, talk, talk—take precedence over people, happenings, or relationships? Even though "talk is cheap," most children won't pay the price of listening if there is no action to back up your words.

Words mean little if there is no action to back them up.

"Gee, Dad. I didn't hear you say that."
"Oh, did you call me?"
"You never told me to do that."
"I didn't think you really meant it."

Children soon learn that parents don't always mean what they say or often don't follow through. "Tuning out" is one of the skills a child develops early when talk is not followed by action.

Eddie, age four, asks his mother if he can have an orange that he sees on the kitchen counter. Mother says no, that it is too close to dinner. Eddie whines, reaches for the orange and says, "I WANT AN ORANGE!" He starts to climb up on the counter to get it. Mother takes him down and says, "No. They are too messy." Eddie waits a few minutes until mother is doing something else nearby, then climbs on the counter, gets the orange,

takes it into the living room, sits down on the rug, and begins to bite off the peelings and spit them out on the floor. Mother sees him, decides it is not worth the effort to stop him, and says, "If you're going to eat that orange, Eddie, don't be messy." But he continues eating the orange, stuffing it into his mouth, juice running down his face and arms and dripping on the rug. When he is half finished, he grows tired of it and leaves it and the peelings on the rug. Mother sees the mess and says, "Eddie, since you made the mess, you'll have to clean it up." She gives him something to put the peelings in, takes a washcloth and wipes off his face and arms, and then proceeds to pick up the peelings herself.

A parental evaluation can show if this is a problem. Ask yourself the following questions:

Do I mean what I say?
Do I follow my words with actions?
If I tell my child to expect a certain consequence for misbehavior, do I act or am I just talk?
Do I keep my promises?

Here are a few more questions to evaluate yourself in your parental role as a counselor:

Am I good at giving advice?
Do my words become preachments? Do my children get that "No, not again" look when I start talking.
Do my children even come to me for advice any more?

Almost always the best way parents can give meaning to their words is through actions. That's where much of the meaning lies. The old saying—"actions speak louder than words"—is very true in effective parent/child communication. It's an unusual person who can talk a grizzly bear out of attacking him. And it's an equally unusual parent who can effectively **talk** a child into becoming a successful adult.

DON'T USE WORDS TO SAY WHAT YOU REALLY DON'T MEAN.

What you say will be determined by whom you're saying it to.

Honest encouragement given a small child—"You sure are getting big and strong. I know you can do it"—would seem phony to an older child.

More Words on Words

Don't let the previous statements about words suggest that without action, they have no meaning, no strength. Words alone do have influence—a very negative one—when used to flatter, as reverse psychology, to show sarcasm, or when used in anger.

Don't use flattery. Don't say it if you don't mean it. Children are perhaps more perceptive to the dishonesty in others than they are to their own. Don't "butter-up" or "soft-soap" your child. (Someone has said that flattery is soft-soap and soap is 99% lye—lies.) Don't praise him if your next step is to ask him if he'd like to do something for you. Honest encouragement is very valuable to a child; insincere praise can only hurt him.

Don't say the opposite of what you mean, hoping you can get the child to do what you wish. A parent might think that because a child sometimes does the opposite of what is asked, intentionally asking him to do the opposite of what is really wanted will produce the desired result in the end. Your request may backfire. Such "reverse" communication will condition your child to tune out all your messages—even the honest ones. Be straightforward and honest in your requests.

BE STRAIGHTFORWARD AND HONEST IN YOUR REQUESTS.

Don't be sarcastic or biting. Don't speak in a way that demeans. Words should never be used against a child. It is the act, not the child, that should receive criticism, if any. Parents may remember a saying from their childhood—"Sticks and stones will hurt my bones, but names and faces will never hurt me." They were said as perhaps the only means available of "striking back" at an injury. They were not true then. They are not true today. Sarcasm—"names and faces"—and other demeaning words do hurt. Their bruises endure after the bodily ones are long gone.

SARCASM AND DEMEANING WORDS DO HURT.

Don't speak or reply in anger or frustration. Delay your reply. We say things we don't mean when we are not in control. The frustrations of parental problems should not cloud the messages sent to the child. Such frustrations (about today's golf game, disagreement with the boss, an overdrawn bank account) are interpreted by the child as frustrations about him. The judge may tell the jury to strike that last statement from their minds; the parent may say "I'm sorry." You can take the words back, but their meaning remains.

Don't use a double standard of communication. Perhaps you are not aware that you do. Do you speak differently to your boss than you do to your children? Do you speak more loudly and harshly to them? Are you more demanding, more impatient? Try the following: Listen to yourself as you speak to a misbehaving or demanding child. Now imagine you have just been talking to your boss instead. How would you feel? How would your boss feel? (Would you still be working there?) Our spouse and our children should be more important than our job. They deserve the same kind of consideration (if not better) we show others through our speech and actions.

MISCONCEPTIONS PARENTS HAVE ABOUT THE CHILD
(Message Receiver)

Our understanding, or lack of it, of children—their world, their friends, their feelings, their capabilities, everything about them—affects our communication with them. Parents must try to see a child's world through a child's eyes, not just through parental eyes. The following patterns of miscommunication and misunderstanding develop because parents fail to consider both worlds—the child's and their own.

137

**JUMPING TO CONCLUSIONS
CAUSES A CHILD TO:**

• not admit to wrongdoing
• blame another person for it

Jumping to Conclusions

Good communication and positive relationships with children are weakened when a parent speaks or acts on assumptions rather than observations or knowledge of misbehavior. Assumptions *(jumping to conclusions)* motivate a child to either (1) not admit to a wrongdoing or (2) blame another person for it—both forms of dishonesty.

Let's look at an example:

Arguing voices are coming from the next room. "It's your fault!" shouts Jeremy. "No, it's yours!" responds Jeffery. You investigate. The five-year-old twins have been painting with watercolors. The glass of water they were using to clean the brushes is on the floor, its muddy contents soaking into the throw rug. (They have been told before never to use watercolors in that part of the room, where the rugs are.) You know the glass didn't tip over by itself. Who did it? "It was Jeremy's fault!" "No, he did it!" The mutual blaming continues.

What do you do: You might assume it was Jeremy's fault—he **always** was the clumsy one. Jeffery's accounts of previous "accidents" and "wrongdoings" often have proved to be correct, so perhaps he's right again in accusing his brother. He must have done it. And so you assume—jump to conclusions—Jeremy is the culprit and . . .

There are two things to consider here: (1) what should be done now and (2) how to "get the facts" about future problems.

The immediate solution. First, analyze the problem: (1) there was an accident (spilled water), (2) there was an initial misbehavior (painting in the wrong place), and (3) there was a second misbehavior (the child having the accident and/or initial misbehavior failing to admit to it).

You have separated the accident from the misbehavior. (It isn't so important that an accident occurred. Life is full of them—little and big.) As long as you don't know who spilled the water and neither child will admit to doing it, both should be required to clean up the mess. That should take care of the accident. It is the misbehavior—painting in the wrong place—that must be considered and dealt with. Because of their misbehavior you might have them **both** put the paints away and then **both** experience a consequence suitable to them and the situation. (Fill out an *Outline for Action* form to analyze this particular problem with its appropriate rewards and penalties.) **Note:** While it is appropriate to have two or three children suffer the consequences for misbehavior as in the previous example, it is not advisable to use such punishment on a larger group. For instance, if one child in a classroom full of children misbehaves, do not punish the whole class for the misbehavior. When the quantity of innocent individuals greatly outnumbers the guilty, it is unfair to make them all suffer the consequence.

The long-term remedy. If children always told the truth about their actions, then parents could not jump to conclusions, or so one might hope. It would seem, then, that the child is the solution to this parental fault. It is not that easy. It still needs a parental remedy.

Why doesn't a child (or other person) tell the truth? Because of the payoffs or consequences. Honesty often brings punishment rather than rewards; withholding the truth eliminates or delays punishment.

Jeremy has learned from previous experiences that when he told the truth he was still punished. His parents do not separate the misbehavior from the admission of it. He interprets his punishment to be for both.

Here are some suggestions for preventing assumptions from directing your behavior and for dealing with the problem assumptions breed—dishonesty.

1. Separate accidents from misbehaviors.
2. If more than one child (but not a group) is involved and neither admits to the problem, all involved should receive the consequence of the misbehavior.
3. Vary the degree of punishment depending upon the manner in which the "owner" of the misbehavior is made known. If appropriate evidence shows Jeremy is at fault his punishment is greater if he does not admit to his error. If, after confrontation by parents, he admits to the wrongdoing, the punishment is less severe. If he admits to the problem without parental probing, the punishment is even less. An alternative here would be to allow him to choose his own punishment. Varying the degree of punishment as suggested can show him that honesty pays.

Parental participation in dealing with problems should be that of finding fair solutions, not one of creating more problems in the future by assuming or jumping to conclusions.

Indiscrimination

Indiscrimination is simply the failure to discriminate or to separate like things from one another. If you have a negative attitude toward teenagers who ride motorcycles and your son's new friend owns a motorcycle, you might be inclined to ask him to be more careful with whom he runs around. Many parents have the attitude that almost all teenagers like loud music, use drugs, rebel against adult authority and show disrespect to their parents and other adults. *"Oh, you kids nowadays are all alike."*

We shouldn't be guilty of neglecting the individual differences of others, especially our own children. We must realize that just because one person or group likes or dislikes something or acts in a certain fashion that not all others follow suit.

It is important to recognize the individuality of each of our children and be sensitive to these differences. One child should not have to live up to the successes of an older brother or sister, nor should a child be judged by the previous good or poor behavior of someone who has preceded him.

MAKE SURE YOUR CHILD IS NOT PUNISHED FOR BEING HONEST.

SEPARATE ACCIDENTS FROM MISBEHAVIORS.

There are better ways to exercise than "jumping to conclusions."

OH, YOU KIDS ARE ALL ALIKE!

139

Look for the good in your child and his friends—you'll find it. Expect the bad, and you'll probably get it, too. We all tend to live up (or down) to the expectations of others, especially our parents.

Indiscrimination, then, is when a parent classifies or pigeonholes everything into "neat" categories. Someone has called it a "hardening of the categories." Such attitudes make parents inflexible to good understanding and communication.

Using Generalizations

This, like indiscrimination, is a form of passing judgment. Using generalizations is a form of exaggeration. It weakens communication because it fails to deal with specifics.

"If I've told you once, I've told you a thousand times!"
*"You **always** talk back."*
*"You **never** make your bed."*
*"I can **never** depend on you."*

GENERALIZATIONS ACCENTUATE THE NEGATIVE AND SUGGEST THERE NEVER WAS ANY GOOD BEHAVIOR.

Generalizations accentuate the negative, suggesting that there never was any good behavior. Using generalizations and other judgmental terms has become a habit for many parents. The "nos," the "can'ts," the "bads," the "nevers" by far outweigh their opposite—"yes," "can," "good," and so forth. Try the following to help replace the negative with some positive: consciously listen to your words. Each time you make a negative comment or speak critically, as soon as possible and before you make a second such remark, say something complimentary, something positive. Then change the ratio—one negative to two positives; then one to three, one to four . . .

Once a Problem, Always a Problem

In a land of choice, we are all capable of moving from success to failure and back again.

Should the previous misbehavior of a child cause a parent to expect similar behavior again? Once bad, always bad? Parental assumption of non-change in a child's behavior will not help in changing it for the better. In a land of choice we are all capable of moving from success to failure and back to success again, whether we be a parent or a child. It is the assumption that a non-compliant or misbehaving child (or an unsuccessful or frustrated parent) must remain so that causes such to happen. Parents should not let attitudes get in their way or that of their children in making an "about face" toward success.

Some parents bring up a child's previous misbehavior as a reason why a current misbehavior occurs. Such judgments take the form of generalizations (previously mentioned) such as: "You **always** do it wrong." Remember Jeremy and the spilled water: "—he **always** was the clumsy one."

Another variation is letting a child's previous bad actions become a parental reason for disallowing certain privileges, activities, or responsibilities. *"I can't trust you any more after what you did last week."*

In place of assuming non-change in a child (or in yourself as a parent) consider the circumstances surrounding the "problem": the timing, the place, other individuals involved—all the variables that might have been an influence. Then remember—they may never be the same again. Move forward and deal with the variables of the present.

Guilty by Association (Labeling)

Here is a slight variation of making incorrect or unkind judgments. It has to do with putting labels on people—especially children. The two-edged sword called "expectations" can strengthen or kill the spirit of a child. Positive expectations, supported by well-balanced parental help and encouragement helps produce happy and successful children. The cutting edge of negative expectations—living up to labels—produces "dumb" and "lazy" children. A parent who labels his child "dumb" soon has a dumb child. A "lazy" label produces a lazy child. Don't let the label obscure the "product."

Assess your child's abilities and encourage his expectations for developing them. Help him determine and develop **his** expectations for himself and support him in achieving them. Ask yourself—are these my expectations or his? Are they positive rather than negative?

Positive labels, if unrealistic, may put pressure on a child to be what he is not yet capable of becoming.

MISCONCEPTIONS PARENTS HAVE ABOUT THEMSELVES (Message Sender)

The way parents communicate with their children is influenced by the way they feel about themselves and how they interpret their past.

"Now, when I was your age I had to milk thirty cows before breakfast and walk four miles to school through three feet of snow."
"This is how we did it when . . ."

A father's employment responsibilities (his place on the corporate ladder) may affect his communication approach:

"Why, as president of Ajax Enterprises, I ought to be able to successfully supervise a wife and a bunch of kids. Just let them know who's boss."

Here are several examples where parental concepts about themselves or their role as parents affect flexible and considerate communication.

It's difficult for anyone to talk to someone who has ALL the answers.

The Know-It-All

Children learn to "tune-out" a parent who has all the answers, knows all there is about the subject under discussion, who only listens to his side of the story, or who must always have the last word. Such a parent robs the child of a desire to do what is asked and to respond positively to a parent's suggestions and requests.

141

Parental superiority and infallibility manifest themselves in the following ways:

"Here, let me do that. I've done it a thousand times." (There's another generalization.)
"That's so simple. I could do it with my eyes closed."
"You're 16 and can't even . . . Why, when I was only 11, I was . . ."
"Just ask your ol' dad. I wrote the book about that one."

Children shouldn't be expected to know as much as an adult (unless it's about computer games.)

These examples of parental superiority don't take into account that children shouldn't be expected, with their fewer years of experience, to know as much as an adult (although with today's new technology, it is easily possible for some children to know a lot more about some things than their parents). Comments like those previously mentioned squelch the youthful desire to please.

"The matter's closed! I've told you how it is—no more discussion."
"I don't need to know your side of the story. I've already made up my mind."

Some parents permit no point of view other than their own. Like the blindmen in *The Blindmen and the Elephant,** their judgments are based only on what they see or believe—their side of the story only.

Here are a few suggestions:

SAYING "I DON'T KNOW" MAKES YOU NO LESS A PARENT.

1. You are no less of a parent if you say "I don't know."
2. Don't expect your child to know everything you know.
3. Accept the fact that your child may know more about some things—computers, lasers, or holograms and so forth. Such things may not have been a part of your growing-up world.
4. Appreciate a child for where he's at and don't judge him on the basis of where you are.

Appreciate a child for where he's at and don't judge him on the basis of where you are.

The Either-Or Approach

It's either good or it's bad. I'm right and you're wrong. I win and you lose. Are there many "either-ors" in your family? This approach categorizes activities and behaviors into two opposite extremes, allowing no variation in between. While there are some things in our lives that are well-defined (and so they should be—everyone needs the certainties of specific guidelines),

IT'S A SNAKE!

The Blindmen and the Elephant is a poem of eight verses. In each of six verses a different blindman approaches an elephant, feels a part of it and describes it as he "sees" it. Thus, the elephant becomes six different things: a wall (its side), a spear (its tusk), a snake (its trunk), a tree (its leg), a fan (its ear), and a rope (its tail).

there are many times in parent/child communication where flexibility is essential. In a world of choice there are so many directions we can go and, granted, some will always be better than others, some worse. Children must be allowed, in the apprenticing process of the Presiding Structure Plan, to have greater and greater flexibility of choice as they move upward through their apprenticeship.

A child, asked to write her definition of a parent, wrote: *"A mother is to say 'no'."* Parents should no more be thought of always saying "no" than children must always want or need a "yes." Certainly, there must be "nos" and "yeses" for there are times when only that kind of option is or should be available.

Here are some ways to lessen the either-or-tendency:

1. Parents must realize that to say yes to a child does not make them any less a parent. Just because a child's idea or request is accepted, does not suggest parental weakness. However, overpermissiveness— letting the child have free rein—would suggest that a parental pygmy is present.

2. Consider giving a child some options between **everything** and **nothing, either-or,** or **yes** and **no.** A wise mother on a train said, "You may walk up and down the aisle but you may not play on the stairs." This mother recognized her small child's need for freedom and movement, but also recognized that the narrow stairs were frequently in use. And, wisdom added upon wisdom, she followed her words with actions—the child did not play on the stairs.

MISCONCEPTIONS ABOUT THE ENVIRONMENT OF COMMUNICATION
(Atmosphere, Time, and Place)

Advertisers are aware of the advantage of "prime-time" and are willing to pay thousands of dollars for a "30-second spot." Parents (and children) should become aware that there are some "prime times" for effective communication and then be willing to pay whatever price is necessary.

Poor Timing = Poor Communication

So often parents and children fail to benefit from potentially good communication because of timing. A wise parent will be aware of the importance of "the when" of communication and will help the child to learn this importance also. Good communication needs:

1. time to talk, time to listen;
2. time to consider, time to investigate;
3. time to act on some previous communication.

> Children must be allowed to have greater and greater flexibility of choice as they move upward through their apprenticeship.

> YOUR CHILD SHOULD BE IMPORTANT ENOUGH TO RECEIVE SOME "PRIME-TIME" COMMUNICATION.

143

Consider the importance of timing and you will take a big step toward improved communication.

Time to Talk—Time to Listen

Ken dashes excitedly into the kitchen. His dad is nearly late for a meeting and is hurriedly eating a sandwich.

Ken: *Did you know that we beat Madison last night?*
Dad: *Mumble, mumble.* (His mouth is full. He keeps his back to his son.)
Ken: *Rich and I were talking about going to the semi-finals tonight and—*
Dad: *Don't bother me now.* (He takes another bite.) *Can't you see I'm . . .mumble, mumble.*
Ken: *—and I was wondering if I could* go. *Rick was going to—*
Dad: *No. I haven't time to discuss it now. Later. We'll talk about it later.* (He picks up his briefcase and heads out of the kitchen.)
Ken: *But then it'll be too late and—*
Dad: *I said 'NO!'* (He slams the door, taking his frustrated mood with him to his meeting.)

Let's look at this father/son problem. Ken's father would not have been opposed to Ken's going to the game. Ken didn't need the car; he was going with Rick. The main problem was timing. Ken approached his dad at the wrong time—his dad didn't feel he had the time to listen. Two things could have turned this communication failure around, one controlled by Ken, the other by his father.

1. Ken could have approached his father a bit earlier, when he wasn't so rushed. Perhaps, however, this was not possible. He knew only a moment before that he might go with Rick. He could still have made a difference and had more control of the conversation if he had been more aware of this father's rushed situation.

2. If Ken's father had employed silent listening while eating his sandwich, rather than mumbling some negative responses, he could have heard all of Ken's message, replied in the affirmative, and been done and out the door a bit sooner.

Time to Consider—Time to Investigate

"I need an answer this minute!" Ever hear that? Sometimes circumstances are such that an immediate reply is needed. But most of the time it is a child's impatience that demands an instant reply. A parent might respond, "I need a bit of time to check with Pattie's mother first." If a child still insists, the reply might change to, "If I must give a 'yes' or 'no' answer right now, the answer will have to be 'no'."

Time to Act on Some Previous Communication

"Did you call Pattie's mother? Can I go?" Your child has not given you enough time to make the phone call. You have had several other small interruptions. Children need to be taught to be patient.

One of the best ways to help your child learn the value of timing when making parental requests is to teach them what you learned in Unit Three about the *Situational Planning Method*. Just as you learned that a parental request to empty the garbage after a TV program is over, rather than in the middle, will get a better response, so should you teach children that they'll realize better results if the "time is right."

Here are some other timing tips:

1. Allow yourself time to "cool-off" when angry. Help your child to learn to do the same if the anger is coming from his corner.

2. Establish a set time each week for each child in which parent/child communication can take place. Let this be "our time." It should be a time without pressure, without hurry, without anger. It should be a positive time. It should be a time when parental pressures are not allowed to intrude. When Robert or Jenny can see that you can be fair in a non-crisis situation, they are more likely to find you approachable and understanding when a crisis does arise. (Unit Thirteen talks more about these parent/child "one-on-ones.")

3. The place of communication can be important—one that provides quiet and privacy, a pleasant place. A man once related, with much fondness, the special father/son relationship he had when a boy. The place was very important. It was the woodpile (not the woodshed, which is often associated with communication of a more forceful and negative nature). The woodpile was selected as a place where either the father or the son could go when something of importance needed to be said and listened to. Either the father or the son sitting on the woodpile was a silent signal: *"Let's talk."*

"Comunicatus Interruptus"

This species can be either a parent or a child. It is distinguished by its presence, with open mouth, between two people who are already speaking.

How often is a parent annoyed by a child's urgent interruption, while the parent and another person are speaking? Many a parent fails to realize that he or she is guilty of the same fault—parent one wanting to talk to parent two while parent two is already talking to a child.

Parents usually "solve" this problem by:

1. ignoring it. (Perhaps it—the child—will give up and go away.);

2. becoming angry at the interruption and the child's impatience to be heard;

3. acknowledging the presence of the child with "just a minute, dear. Can't you see Mommy's talking?" (Many parental "minutes" are open-ended.)

SCHEDULE A REGULAR TIME (WEEKLY) WHERE POSITIVE COMMUNICATION CAN TAKE PLACE.

**HOW LONG ARE YOUR
"JUST A MINUTES"?**

Here are some suggested acceptable replies:

"I am talking to Julie now. Can you wait a minute?" (Then mean what you say.)

If the child indicates that the message cannot be delayed, ask, "What do you need?" Allow sufficient time to find out if Johnny has fallen out of the apple tree, if someone is at the door, if the toilet bowl is overflowing, or if some other real problem needs immediate attention. If you find the problem is merely a child's impatience or need for attention, explain you will listen to her shortly.

As soon as children know they have access to mother's listening ear and that she means what she says with "just a minute," they are most likely to decrease their immediate needs for her attention.

Knock, Knock—Are You There?

A child's reaction to this type of parent might be: "Do you hear me? Are you in there?" Too often, in much of our communication, we become so involved in thinking ahead about our next comment or defense, we fail to listen to what is being said. Or we are thinking about our problem rather than the child's.

"Tuning-out" is something both parents and children may have learned to do. "Tuning-in," if it is not yet a part of your communication process, must also be learned. Do the following:

1. Take an inventory of how you listen to others. Are you looking at them? Could you repeat back to them, word for word, the sentence they are speaking? Do you find yourself saying, "Would you say that again," or "I didn't catch that last bit?" Whose problem are you listening to—the speaker's or yours?

2. Now, act on your inventory. Look your child in the eye (silent listening). Parrot or paraphrase back what you hear him say. Make his problem yours. Do other "together" things along with your listening such as walking somewhere together, touching—a hand on his shoulder or arm, or any other thing that says, "I'm here, **really** here." You must be "here" to hear.

Following are some additional ideas to help you improve communication in your home.

MORE TIPS AND REMINDERS FOR IMPROVING COMMUNICATION

Be consistent, but flexible.

Children, and parents, need the freedom to speak and move. However, there should be guidelines, rules, plans, understandings (whatever you wish to call them) that strengthen such freedom through consistency and fairness (which are inseparable).

Complain quietly.

Establish a family policy of writing down complaints and posting them on a bulletin board. (Voiced complaints about what's for supper can drive a mother to tears and generate a negative atmosphere for one of the most important times a family can benefit from—eating together.)

Brainstorm solutions.

The key to successful brainstorming is to enforce the rule that no negative comments about another person's suggestion or idea will be allowed. All ideas get an equal hearing.

Consider future results of today's decisions.

Both parents and children need to ask—what will be the effect of today's decision tomorrow, next week, next month, next year, five years from now and so on. Today's momentary benefit may not outweigh the future effects.

Use your spouse to "soften blows."

Sometimes the necessary firmness of a parent in dealing with a child creates a barrier between that parent and the child. Your spouse can be an effective go-between—the person on the outside of the problem who can see both sides impartially. Such a parent is in a position to be heard by a child even if that parent is saying much the same things the other parent wanted or needed to say, but couldn't get a hearing.

Understand the "praise problem."

Praise, given at the wrong time, will stifle communication. For example, if your daughter has a problem or has done something wrong and wants to "unload," she is hampered in opening up if, in trying to cheer her up, you praise her for being such a "cheerful girl" or such a "good daughter." How can she talk about her "bad" behavior or her problem to a parent who has just praised her for her "goodness?" To admit to her problem is going against her parent's image of her. Use praise, but watch your timing.

Praise a child who helps keep communication open.

Make talking with and listening to mom and dad an enjoyable experience. Be positive, be appreciative. And let humor be an important ingredient. Communication does not have to be "heavy."

Be positive about the negative.

Just because a parent and child talk about negative things, neither has to be negative. Implement the various suggestions in this and the previous unit to help maintain a positive posture of communication.

A SPECIAL TIP FOR ALL FAMILY MEMBERS:

Leave silent, written messages of thanks, praise, or encouragement pinned to hanging clothes, under pillows or on beds, in lunch boxes or in dresser drawers or . . .

SO, HOW DO YOU TAKE THE "MIS" OUT OF MISCOMMUNICATION?

The Message

"When I use a word," Humpty Dumpty said, in rather a scornful tone, "it means just what I choose it to mean neither more nor less."

"The question is," said Alice, "whether you can make words mean so many different things."

"The question is," said Humpty Dumpty, "which is to be master—that's all."

from Lewis Carroll's
Through the Looking Glass

Words do not have meaning. They only **carry** the meaning of the sender or the receiver. The person has the meaning.

Say what you mean and mean what you say. Words supported by action have positive power.

Words by themselves usually have negative power, especially when used to flatter, when spoken in anger or with sarcasm, or used as reverse psychology.

Don't have a double standard of speaking. Be as considerate of family as you are of others.

The Receiver (Child)

Don't assume wrongdoing. Act on facts. Use equal consequences for participants if wrongdoer remains unknown.

Separate accidents from misbehaviors. Separate the child from the act (misbehavior). Punish the act, not the child.

Make honesty worthwhile. Reward, not punish, for honest responses.

Recognize the individuality of each child. Don't put children in categories or compare one against another.

Don't exaggerate a child's misbehavior. "You **always** . . ." "You **never** . . ."

Give the child opportunity to change. Don't assume nonchange.

Don't put labels on children—good ones or bad ones.

Encourage a child to work toward **his** expectations, not yours.

A child's ideas must be considered of value and importance.

The Sender (Parent)

Parents don't have to know all the answers. Be willing to say, *"I don't know."*

Don't expect your child to know all you know, and recognize that your child may know some things that you don't.

Appreciate your child for where he's at, not on the basis of where you are.

If you must have the last word, let it be *"thanks."*

Not all answers must be "yes" or "no." The world is full of options. Allow your child some.

Children need guidelines. Too many options (overpermissiveness) can create insecurity.

Environment of Communication

Timing of communication is important. Sender and receiver should each work toward a greater awareness of each other's time patterns and needs.

Set aside some "prime time" for communication on a weekly basis.

Have a regular place, quiet and private, for parent/child communication.

Teach children how to time their requests for a more listening ear.

Make sure *"just a minute"* means what it says.

Teach children not to interrupt by being a good example yourself.

Show your child you are listening. (See Unit Seven.)

A FINAL WORD (Words)

Parents should want the optimum conditions for effective communication in the home. Some of the patterns of miscommunication just mentioned in this unit may be preventing that from happening in your home. An awareness of a problem is often its own best solution. Hopefully, your new awareness, plus the use of some of the suggestions given, will help you improve the communication that takes place between you and your child.

However, the **most** important thing about parent/child communication is that **it take place.** Worse than poor communication is no communication. There is too often much that is left unsaid between parents and children—feelings and concerns, hopes and fears, problems and successes to be shared.

An excellent idea (seen on bumper stickers) for improved parent/child communication:

HUG YOUR KID TODAY!

TAKE TIME TO COMMUNICATE

Exercise 9.1

COMMUNICATION QUESTIONAIRE FOR THE PARENTS OF _____

Read each question carefully. Circle the number which best describes your true feelings.

	Never	Almost Never	Some-times	Almost Always	Always
1. Are you interested in the things your child does and is interested in?	1	2	3	4	5
2. Do you stick to the subject when you talk to your child?	1	2	3	4	5
3. Is your child able to say what he feels around home?	1	2	3	4	5
4. Do you interrupt your child before he finishes talking?	1	2	3	4	5
5. Do you talk to your child as if he were younger than he is?	1	2	3	4	5
6. Do you find yourself thinking about other things while you are talking to your child?	1	2	3	4	5
7. Does your family talk things over with each other?	1	2	3	4	5
8. Does your child disagree with your opinions?	1	2	3	4	5
9. Do you listen to and value your child's opinion?	1	2	3	4	5
10. Do you make clear the things you mean to say?	1	2	3	4	5
11. When your child has personal problems, does he discuss them with you?	1	2	3	4	5
12. Do you ask to hear your child's side of things?	1	2	3	4	5
13. Do you discuss matters of sex with your child? (when at the appropriate age)	1	2	3	4	5
14. How often does your child criticize you and point out things that are wrong?	1	2	3	4	5
15. How often does your child praise you and express appreciation?	1	2	3	4	5
16. Are there times when you feel your child can't do anything right?	1	2	3	4	5
17. Do you trust your child?	1	2	3	4	5
18. Do you have confidence in your child's abilities?	1	2	3	4	5
19. Do you usually stay calm when you talk about a problem?	1	2	3	4	5
20. Do you explain your reasons for objecting to something your child wants to do?	1	2	3	4	5
21. Do you feel that you and your child seldom talk except when someone is upset or angry?	1	2	3	4	5
22. Do you find your child "tuning you out" instead of talking with you?	1	2	3	4	5
23. Do you feel your child shows respect for your ideas and opinions?	1	2	3	4	5
24. Do you wish that you and your child could communicate better?	1	2	3	4	5

Now complete the following statements:

25. When I think about the future, I worry about

26. The best thing about our family is

27. I would like to be able to talk to _____ about

28. Most children don't realize that

NOTE: Copies of this questionaire are available from Lion House Press. If you wish, you may make copies.

150

Exercise 9.2
COMMUNICATION QUESTIONAIRE FOR _____

Read each question carefully. Circle the number which best describes your true feelings.

	Never	Almost Never	Some-times	Almost Always	Always
1. Do your parents seem interested in the things you do and are interested in?	1	2	3	4	5
2. When your parents sit down and talk to you about a specific problem, do they bring in a lot of other issues by the time they're through?	1	2	3	4	5
3. Are you able to say what you really feel around home?	1	2	3	4	5
4. Do your parents keep you from finishing what you have to say to them by interrupting?	1	2	3	4	5
5. Do your parents tend to talk to you as if you were much younger than you actually are?	1	2	3	4	5
6. Do your parents seem to be thinking about other things while you are trying to talk to them?	1	2	3	4	5
7. Does your family talk things over with each other?	1	2	3	4	5
8. Do you hesitate to disagree with either of your parents? Which one? _____ Both? _____	1	2	3	4	5
9. Do your parents listen to and value your opinion?	1	2	3	4	5
10. Are you sometimes confused about what your parents really mean by what they say?	1	2	3	4	5
11. When you have personal problems do you discuss them with your parents?	1	2	3	4	5
12. Do your parents ask to hear your side of things?	1	2	3	4	5
13. Are you able to discuss matters of sex with your parents? Which one? _____ Both? _____	1	2	3	4	5
14. When your parent talks with you concerning your actions, are the comments criticizing you?	1	2	3	4	5
15. When your parent talks with you, how often does he/she praise you for good actions?	1	2	3	4	5
16. Are there times when you feel your parents think you can't do anything right?	1	2	3	4	5
17. Do you feel that your parents trust you?	1	2	3	4	5
18. Do your parents have confidence in your abilities?	1	2	3	4	5
19. Do your parents often become upset when they talk to you about some problem?	1	2	3	4	5
20. Do your parents let you know their reasons for objecting to something you want to do?	1	2	3	4	5
21. Do you feel that you and your parents seldom talk except when someone is upset or angry?	1	2	3	4	5
22. Do you find yourself "tuning out" your parents instead of talking with them?	1	2	3	4	5
23. Do you feel that you show respect for your parents' ideas and opinions?	1	2	3	4	5
24. Do you wish that you and your parents could communicate better?	1	2	3	4	5

Now complete the following statements:

25. When I think about the future, I worry most about

26. The best thing about our family is

27. I would like to be able to talk to my parents about

28. Most parents don't realize that

NOTE: Copies of this questionaire are available from Lion House Press. If you wish, you may make copies.

151

QUESTIONS and ANSWERS

Q. As a school teacher I run into many children who don't seem to listen to what they are told. Is there a particular reason for this? Do such children usually have hearing handicaps?

A. When children do not seem to listen, it is usually because they have learned that people do not mean what they say. We ignore cries of "Wolf!" when such cries are false. If people warn us, yet the warnings do not reflect what is actually true, we ignore them. When children fail to listen, it is invariably because listening does not **pay off**.

Q. I have heard "Think before you act" and "Rewards and penalties are more effective if given immediately." Which is correct?

A. Both are correct. Parents should take time to sit down together and categorize their children's actions so they agree on what types of rewards and penalties should be given for certain types of actions. (This idea of categorizing is easier than it sounds and is not contrary to the type of classifying referred to earlier in this unit.) In this way parents can give consequences immediately, but with forethought.

Q. How important is telling your child that you love him/her?

A. I think the following quote from a magazine answers this best. "A friend of mine recently shared what he considered to be a choice learning experience. It was provided by his young son. Upon returning home from his day's work, this father greeted his boy with a pat on the head and said, 'Son, I want you to know I love you.' The son responded with, 'Oh, Dad, I don't want you to love me, I want you to play football with me.' " (*Ensign*, 1975, p. 108). Telling in words that we love a child is important. But, as this little story illustrates, there are other important ways also.

Q. In this unit it is said that parents may wrongly classify a child because of the company he/she keeps. I watch who my daughter's friends are to get an idea of how and what she is doing. Is that wrong?

A. No. I advocate that parents very much watch who their child's friends are. Who a child associates with is generally a good indicator of the child's own values. However, be careful you don't judge and convict your child without a fair evaluation. And be very careful about negatively labeling a child. Children (and adults) often grow to fit their labels.

Improving Your Child's Self-Worth

> How can we help a child develop a positive self-worth? Unit Ten explains the main ingredients (unconditional love, resultant love, consequential focusing, skills for handling mistakes) parents should know how to use to strengthen a child's feelings of self-worth. This unit also discusses the most important **do's** and **don't's** for parents wishing to help their child. The unit closes by introducing parents to the RUN system, a system for determining whether parents are too negative with their child.

I HAVE A LITTLE SHADOW...

Name something you have with you all the time. That's right. It's "yourself." You are always with you. You are the most important thing in your life. You are always around when you are in trouble. You are always around when you do good. Without you, you have no life. Nothing in life will have more influence on you than you, yourself.

But who are you? What is this thing that is the most important of life's ingredients? Is your *self* the same from the day you are born to the day you die? Few people have difficulty answering that last question. Obviously not. We change through life's daily experiences. In fact that is the reason for life—to develop that *self* of ours.

Our *self* is quite changeable. Every experience we have in life has some impact on our *self*. Good habits such as honesty, cleanliness, and helpfulness are part of *self*. Good attitudes are part of *self*. And as we earlier concluded, habits and attitudes are not determined by instincts, they are learned. So we see **the self is learned.** It is something that life's experiences mold and develop. A person's *self* can be almost anything. Mother Nature did not even restrict our freedom of choice to the extent that we can only develop a *good self.* Life does not restrict us from developing a *bad self* (people can learn to feel good about hurting other people as we see with bombings in airports where innocent people suffer). Each person is an *individual.* No two people have *selfs* that are exactly the same.

A PERSON'S SELF IS LEARNED AND CAN BECOME ALMOST ANYTHING.

153

Because the *self* is such an important part of life, it must have some substance to it. It cannot be too changeable like the wind, first going one direction, then another. We pointed earlier to the fact that daily experiences affect the *self*. So what keeps the *self* from changing dramatically with each new experience? To answer this question, three major steps in the development of self need to be considered.

Step One: In previous units we emphasized the role of consequation in our lives. Consequences are the guideposts in life that direct our thoughts and actions. Learning from the consequences produced by our daily successes and mistakes is what allows us to rise above Mother Nature's other animals who are guided by instincts. We learn from experiences while those ruled by instincts do not. The experiences in our lives become the mechanism for teaching. We can arrange experiences in the lives of our children that can teach them **good** and **bad** ways to think and act.

We can arrange experiences in the lives of our children that can teach them good and bad ways to think and act.

By way of review (since *consequences* and *consequation* were discussed in previous units) *consequences* are the results or effects, either positive or negative, of our actions. *Consequation* is the process of controlling the action by controlling the effect or result of the action.

Step Two: As a child repeatedly experiences certain consequences, he begins to learn relationships.

> *"If I smile, Mommy picks me up."*
> *"If I scream, Mommy picks me up."*
> *"If I reach out my hand and fingers, I can grab the rattle."*
> *"If I act sweet and nice, I can convince Mother to let me stay up."*

Through receiving consequences for our different actions we learn that some things (being picked up by mother) can be *attributed* to some of our actions (screaming and crying). So, from our past experiences we learn to *expect* certain things.

> *"If I scream, I will get what I want."*
> *"If I try, I will just fail, so why try?"*
> *"If I try to do good, nobody cares."*
> *"If I do what I should, Mom and Dad will be proud of me."*

In Unit Two the point was discussed that desires can stimulate a child to action. It was also pointed out that desires develop from the expectancies a child develops as his actions produce satisfactions.

> *"When I get hungry, hotdogs satisfy me. I'm hungry now, so I expect a hotdog will satisfy me. I desire a hotdog now."*

> *"If I scream, my past experience tells me I can expect to get spanked for my screaming, so I do not desire to scream."*

"My past family activities have been more fun than activities with my friends, so I have a stronger desire to do things with my family than with my friends."

So a child begins to attribute certain results to specific actions and, consciously or unconsciously, sees a relationship between the two. The relationship becomes stronger and stronger as a child has repeated experiences, the consequences of which suggest that the relationship is true. The more experiences a child has that have the same outcome, the stronger the child attributes certain results or consequences to certain actions.

The process of recognizing the relationship between an action and its consequences and expecting those consequences to follow that action is called *attribution*. When we attribute or expect a result or consequence from an action, we learn to either repeat or shy away from it.

ATTRIBUTION:

Recognizing the relationship between an action and its consequences and expecting those consequences to follow that action.

Step Three: *"You can't teach an old dog new tricks."* This is a common quote in our society that suggests people are harder to change the older they get. Through life we develop habits and it is generally true that the stronger the habit, the harder it is to break. Often we find ourselves mad because this is true. We all have bad habits we would like to get rid of and we get frustrated because they are so tough to change. But look on the bright side. If bad habits are tough to change, then notice that *good habits* are hard to break also. So it's true that we do become *set* in our ways as we grow older and have more experiences. Mother Nature knew we needed some stability through life. Just as cement hardens or *sets*, so do our habits. And if we have been developing good habits, the tendency is for our *self* to harden and *set* into something that is good. If that *self* develops some bad habits and attitudes, then at least Mother Nature has allowed us ways of changing—difficult though they may be.

HABITS

The word *set* as used in the previous paragraph, refers to the process of our actions becoming strong and firm habits. "He is becoming set in his ways." It is used as a verb and suggests a certain hardening or inflexibility. The word *set* is also used in another way (as a noun). We say, "I have a set of dishes," meaning we have an assortment or arrangement of related or like pieces of china or other type of table-ware. We also might say, "He has a definite set of ideas on that subject." We can have a set of ideas, a set of feelings or a set of attitudes about ourselves, some other person, or some object. Sometimes just the word *set* is used such as: "We develop a negative set or a positive set about ourself or someone else." What we are really saying, using more words, is that we have developed a firm and definite collection or set of ideas, attitudes, and feelings about ourself or someone else.

SET:

The solid feelings and firm ideas and attitudes we have about something or someone.

155

DEVELOPING OUR SELF

As each of us travels along life's road we find ourselves depending heavily on *consequences, attribution,* and *set* as to what we think and do. If we receive unpleasant *consequences* because of our experiences with "Uncle George," then our mind records our actions with Uncle George, **and** the fact that they were unpleasant. As repeated unpleasant experiences with Uncle George occur, our mind begins to *attribute* that unpleasantness to Uncle George and it develops a belief about what we can expect if we interact with Uncle George in the future. As even more experiences occur, those *attributions* or *expectancies* harden into a *set* that will be difficult to change, even if we recently have one or two positive experiences with Uncle George.

Well, developing a strong set about our own *self* occurs the same way we develop a set about George, or anything else in our world. If we are around Uncle George when positive things happen to us, then Uncle George becomes positive in our mind. If we are rewarded around Uncle George when we behave properly, then we will most likely feel good about behaving properly around Uncle George in the future.

The sets or solid feelings we develop about ourselves come through the process of association.

The *sets* or solid feelings we develop about ourselves come through the process of *association.* If we are always failing we will develop a view of our *self* as a failure. If we are always being rebuked for doing something wrong we will see our *self* as bad and "wrong." Our child's *self* will become what we let our child associate with. The following poem by Dorothy Law Nolte says it well:

CHILDREN LEARN WHAT THEY LIVE

If a child lives with criticism,
he learns to condemn.

If a child lives with hostility,
he learns to fight.

If a child lives with ridicule,
he learns to be shy.

If a child lives with shame,
he learns to feel guilty.

If a child lives with tolerance,
he learns to be patient.

If a child lives with encouragement,
he learns confidence.

If a child lives with praise,
he learns to appreciate.

If a child lives with fairness,
he learns justice.

If a child lives with security,
he learns to have faith.

*If a child lives with approval,
he learns to like himself.*

*If a child lives with acceptance and friendship,
he learns to find love in the world.*

From what we have discussed it should be apparent that a child's *self* becomes what it is associated with and it grows and hardens as it collects experiences.

A child's self becomes what it associates with and it grows and hardens as it collects experiences.

DEVELOPING GOOD SELF-ESTEEM IN A CHILD

So what do parents do to improve a child's self-worth? Or, how is good self-worth started and developed in a small child? The answer to both questions is the same. **Start today** using the following guides:

Unconditional Love. Stick a piece of chalk in some perfume or air freshener liquid and that chalk becomes an enjoyable air freshener to you. Stick the chalk in a smelly substance like sulfur gas and then see how you feel about that chalk. Our *self* is like a sponge (or chalk). It takes on some of the attributes of things around it. A woman dressed nicely and wearing perfume has a better feeling of *self* than if she is in tattered and dirty clothes.

UNCONDITIONAL LOVE:

Affection, interest, attention, acceptance shown to someone regardless of behavior, good or bad.

The first key to better child self-worth is to provide positive things for the child—hugs, a piece of candy, positive conversation, a clean and warm bed—irrespective of what the child does. We call this *unconditional love*. Unconditional love is those signs of affection, interest, attention, love, or acceptance we show another person regardless of his or her actions or behavior. Such signs say "I like **you**." "I love **you**." "I accept **you**." "**You** are important to me." They have nothing to do with the actions or behavior of the person (child).

Examples of unconditional love are:

Dad putting his arm around little Jimmy as they walk.
Mother bringing all the kids a treat when she comes home from work.
Mother ruffling Andy's hair as she passes his chair while he reads a book.
Dad cheering when Chris comes up to bat at the ballgame.
Mother reading to Julie at bedtime.
Dad leaving a little present on David's bed with an unsigned note saying, "From someone who loves you. Thanks for being you."

...THEN THE THREE BEARS...

WHEN YOU ARE IN A POSITIVE, PLEASANT ATMOSPHERE, YOU FEEL BETTER ABOUT YOURSELF.

Expressions of unconditional love in a family are automatically absorbed by that child's *self*. **When you are in a positive, pleasant atmosphere, you feel better about yourself.** Keep in mind, however, that unconditional love helps a child's self-image, but **does not** automatically influence a child's actions. Unconditional love does not direct a child's actions with the power resultant love does.

WARNING: Most parents, in a situation where the child has misbehaved, find themselves wanting to sit down with the child and have a positive talk, or express some *unconditional love*. What they are doing is **not** unconditional love. They are actually rewarding the misbehavior. Be sure your expressions of unconditional love are not given right after a child misbehaves. Give it when the child is either doing something good or doing something that may be considered neither good or bad—just sitting and thinking. Unconditional love should not be given only when the child is good. Three daily expressions of unconditional love is a good rate.

Resultant Love. Showing love and appreciation to a child when he or she acts properly is what we call *resultant love*. It is the key to developing proper actions. This has been the theme throughout the NAP Handbook. Mary learns what actions are good by the consequences her actions produce. If she is quiet and courteous, but her misbehaving brother Andrew is the one who gets mom and dad's attention, guess what Mary's future course of action will be?

RESULTANT LOVE:

Affection, interest, attention, acceptance, or appreciation shown to someone because of good behavior.

When good thoughts and actions pay off, they become part of the child's *self*. When bad thoughts and actions pay off, they also become part of the child's *self*. If Jeanie behaves well and receives love and appreciation, she learns to do well and feel good about her *self*.

However, if Jeanie misbehaves and her misbehavior pays off with attention and loving concern, while being told that what she did was bad, her *self* is in conflict. She sees that what she does is good because it pays off with attention, yet others tell her it is bad. The more consistently the child finds that bad actions don't pay off while good actions do, the better *self-image* the child will develop.

Examples of resultant love include:

Thanking a child who did the dishes without being told and letting that child stay up a little later that night.
Thanking a child who gets you the paper.
Giving a two-year-old a hug and cookie for picking up his toys.
Disciplining the teenager who took the car without asking.
Showing appreciation when the child cleans up the mess he made.

A healthy self is based on feelings of success and accomplishment.

Another important reason for resultant love is the emphasis it automatically puts on success and accomplishment for the child. **A healthy self is based on feelings of success and accomplishment.**

Fathers often, unintentionally, thwart such feelings in their sons when trying to teach them to be strong and manly and physically handle themselves For example, in wrestling they might show their son how to pin an opponent this way or that way. But, because of the father's desire to feel successful, the boy is always losing and being pinned. The wise father, when wrestling with his son, will sense when little Johnny is about to give up and will "give up" first. A wise dad needs to let Johnny win some of the time. "Boy, Johnny, I give up. You sure are a little toughie." (Don't be such an obvious loser that your efforts become insincere and ineffective.)

Too often fathers are inclined to try telling a funnier joke than their child. Too often mother has to remind Debra (who just picked out a skirt and sweater outfit) that mother is really a wiser shopper. Giving children resultant love as they exert effort and make choices is an important part of helping their feelings of self-worth. Parents, be sure your needs for a better feeling of self-worth do not rob those of you child. Be sure those expressions of resultant love you think you are making really are. **Getting positive expressions and rewards from mom and dad when trying to do positive things plays a very important role in helping develop a child's self-worth.**

Keep in mind that resultant love includes imposing penalties as guidelines for misbehavior. Sometimes a real love for the child requires parents to follow through with unpleasant consequences that parents would rather not do.

Handling mistakes. Because Mother Nature allows us to make mistakes in life, we will. We won't always be right in what we do. One of the biggest problems children have in developing a good *self* image is knowing how to handle mistakes. Some children have poor *selfs* because they are rebuked for making mistakes, yet they have not been taught how to deal with them. Often parents make matters worse by not admitting their own mistakes and trying to cover them up so others—including their children—won't see them.

Ever heard the saying: *"Parents, have you hugged your child lately?"* Well, here is another saying that is just about as important:

Parents, has your child seen you make a mistake recently?

Parents should let their children see them make mistakes. We all make them. And parents should let children see that mistakes require: (1) admission of doing them, and (2) attempts to rectify the mistake. Through example and guided experiences children should learn that making a mistake is not totally bad with no chance whatsoever for correcting it.

Suppose a parent makes a mistake. For example, father promises to pick up his daughter, Desiree, from school, but he forgets. He should not blame the situation on being too busy. He made a mistake. In one such situation a father forgot to pick up his daughter. Later, he did not try to hide his error. He admitted that it was his fault and then gave her a slip of paper listing

Children should learn that making a mistake is not totally bad, with no chance to correct it.

159

several favors from him that she might choose from. She had a choice of: 1) a later bed-time for one week, 2) dad taking her shopping on Saturday instead of his going golfing, or 3) dad doing her dishes for two days.

Learning to accept one's mistakes and learning that we need to make retribution for our mistakes (without being reminded forever) are some of the best secrets for building self-esteem. Provide your child with an environment where: (1) making mistakes is considered a natural part of life, (2) retribution for mistakes is required, and (3) mistakes a person makes are forgotten when retribution is made. Almost every child with poor self-esteem is deficient in skills for dealing with mistakes. When someone is not perfect (and that includes all of us), knowing how to handle mistakes is an integral part of developing good self-worth.

Almost every child with poor self-worth has not learned how to deal with mistakes.

Consequential Focusing. What is the real key to success? What is the one secret for good housekeeping? What is the one key to being a baseball superstar? Ever notice how so many of us try to find that one ingredient that is "the answer." Well, the key to developing good self-esteem is *consequential focusing.* If there is one thing that comes closest to being the one best answer, it is consequential focusing.

To explain consequential focusing let's take a common situation that happens repeatedly in every home. Little Johnny misbehaves. Mother, who has been getting fed up with his actions, finally lets go and reprimands him strongly. Being quite upset, mother continues to be mad, even after the discipline has been given. So often we parents can't calm down after discipling a child. After all, that child has to see just how mad we really were.

Now, invariably after a child misbehaves and is disciplined, that child will do something right. But mother is still mad. Johnny did something wrong, then did something right, but the emotional reaction from mother is still the same. Such situations cause him to draw one of two conclusions: (1)"Mother is unfair" or (2)"I must be a bad child." Johnny's actions changed, yet the emotional result was the same. So he concludes the emotion and discipline received from mother can't be due to his actions—they changed. Therefore, he thinks, those unpleasant things he just received must have come because **he** is bad.

Whenever we discipline children, we have to be sure we focus the discipline specifically on the misbehavior of the child. If we let our discipline mood "spill over" onto the good behaviors (which surely follow), then we weaken the child's self-esteem rather than weaken the misbehavior of the child.

Disciplining a child does not automatically reduce the child's self-esteem **if** you focus that consequence on the **action** of the child. Discipline for misbehavior can be a strong and healthy road sign from which the child can learn.

Consequential focusing—making sure the consequences you give your child for misbehavior or good behavior do not spill over

to some other action—is very important for developing good self-esteem in children.

Real-world Experiences. Often times parents distort the world of the child. In some instances we try to be totally positive and protect our children from all unpleasant consequences of life. In other situations a child is dealt with in mostly negative terms. Some children receive mostly criticism because mother and dad become so busy that they only notice the child when misbehaving. The real world is actually a combination of both pleasant and unpleasant experiences. Not being guided by instincts to always do good, children will make mistakes. Those should produce unpleasant consequences. But don't forget also those positive consequences for good actions. And remember, if a child is being properly directed by consequences, he should be doing many more good things than bad. So, in your family be sure you are dispensing more positives than negatives to your child. A child's *self* is healthier when that child knows how to deal with society's ups and downs.

The child must learn that the real-world is a combination of pleasant and unpleasant experiences.

DO'S AND DON'T'S
FOR DEVELOPING A CHILD'S SELF-WORTH

Give your child *unconditional love.*
Give your child *resultant love.*
Teach your child to *handle mistakes.*
Use *consequential focusing.*
Prepare your child for *real-world experiences.*

ONLY IN A WORLD OF LOVE CAN A CHILD UNFOLD AND BLOOM.

These are five important guides for parents concerned about developing a healthy self-worth in their child. With these guides in mind, here are a number of parental **do's** and **don't's** for developing a child's self-worth.

DO'S

1. Show unconditional love to your child (perhaps three times a day).
   Give resultant love to your child (perhaps three times a day).
   Help arrange successful experiences for your child.
   Help children think positively about themselves. Make comments like *"Hey, Jeffrey, you sure look nice. It makes me feel good to see you like that. How does it make you feel?"* (Be sure to praise positive responses of the child and ignore negative ones if they make them.)
5. Discipline your child with consequences for misbehavior (sit on a chair, take away privileges, spankings).
6. Be sure to use consequential focusing—focus rewards on specific positive actions and focus penalties on specific misbehavior of the child. **Be prepared to reward good behaviors that quickly follow misbehavior.**
7. Help children realize that all people have problems and make mistakes.
8. Teach your child that mistakes need to be paid for and corrected.

Focus on what a child does, not on him, when disciplining.

Want to improve your child's self-worth?

RUN with it!

9. Identify at least one mistake your child makes each week and help him or her work out a proper way of handling that mistake.

10. Each week point out at least one mistake you make and let your child see how you handle it.

11. Focus on a child's bad action, not his character, when disciplining.

12. Express appreciation to children when they do what you request of them.

13. Have clear rules and guidelines in your home. Stability in the home helps the child feel more comfortable in identifying his or her own *self.*

14. Make sure child experiences daily successes.

DON'T'S

1. Do not demean your child when he or she does something wrong. Avoid comments like *"You dummy. You did it again."* or *"Now that was a stupid thing to do."*

2. Do not hold grudges. Children should pay for misbehavior only once. If you hold grudges, children will begin to do the same.

3. Do not argue or debate with a child when disciplining him or her. State what the misbehavior was and what the penalty is. Then carry out the penalty. Discuss the discipline at some later date. Have a weekly family meeting where children can voice honest concerns about discipline procedures in the family.

4. Do not repeatedly remind children of past mistakes.

5. Do not sympathize with a child who makes self-defeating comments—*"I'm no good." "I can't do it."* Act neutral and uninterested in such comments, while being supportive of positive comments about self from the child.

USING THE "RUN" SYSTEM FOR IMPROVING SELF-WORTH

There is a special Outline for Action form (following these instructions) that parents can use to help improve their child's self-worth. This form is to be used with the *RUN System.* It is a system for checking to see to what extent parents are providing unconditional love, resultant love, and negative comments to their child. Figure 10.1 shows the *RUN System* weekly chart. The chart is divided into three main parts—one each for mother, father, and child. In most situations only the mother and father sections will be used. Basically the *RUN System* involves both the mother and the father using one of these forms. During a specified week the mother monitors both her and her husband's reactions to the child, while the father monitors himself and his wife.

The chart has three columns of circles, arranged into groups for each day of the week. For each day there is an "R" column, a "U" column, and an "N" column. "R" stands for resultant love. "U" stands for unconditional love, and "N" stands for any negative comment or discipline given to the child.

For one hour each day (and that hour is chosen independently by husband and wife) each parent records the number of resultant loves, unconditional loves and negatives they themself **and** their mate give their child or children. For every occurrence of one of the three types of interaction with the child that parent fills in a circle above the appropriate letter. Both parents keep their charts without showing it to their mate until the end of the week. At that time they sit down and compare how they monitored themselves against how their mate monitored them. This is done in a spirit of providing information only.

Filling out a weekly *RUN* chart every month for a few months has several positive effects. First, it makes each parent more aware of giving these three kinds of responses to their child. Second, it often points out that parents are dealing more negatively than positively with their children. A healthy ratio for developing self-worth in a child is for parents to give at least twice as many "R's" and twice as many "U's" as "N's" to their children. In families with strong parent-child conflict problems, the "N's" typically equal or exceed the number of "R's" and "U's" given.

An additional insight parents often receive from using *RUN* charts is that parents often give comments they consider "U's" or "R's," yet their children or their mate interpret them as "N's." For example, a father may tease a child and with a half-smile say something like *"Johnny, you little toad."* Now father may feel he has just been positive with his son and given him an unconditional love, yet mother may spot that Johnny took the comment as being negative. By monitoring each other's behavior, parents can help each other give their children better and more positive responses.

The *RUN* chart includes a place to write down the exact hour each day that a father (or mother) monitors himself and his wife. Mother and father won't always pick the same time to monitor, but during the week at least one or two of the hours will overlap. In those cases parents can directly compare how they rated themselves in contrast to how they were rated by their mate.

At the top of the next page is an example of how a run chart might look at the end of the week. You should always start at the bottom when filling in the circles. At the end of the week your chart will look like a graph, with columns of darkened circles of varying heights. In order to be more aware of any increase or decrease of positive or negative responses draw a line connecting the uppermost filled-in circle of all the "R" columns. Then do the same for the "U" columns and the "N" columns. The example on the following page shows this partially done.

Try the *RUN System* with your mate. It can provide you with a better picture of what you as a parent do, **plus** it can help you better support and strengthen your child's positive feelings of self-worth.

MAKE SURE YOUR POSITIVE RESPONSES TO YOUR CHILD FAR OUTWEIGHT THE NEGATIVE ONES.

JOHNNY, YOU LITTLE TOAD!

Person being monitored *Mom* ☐ Self-monitoring

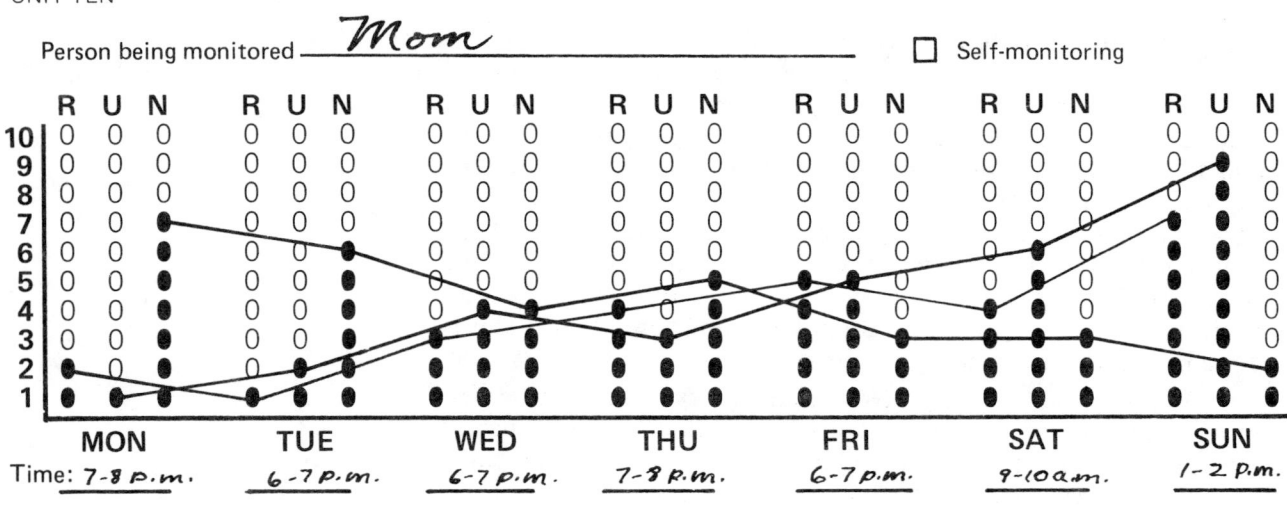

MON — Time: 7-8 p.m.
TUE — 6-7 p.m.
WED — 6-7 p.m.
THU — 7-8 p.m.
FRI — 6-7 p.m.
SAT — 9-10 a.m.
SUN — 1-2 p.m.

OUTLINE FOR ACTION — **RUN** SYSTEM CHART

Person being monitored _____ ☐ Self-monitoring

	R	U	N	R	U	N	R	U	N	R	U	N	R	U	N	R	U	N	R	U	N
10	0	0	0	0	0	0	0	0	0	0	0	0	0	0	0	0	0	0	0	0	0
9	0	0	0	0	0	0	0	0	0	0	0	0	0	0	0	0	0	0	0	0	0
8	0	0	0	0	0	0	0	0	0	0	0	0	0	0	0	0	0	0	0	0	0
7	0	0	0	0	0	0	0	0	0	0	0	0	0	0	0	0	0	0	0	0	0
6	0	0	0	0	0	0	0	0	0	0	0	0	0	0	0	0	0	0	0	0	0
5	0	0	0	0	0	0	0	0	0	0	0	0	0	0	0	0	0	0	0	0	0
4	0	0	0	0	0	0	0	0	0	0	0	0	0	0	0	0	0	0	0	0	0
3	0	0	0	0	0	0	0	0	0	0	0	0	0	0	0	0	0	0	0	0	0
2	0	0	0	0	0	0	0	0	0	0	0	0	0	0	0	0	0	0	0	0	0
1	0	0	0	0	0	0	0	0	0	0	0	0	0	0	0	0	0	0	0	0	0

MON TUE WED THU FRI SAT SUN

Time: _____

Person being monitored _____ ☐ Self-monitoring

	R	U	N	R	U	N	R	U	N	R	U	N	R	U	N	R	U	N	R	U	N
10	0	0	0	0	0	0	0	0	0	0	0	0	0	0	0	0	0	0	0	0	0
9	0	0	0	0	0	0	0	0	0	0	0	0	0	0	0	0	0	0	0	0	0
8	0	0	0	0	0	0	0	0	0	0	0	0	0	0	0	0	0	0	0	0	0
7	0	0	0	0	0	0	0	0	0	0	0	0	0	0	0	0	0	0	0	0	0
6	0	0	0	0	0	0	0	0	0	0	0	0	0	0	0	0	0	0	0	0	0
5	0	0	0	0	0	0	0	0	0	0	0	0	0	0	0	0	0	0	0	0	0
4	0	0	0	0	0	0	0	0	0	0	0	0	0	0	0	0	0	0	0	0	0
3	0	0	0	0	0	0	0	0	0	0	0	0	0	0	0	0	0	0	0	0	0
2	0	0	0	0	0	0	0	0	0	0	0	0	0	0	0	0	0	0	0	0	0
1	0	0	0	0	0	0	0	0	0	0	0	0	0	0	0	0	0	0	0	0	0

MON TUE WED THU FRI SAT SUN

Time: _____

Figure 10.1 RUN System Chart

UNIT TEN: IMPROVING YOUR CHILD'S SELF-WORTH
Exercise 10.1

1. Parents have certain actions they do that they feel help their child have stronger feelings of self-worth. Sometimes we teach our children and think that our teasing is viewed in a positive way by the child. Sometimes a parent "lectures" a child, believing those lectures help him/her. List something your mate does which he/she feels is upbuilding for the child, yet you note that the child takes negatively.

_____

_____

_____

_____

2. List two things that were not mentioned in this unit that you could do to show unconditional love to your child.

_____

_____

_____

_____

3. Five things were mentioned in this unit that can help improve a child's self-worth. Give specific examples of what you could do with those five things to help your child.

   (a) Unconditional Love
   Example: _Put my arm on my six year old son's shoulder while we walk._

   _____

   _____

   (b) Resultant Love
   Example: _Smile and say "thanks" to my daughter for bringing me the paper I asked for._

   _____

   (c) Handling Mistakes
   Example: _I failed to get home when I promised. I should not try to make an excuse, but make amends to my wife for not doing what I promised._

   _____

   _____

Continued on next page.

165

(d) Consequential Focusing

Example: _I punished my 13 year old for not mowing the lawn; 15 minutes later I praised him for cleaning his room._

(e) Real-world Experiences

Example: _We help our daughter who dislikes teasing, to adjust to it, rather than complain to parents of children who tease her._

QUESTIONS and ANSWERS

Q. **The unit mentions that unconditional love does not give direction to a child's behavior. Doesn't it do anything besides make the child feel good?**

A. Yes. In some cases unconditional love motivates a child. Unconditional love can pep-up a child and excite him to do something, but it does not necessarily direct the child as to what he should do. Too many parents sadly find out that unconditional love is not enough to successfully raise their children.

Q. **I am a bit confused about consequential focusing. The unit mentions that parents should reward good behavior that immediately follows bad behavior which has just been punished. In an earlier unit something was said about making sure parents don't reward a child right after he/she has been punished for doing something wrong. Which is correct?**

A. Both are correct. Do not punish a child for lying, then immediately hug him and tell him you are sorry you had to punish him. In such cases the parent has both punished and rewarded the child for lying. And that is not good because the hugs and affection diluted the effect of the punishment. On the other hand, you could punish a child for lying and then immediately reward him for picking up his clothes. In the second case you are administering the reward to a different behavior than the one that was punished. See the difference?

Q. **Do children develop better feelings of self-worth in families where parents are the boss or in families where children have a great deal of freedom to do what they want?**

A. Self-worth is not dependent on freedom, intelligence, or having superior talents or a superior position in a group or organization. Janitors can feel more self-worth in keeping a school clean than a principal does in his duties. The president of a country does not necessarily have better feelings of self-worth than citizens of the country. A child's self-worth is strengthened more when he learns to better use what he has than dreaming about what he could have. Families based on presiding structure teach the child that each person has his own role to play in the family and in life in general. The engineer may run the train, but he has only one of several important roles necessary to make the train function properly. A child does not have to feel he/she is running the family in order to have a strong feeling of self-worth.

Q. **Can the RUN System Chart be used by anyone else in the family? I would think a parent could monitor a child or a child could do some self-monitoring.**

A. Certainly. Parents are not the only ones who can improve by increasing the "R's" and "U's" and decreasing the "N's." Other family members can also benefit from using the chart. Speaking of increasing and decreasing some actions, did you notice how the lines of the graph on the top of page 164 sort of cross in the middle and form an "X" because the positive approaches were increasing and the negative aspects were decreasing? When you see some type of an "X" shape, you'll know you're moving in the right direction.

Helping Children Develop Values

How are values developed? Are they changeable? How can parents increase their influence on a child's values? Do children just naturally develop good values? In this unit four major types of values are discussed: object value, experiential value, life values, and parent value. Common parental mistakes in value development are mentioned along with how to get a child to do the right thing for the right reason.

"EASY-LISTENING" VS. "HARD-ROCK"

"I want Richard to be honest."
"Marilyn seems to like everything I don't."
"I want Jason to do things for the right reason."
"I would like David to appreciate good literature."
"I would like Maria to enjoy playing the piano."

What do all five of the preceding statements have in common? They are all concerned with *values*. The first statement expresses a parent's desire that Richard will consider honesty to be important. The second points out the frustration parents feel when their child is developing values different from theirs. The third suggests that parents want children to do things, such as help others, for altruistic, rather than materialistic reasons. Every parent becomes aware, on an almost daily basis, that their child has different values than they do. For example, parent/child tastes in music differ. The "easy-listening" music preferred by Marilyn's parents may be as unacceptable to her as the pulsating, "hard-rock" sounds she likes is to them.

But why? Why do people have different values? Where do values come from in the first place? And can a child's values be changed?

167

ARE WE BORN WITH VALUES OR ARE THEY LEARNED?

CHILDREN ARE BORN WITH VALUES and THEY LEARN THEM.

Are children born with values or do they learn them? That is a double question many parents ask and the answer to both of them is: Yes, children are born with values **and** they learn them. If that answer makes you feel uncomfortable, continue reading. Further explanation will make this issue much more clear.

Did your aunt or grandmother or mother ever have an old corsage they had pressed between the pages of a book of remembrance? Did you notice how that old dried-up hunk of foliage meant a great deal to them, but had no meaning to you? The difference in music tastes has already been mentioned. From hundreds of daily experiences like these it was not hard for psychologists to figure out that everyone does not have the same values. If that were the case, it would be easy to conclude that we are born having certain values rather than learning them. Realizing that people often have widely varying values, it must be that most, if not all, of these values are learned through experience.

Mother Nature designed us with a few basic values built in. As infants, we liked warmth more than cold and we enjoyed being held. We did not like being hungry or being shaken quickly. These initial likes and dislikes we had were our basic, limited value system. We had no fondness for certain kinds of music, or basketball, or playing cards, or having money or stylish clothes. We learned to like (or dislike) such things as we had more experiences. We were started off with very few likes and dislikes, but were equipped with a system that allowed us to learn to like or dislike almost anything.

Values come from our experiences. We learn to like and dislike as a result of those experiences. Except for those very few we were born with, our likes and dislikes develop from consequences we receive from our experiences.

BUT WHERE DO THE NEW FEELINGS OF LIKING AND DISLIKING COME FROM?

If six-year-old Billy did not automatically like throwing a ball when he was born, how did he develop an interest in throwing balls? If teenager Debbie was not born liking to cruise main street with her friends, how did she develop that interest? If Steven was not born liking math, how did it develop?

WE LEARN TO LIKE AND DISLIKE THINGS BECAUSE OF OUR EXPERIENCES.

Each one of us is born with a reservoir of feelings inside us. We are born with the ability to feel happiness and joy or sadness and pain. But when we are born, our emotional system—that system of feelings in us, is not completely developed to its fullest capacity. As an infant, few things in life can make us feel happy or hurt. Things such as books, trees, fishing, TV, or stylish clothes don't affect us one way or another. They will stimulate no particular happy feeling within us. Only our immediate concerns—being hungry or cold, needing to stretch—are the main things we care about.

Not only do few things cause us to have feelings when we are young, but also the feelings we do have are quite basic. A cave man would not appreciate a finely cooked meal placed before him. In like manner, a child's emotional system is quite primitive and does not yet allow him to have more refined and in-depth feelings. Such feelings are possible as he matures and accumulates more and more experiences. These increased experiences help him "get in touch" with his feelings.

Another point to keep in mind in understanding how to influence a child's values is that **children are programmable.** Most people are aware that you can buy *programmable* and *non-programmable* calculators. Non-programmable ones are those that are built in such a way at the factory that they will perform certain functions—add, multiply, determine percentages, and so on, but will not do anything else. They are very limited. However, the programmable ones are built to allow the user to modify and change the programs or functions they can perform.

Animals, with their instincts, are like non-programmable calculators. Mother Nature built them with certain likes and dislikes (or values as they might be called) that can't be changed. Mother bears will attack you if you get between them and their cubs. Rabbits run, rather than fight.

Human beings, with just a few likes and dislikes at birth, are like programmable calculators. Mother Nature built us so we could change what we like and dislike. Parents can arrange conditions so children will develop certain likes and dislikes. In fact, children can program themselves to like or dislike certain things. When you stop to think about it, the ability to like or dislike almost anything is one of the best gifts of Mother Nature. To be able to change our values provides us with the ability to change the direction of our lives, for we seek those things that are of value to us. Some people learn to value and collect salt and pepper shakers, bottle caps, coins, or stamps. Others learn to value art, opera, baseball, skiing or working. We have the ability to learn to value almost anything.

SO HOW DOES SOMETHING TAKE ON VALUE FOR A CHILD?

Mother Nature's process for developing values is so beautifully simple that many parents question its ability to produce them. Remember, all the thousands of colors on our earth come from just three basic ones, so do not be fooled by the simplicity of the process for developing values.

The key to developing values is *association*. Associate what you want your child to like with something the child already likes. Ask a man what he thinks about when he smells a soft fragrance of perfume. The flower it perhaps came from? Breakfast? No, he most likely thinks of its wearer—a woman. He associates or *pairs* the two—the perfume and the woman. Women wear perfume and men wear after-shave or cologne because they associate a pleasing response or reaction to such scents. They, then,

CHILDREN ARE PROGRAMMABLE.
Their thoughts and actions can be changed.

IT'S MY COMIC BOOK COLLECTION.

KINGSLEY 83

We have the ability to learn to value almost anything.

The key to developing values is ASSOCIATION.

believe themselves to be more pleasing to others. Because many children associate dentists with pain, they place a negative value on dentists.

By taking an object that a child finds of positive value and placing it with another object that a child has not seen and not yet developed a value judgement on, we can help the new object acquire a positive value. The ability of one object to pass on value to another by being associated with it is the key parents can use to develop values in children. An association with something positive creates a positive value, while an association with something negative produces a negative value.

If you want the ability to work to be of value to Greg, pair work with things that are positive to him.

If you want Brenda to like certain clothes, make sure those clothes are identified with people she looks up to.

If you want Matthew to be honest, make sure honesty pays off for him.

If you want Karen to like playing the piano, make sure enjoyable things are associated with piano playing.

If you want Larry to dislike smoking, make sure unpleasant things are associated with smoking or pleasant things are associated with not doing it.

Advertisers know and use this principle of association very well. By associating a well-like movie or TV star or sports celebrity with a certain product, people's positive feelings about buying the product increase. The product may become instantly desirable simply by being associated with someone the paying public considers desirable.

Through association the value of one object can be passed on to other objects.

YES, FOLKS, YOU ALL RECOGNIZE THIS YEAR'S U.S.A. CHAMPION TENNIS PLAYER, DAN SMITH, WHO DOESN'T USE JUST ANY RACQUET, NO, HE USES ZEBO!

ZEBO

CAN A CHILD'S VALUES BE CHANGED?

Most certainly. Because they are learned in the first place, different ones can replace them, using much the same process in which they were initially learned. If you want your child to like object "C" instead of object "B," pair "C" with good things the child likes and make sure "B" becomes associated with things the child does not like. (Using the inventory of likes and dislikes you filled out in Exercise 2.1 and also referring to those things you listed as rewards and penalties on an Outline for Action form will help you to identify things you can use in this value-changing process.)

BECAUSE VALUES ARE LEARNED, THEY CAN BE CHANGED.

CAN PARENTS REALLY HAVE AN IMPACT ON A CHILD'S VALUE SYSTEM?

Yes! Many parents do not realize the strength, the power, and the value they have in the lives of their children. But their peers? Aren't their peers the ones with real power—the ones they value. Next to the family, peer pressure is usually the most powerful influence in a child's life. Often it **is** the most powerful, but

Parents do not often realize the strength and power they have in the lives of their children.

170

it does not always have to be. Shortly we will see how to increase parental (and home) value.

IS HONESTY SOMETHING THAT CAN BE PRODUCED THROUGH PARENTAL GUIDANCE?

Definitely. Honesty, courtesy, responsibility, and other life values can be taught by increasing the worth of such actions. Some suggestions for doing so follow later in this unit.

ISN'T IT JUST NATURAL FOR CHILDREN TO LIKE THINGS DIFFERENT FROM WHAT PARENTS LIKE?

No more so than it's natural for parents to like things different from what their children like. Parents may often feel that their teenagers intentionally like things that they don't like—that kids nowadays do things contrary to parental likes just to be rebellious. While this does happen, it is not the major reason for differences in likes and dislikes of parents and children. Many children like the things they do simply because they are available to develop a liking for. It's just that simple. To further explain: video and computer games are very popular today. They're available, they're here. So today's kids like them. Parents, who were teenagers ten or more years ago, never learned to get a kick out of such electronic activities. They got their "kicks" in other ways, ways that were perhaps not too acceptable by their parents. So, it isn't so much a matter of natural or unnatural. It's a matter of availability. If parents want their children to accept parental interests and values, they must make positive consequences more available and desirable than those their children are presently attracted to.

Kids don't naturally dislike things their parents like.

WON'T CHILDREN JUST NATURALLY DEVELOP GOOD VALUES?

Do carrots just naturally develop in the package? Good values are like seeds. They need to be planted, nourished, and taken care of. First, they have to be planted; they have to be taught and example is the best teacher. Children, through parental example, must see the positive results of good values. Adherance to values must be rewarded and nourished. If one set of values will more adequately meet a child's needs and desires than another, that is the set he will follow. The power of association determines a child's acceptance or rejection of parental values.

HOW'S YOUR UNCLE BILL?

Because the *principle of association*, as first mentioned in Unit One and earlier in this unit, is so important in value development, it would be well to refresh our understanding of it.

We are often unaware that, as part of our thinking process, we are always comparing one thing to another, one activity to

171

YOU KNOW, YOU LOOK JUST LIKE ROBERT REDFORD. CAN I HAVE YOUR AUTOGRAPH?

another, one person to another. The remark *"Doesn't he remind you of Uncle Bill?"* is a comparison. If you have a good feeling about Uncle Bill, you are, in effect, saying that you do or can feel that same way about this person. If your opinion of Uncle Bill is negative, your remark will suggest a negative feeling or attitude. By associating—in other words, pairing—one item, event, or person with another, the value of the one takes on the value of the other. It is these comparisons, these judgments that direct our choices through life.

DIFFERENT KINDS OF VALUES

The values we develop during our lives could be placed into four major classifications: *object value, experiential value, life values,* and *parent value.*

OBJECT VALUE: Children can learn to value objects. Bicycles, food, toys, books, trees, dirt, rocks, gum wrappers, birds, and bugs are just a few of the millions of objects on this earth children can learn to like, to dislike, or to not care about at all.

EXPERIENTIAL VALUE: Objects are not the only things that can have value to a child. Experiences can have value also. In fact, many children enjoy activities more than objects. Going fishing, playing basketball, watching a movie, studying, running, telling jokes, being scolded, or talking to someone you hate are all experiences a child can put a positive or negative value on.

LIFE VALUES: Some dimensions of life are what might be called life values. Being honest, trustworthy, considerate, and dependable and following a work ethic are examples of life values.

PARENT VALUE: Parents are seen by children as both objects and actions. They do things for the child. Parents are the most important outside force on a child.

WE ALL WANT OUR CHILDREN TO DO THINGS FOR THE RIGHT REASON.

There is a fifth area of value development that also should be considered. That is what is called *value shifting.* Have you ever asked yourself: "How can I get my child to do something for the right reason, such as cleaning his or her bedroom because of feeling good in doing so, rather than for a material reward?" If you have, you have been concerned with value shifting (which was first discussed in Unit Four).

Let's now look more closely at these areas and see how parents can help their children develop positive values in each.

OBJECT VALUE: Any object on this earth can have a value. Some naturally have a positive value. Certain fragrances are automatically pleasant to children, as are many foods and drinks. Certain "fragrances"—skunk, sulphur gas—are automatically unpleasant to children (and adults). Most objects in a child's life, however, mean nothing until they are associated with things the child **already** considers either positive or negative. Forks and spoons are paired with getting food. Binoculars let you see far distances. Clothes can be liked because they keep the child warm or because a friend wears the same kind. Table 11.1 lists several kinds of objects and suggests some ideas parents may use to increase or decrease the value of such objects to a child.

Any object can have value to someone.

Table 11.1   OBJECT VALUE

OBJECTS:	What INCREASES the value of an object:	What DECREASES the value of an object:	What parents can do to influence child's value of an object:
HAIR STYLE	It's comfortable. Child's peers place value on that hair style. It's "in." It's easy and inexpensive to take care of. Parents like it. Parents dislike it.	It's uncomfortable; gets in eyes. Peers laugh at it. It takes time and is expensive to maintain. Parents dislike it. Parents like it.	Encourage and influence your child to choose peers who support your values. Pay for haircuts and styling if style meets your values. Make yourself more valuable to your child. (See *parent value* on following pages.)
NAME-BRAND CLOTHING	Child's peers wear same brand. Parental approval. Parental disapproval. It is comfortable. Such clothing suggests expensive tastes.	Person child dislikes wears that brand. Parental disapproval. Parental approval. It is uncomfortable. Such clothing is expensive to buy on limited allowance.	(See influencing peer choices, above.) (See increasing parent value, above.) Pay for clothes that meet your standards and values.
BOOKS	Praise child who purchases, borrows, or reads books. Have many books in the home. Talk about the value of books. Child sees having and using books as being enjoyable.	Make fun of books and people who have them. Have no books in the home. Speak negatively about books. ("Waste of money!") Child sees no positive experiences with books.	(Follow suggestions in first column to increase value of books.) (Follow suggestions in second column to decrease value of books.) Read to your child. Help him associate books and "book" activities with positive times with parents.
MUSIC	Have experiences in home pertaining to music: have and use piano or other musical instruments. Have stereo, radio, cassette player with records and tapes that are played regularly. Play music at bedtime. Talk positively about music and musicians.	Make children listen to music when they prefer to do "funner" things. Have nothing pertaining to music in the home. Tell children that radio or stereo must be off at bedtime. Speak negatively or not at all about music.	Have music be a part of other pleasurable activities: family meetings, activities, campfires, traveling in car. Show respect for equipment and recordings by way you take care of them. Allow music (parent's choice and volume) to be played at bedtime. (Again, parent value helps here.) (See first column.)
TOYS	They are fun to twist, turn, pull, bite, hold, etc.. They are soft. They make pleasant sounds. They work, are not broken, are kept up. They are bright and cheerful. Parent is with child when he (she) plays with toys.	They are too big or heavy to handle or to bite, etc.. They have sharp edges and points. They pinch. They make loud noises. They don't work well. They are painted ugly colors. Child is scolded often for not putting them away, or putting in mouth, or using improperly.	(See either first or second column for ideas to influence child's object value, either positively or negatively.) Teach child to treat them well and to take care of them by letting him (her) see how you take care of your "toys"—stereo, shop tools, etc.. Teach child to put them away. Have special, accessible place to keep them.

**ONE TYPE
OF VALUE
INFLUENCES
OTHER TYPES
OF VALUES.**

As shown repeatedly in the right column of Table 10.1, the value a child places on a parent and the things a parent finds important and of worth can greatly influence the things—hair styles, clothing, books—a child finds of value. If Jennifer has a positive relationship with her parents, she is more apt to like and dislike the same things. If her relationship is negative, she will possibly like what her parents dislike and the reverse. This is why the "like"/"dislike" and "approval"/"disapproval" are shown in the two columns. So we see that one type of value influences other types of values. Parent value will influence object value, as will experiential value. (Positive experiences in reading will increase the value of books as objects.)

EXPERIENTIAL VALUE: Experiences are an important part of life. In fact, they are the reason for life itself. Wouldn't it be nice if your children learned to like the same types of activities that you do? Well, it's possible. The main reason that it does not happen is that children cannot see the value of many activities in the same way that parents do. We usually look at experiences in terms of what the experiences can do for us, while children like activites that make them feel good at the time. Table 11.2 gives some ideas parents can use to influence the value of playing baseball, studying, and fishing. The ideas given can be just as valuable in developing values in other kinds of activities.

Table 11.2
EXPERIENTIAL VALUES

EXPERIENCE:	WAYS TO INCREASE ITS VALUE:	WAYS TO DECREASE ITS VALUE:
PLAYING BASEBALL	Have child start doing it with someone child loves (father, brother, uncle). Laugh and have fun while teaching child to catch the ball. Praise good catches by the child. Show child you appreciate being able to have this experience with him/her. End baseball experience with a treat or other pleasurable activity.	Be very serious; demand child try harder. Criticize when child makes mistakes. Continue to play after child is tired. Tell child of his/her awkwardness. Tell child you expect him/her to do better—child is not trying hard enough.
STUDYING	Have study time for all members of family so child can see the value for everyone. For parents, the studying may be reading a novel or other book. Start with short study sessions and increase time as child gets older. Start with material child enjoys interacting with; then add more difficult material as child gets older. Provide rewards—praise, material gifts—for good studying and the results of good studying (good grades). Have a scheduled time for studying. End study time with some treat. Have family members discuss what was studied. Have a designated place for studying. Help child, where possible and if necessary, with studies. Thank child for doing his/her studies.	Criticize child for lack of studying. Vary the time when studying should occur. Have haphazard, irregular schedule. Show no appreciation when the child completes studying. Remind child it is simply expected that he/she study. Don't ask about the material the child is studying.
FISHING	Choose fishing spots where child can be successful (catch fish). Talk and joke around while travelling to and from fishing. Help child learn how to prepare his/her own equipment. Talk about the fun times you had fishing as a youngster. Praise child when he/she does something well. ("Hey, that was a good cast!") Thank child for going with you.	Go someplace where there are few fish. Point out the child's faults while travelling to and from fishing. Remind child you are doing child a favor by taking him/her fishing. Ignore the child and think about your own problems or plans. Be short tempered and take offense at everything child does. Don't show child how to fish and complain when he/she does it wrong.

LIFE VALUES: Some values we want our children to develop have to do with things less tangible than objects or experiences. Honesty, work-ethic, courtesy, sincerity, and integrity are the kinds of life values most parents want for their children. While these kinds of values seem much different from values we develop for objects and experiences, the process for developing them is the same. In fact, life values develop from the values associated with objects and experiences. The value of honesty develops from experiences where honesty pays off for the child. The value of dishonesty develops where dishonesty pays off. When dishonesty is associated with success and peer approval, it is what the child will come to value. Table 11.3 lists several ideas parents may use to develop certain values.

Life values develop from the values associated with objects and experiences.

Table 11.3   LIFE VALUES

LIFE VALUE:	WAYS TO INCREASE ITS VALUE:	WAYS TO DECREASE ITS VALUE:
WORK	Start when the child is young. Work beside or with them; don't have child work alone; be a good model. Start with short, easy chores and increase the difficulty and duration over the years. Show children how to make games out of work (try to get so much done in a certain length of time or organize work so that periodically family members change jobs with each other). BE SURE POSITIVE CONSEQUENCES RESULT FROM WORKING. Express positive feelings when work is done and ask child how he/she feels. ("I really feel good seeing this mess clean-up. How does it make you feel, Johnny?") Express appreciation for jobs well done. Post family work roster showing 5 or 6 daily chores for each child. Give allowances for good performance. (rewards) Reduce allowances when work is not done. (penalties)	Make the child work alone. Criticize child's efforts. Remind child how lazy and uncooperative he/she is. Give child more than he/she can handle. Don't explain how you want the job done. Spring work on child without warning, especially when he/she is doing something fun. Do not express appreciation for work done (or work done well); point out it is simply expected.
COURTESY	Be a good example. Show courtesy to child. Express appreciation to child when he/she is courteous. (At least once a week.) Diplomatically point out instances where you see others being courteous. Emphasize treating others the way you want to be treated. (mutual respect) Start when the child is young. Let child experience situations where not being courteous does not pay off.	Don't be courteous; just expect your children to be. Yell at the child when he/she is not courteous. Demean child for not being courteous.
HONESTY	Be a good example; even intentionally set up situations to show honesty. Diplomatically point out situations of honesty. Point out examples of the positive results of honesty.	Let child see you being dishonest. Show them they can get ahead by being dishonest.

PARENT VALUE: In the real sense of classifying values, parents would not be considered in a separate category. For, after all, parents are objects and parents provide experiences for the child. Although parents can be an "extra-important object" in a child's life, there are many who feel their children do not value them very highly. Therefore, one of the main purposes of this section on *parent value* is to provide ideas parents can use to raise the value of themselves in the eyes of their children.

Parents are valued as objects and as providers of experiences.

Parents have little trouble being of high value when their child is young. But, as children get older, more things outside the family catch their attention. Much of modern technology is focused on getting your child's attention.

"Buy this brand of jeans. It makes you attractive to boys!"
"See this movie. It's the greatest!"
"There is no fun better than going to the amusement park!"
"Smoke. It's the adult thing to do!"

Parents of all generations have had to compete with outside influences but never ones as strong as those today. In the past number of years one word keeps cropping up which describes children's (mostly teenagers) attitude of parents: **boring**. Parents get that label for two main reasons: (1) society has more glamorous alternatives to family activities today, and (2) parents make some common mistakes that support such attitudes.

COMMON PARENTAL MISTAKES

ARE YOU:

TOO BUSY?
TOO NEGATIVE?

There are two major mistakes or problems:

1. Being too busy.
2. Being too negative.

Table 11.4 lists several ideas parents can use to increase or decrease their value in the eyes of their child. Notice that all of the ways to decrease parent value have to do with being too busy or too negative. Yet being busy and negative **can** also be positive for you and your child. Being around all the time can make your

Table 11.4
PARENT VALUE

WAYS TO INCREASE PARENT VALUE	WAYS TO DECREASE PARENT VALUE
Have at least twice as many positive experiences as negative ones with your child each week. (Talk with them, play with them, work on a task together, express thanks, give unconditional love, give resultant love.) (Include a constructive criticism in the weekly feedback to the child.)	Have more negative experiences than positive ones with your child each week.
Pair yourself with positive experiences your child has. (Go to the circus, on a picnic, to a movie. Be present when your child is in a school play or at a ball game.)	Demean the child rather than disciplining the misbehavior. Criticize more than you praise.
Let your child see you make mistakes and see you correct them.	Get busy and don't go places with your child.
Treat your child with respect. Discipline child when needed. Use communication skills discussed in Units Seven and Eight.	Tell your child you had planned something special, but because of his actions the opportunity is gone.
If your child doesn't like you now, start associating yourself with the positive things listed above. A child's feelings about you can be changed.	Repeatedly point out the shortcomings of your child.
Arrange it so the child has more fun on activities with you than without you.	Always tell a funnier joke than child does.
TIME PLANNING: When on a busy schedule, do things that can still make you positive to your child. Send cards; leave written messages on pillow; set aside "quality time" for interaction; call him/her on the phone; don't forget special dates—birthdays, holidays; take child with you to work or on business trip—when possible; use chore time as interaction time; talk to them while in car going to and from places.	Always say something wiser than child does.
	Remind child how lucky he/she is to have you as a parent.
POSITIVE PARENT PERCEPTION: Moms and dads should be public relations managers for each other. Make positive comments which remind children what the other parent has done for them.	Hold grudges for past misdeeds of child.
BE POSITIVELY UNPREDICTABLE: Add excitement to your family by bringing unexpected little gifts home and by having occasional, unplanned, unannounced exciting family activities.	Don't help them work out problems; tell them what they should do.

child tired of you. And pointing out negatives to children—if done properly—can help them. Being busy and negative are like salt in your diet—a little is essential but it can be overused.

IDEAS FOR DEVELOPING POSITIVE PARENT VALUES

Table 11.4 includes several ideas parents can use to make themselves of more value to their children. Out of those listed, four points need to be emphasized:

Positives Plus Negatives.

Parents need to give their children both positive and negative feedback in their lives. Provide payoffs for being good and penalties for misbehavior. In doing so, however, make sure you are giving nine positive consequences for every one negative one. We often find ourselves paying more attention to the misbehaviors of our children than to their positive behaviors. Almost every parent would benefit by spending more time and effort on little Johnny when he is behaving correctly.

WE ALL NEED POSITIVES AND NEGATIVES IN OUR LIVES.

Time Planning.

Many busy parents are doing a fine job raising children. Certainly, it is not easy, but it can be done. By planning one's time, parents can provide more time for positive interaction with their children. How about having pleasant talks while taking them to school. What about playing around together while washing the car. Everyday needs and responsibilities provide many opportunities for parents to not only get some things done, but also have positive interaction with their children.

Your everyday needs and experiences can provide opportunity to interact with your child.

Positive Parent Perception.

With so many attention-getting forces attracting children, parents need a public relations program to help them compete. Many children fail to see and appreciate the things parents do for them. Well, parents do have some good public relations help— each other. They can help each other by reminding children in a positive way what the other parent does for them. Take the time to point out such things as:

"Boy, that was a good breakfast. That mom of yours really puts in a lot of time taking care of us, doesn't she?"

"Hey, Debbie, that's a cute outfit. You know, I was watching your mother pick it out for you. She sure does care for you, doesn't she?"

"Billy, I know you and your dad had an argument this morning. You know, he really cares about you. Did you ever think how much easier it would be for him to just let you do what you want? But you mean too much for him to do that."

"Hey, guys. Your mom comes home from work tired, yet she takes the time to fix our supper. Think how much she must love us to do that. Let's do something nice and fix supper for her for a change."

Many children need a reminder once in a while to keep what mom and dad do for them in perspective. It is easy for children to take parents' efforts for granted. Help your children appreciate what their mom and dad do for them, but be careful to do it in the right spirit.

Be Positively Unpredictable.

Add spice to your family life. Everyone realizes that unexpected flowers and cards do wonders for a marital relationship. The same is true for families. Too often parents run a boring family. Nothing exciting seems to happen. Bring surprises home to your children. In some cases the surprise may be nothing more than sticks of gum. In some cases it may be an unexpected trip to the movies. Donuts for breakfast, lemonade for family members working in the yard, notes and treats left on pillows saying things like *"Thanks for being my daughter"*, an unexpected letter from dad who wrote it at the office, unplanned family drives that end up at the ice cream parlor—all these little things are what make a house a home.

VALUE SHIFTING

Throughout the NAP Handbook giving children consequences for their actions has been emphasized. **Make sure your child receives rewards for good behavior and penalties for misbehavior.**

But should that be the case? What about comments like:

"I want Steven to do it because it is right, not because he gets rewarded."
"Mary Lou should just do it. After all, she should be obedient."

Children do not automatically know what is right and what is wrong.

It is important that parents keep in mind the fact that children are not born knowing what is right or wrong. They have to learn to make such judgments and decisions themselves. Such decisions are based on the child's experiences and what those experiences produce.

If parents bought pianos and just waited for the child to learn to play them, very few pianos would be played. Some children would find the natural consequences of playing with the piano keys enough to stimulate them to learn to play. For most children, however, extra support in terms of rewards for effort and practice is needed until they become good enough that the sounds they produce become strong enough reward to motivate their continued playing.

Many of the more important things children could learn to do do not provide enough natural satisfaction for the child to do them. Learning to wait your turn, to jog, to study, to save money, to lose weight, to work, and to help others are a few examples. In such situations, parents may provide additional incentives to help the child learn. Just as the physician may use surgical and medicinal helps to aid the natural healing process, so may a parent add special consequences to help when natural consequences are not powerful enough.

If the child is not picking up the desired actions without special assistance, parents may provide things the child values as additional incentives to learn. These incentives may be food, activities, toys, various objects, affection, and social interaction.

The secret for parents who want to develop positive actions in their child is to: (1) **get the action to occur,** then (2) **get the action to occur for the right reason.** What this means is that parents should use whatever *reward* it takes to get the child to begin doing it, then work on *shifting* from giving the child some material reward such as money or food, to a more intrinsic reward such as doing it because it makes the child feel good inside. *Value shifting* is that process of shifting from giving material rewards to the child (which the child finds of value) to giving verbal appreciation (which the child also finds of value) and then on to getting the child to feel good inside himself for what has been done.

FIRST, GET THE ACTION GOING.

THEN, GET IT TO OCCUR FOR THE RIGHT REASON.

Value shifting is an important skill for parents to learn. Mother Nature provided them with the ability to learn how to use rewards to develop actions in children. The secret to getting actions started in a child is similar to getting a newly planted tree to grow. Initially the tree needs lots of extra nutrients and water to take root. Later, continued application of the same amount of nutrients will be too much for it and will weaken it and may even kill it.

With children it often takes extra attention and rewards to get an action going. We start by rewarding Mary Lou every time she does the desired act. After she is performing the act consistently, rewards should be gradually reduced until very few are needed.

Use extra attention and rewards to get an action going.

Mother Nature never intended parents to reward children every time they perform some act. In fact, doing so will eventually weaken the child's tendencies to act, just like over-feeding a tree will weaken it. *Value shifting* is the basis for this weaning process in children. While it may be accomplished several ways by a trained psychologist, Table 11.5 outlines basic steps for parents interested in using this method.

However, prolonged attention and rewards can weaken a child's tendency to act.

A tape is available that explains in greater detail the principles of value shifting and how to make it work. This tape, *Getting Children to Do It for the Right Reason,* may be ordered by using the address shown on the last page of this handbook.

TABLE 11.5   IDEAS FOR VALUE SHIFTING

ACTIVITY:		MAKING BED.
INITIAL CONSEQUENCE:		Some material reward (food, money, special privilege) given every time child makes bed.
STEPS OF VALUE SHIFTING:	step 1	Give material reward every time action is done.
	step 2	Add verbal praise to the material reward. ("That's good, Johnny" followed by cookie or whatever.)
	step 3	Give verbal praise every time, and give material reward every other time, then every third time, then every fourth . . .
	step 4	Give verbal praise and add comments to make child begin to think about the value of what was done. ("That was good, Johnny. It makes me feel good to see your bed made. How does it make you feel?")
	step 5	Intermittently praise the child for making the bed and ask how he/she feels about doing it. (Every month or so give a special reward, such as an extended bedtime or special treat or activity, for having a good record of bed making.)

SO, HOW CAN PARENTS HELP CHILDREN DEVELOP VALUES?

It is important that parents remember that most of a child's values are learned. And if they are learned, there are things parents can do to influence which values a child learns.

The key principle of value development is *association*. Associate the things you want your child to like with things the child already likes. If you want a child to value a certain object, associate (or pair) that object with other things the child already likes. Make sure the activities you want your child to like result in things the child likes. If you want your child to develop certain life values such as work and honesty, make sure such efforts result in pleasant consequences for your child.

Values can be developed in children and parents should be actively involved in helping children develop good values.

UNIT ELEVEN: HELPING CHILDREN DEVELOP VALUES
Exercise 11.1

1. Pick some object or thing you would like your child to learn to value and explain what you could do to help it take on value.

   Example: Encyclopedias - I would take time to go through looking up interesting topics with them. AND - perhaps have some treat after such activities.

2. Pick some activity you would like your child to learn to value and explain what you could do to help it take on value.

   Example: Learning to preserve fruit. I would start by making sure that my child has fun helping in the bottling of fruit. I would give rewards, and make sure I do not work him/her too hard I would explain the value of bottling fruit. Praise for effort would be included.

3. Suppose your child enjoyed lighting matches all the time. What are some things you could do to reduce the value the child saw in lighting matches?

4. Point out four things you could do to increase your parental value to your child.

QUESTIONS and ANSWERS

Q. The unit mentions that children are born with few things automatically having value. What about things like playing the piano or studying art that some children seem to like to do? Where does the value for doing such things come from?

A. There are many activities in our world that have an intrinsic value that stimulates us to desire them. However, most of them do not have enough value to make us want to do them. Children have to get through the arduous stage of piano practice before piano playing takes on value because of the music it produces. Most important things in life require us to go through a phase of doing without receiving an intrinsic payoff. Getting an education, apprenticing on a job, learning to draw properly—there are so many things in life that we learn have value if only we can somehow make it through those painful, effort-filled dimensions we must encounter before we can reap the benefits of the activity. Wise parents use additional rewards and penalties where natural consequences are not enough.

Q. My two-year-old hates to take baths. Is that a problem of value? And what do I do about it?

A. Yes, this is a value problem. When children fail to do something, it means it is of higher value to the child not to do it. Remember the *principles of least effort* and *profit of action*? Your child could hate taking baths because he has had some fearful bath experiences in the past, or because soap got in his eyes, or perhaps his attempts not to take baths gets him more of mother's attention than willingly taking a bath. Fill out an Outline for Action form referred to in Units Six and Seven (Developing Positive Actions - Form A).

Q. Does the giving of rewards and penalties influence values in a child?

A. That is a very good question. It shows you are starting to get the real idea behind consequation. Consequation, that is the application and/or removal of positives and negatives, is basically changing the value of actions for children by associating those actions with rewards and penalties.

Q. You mention that developing values for things like wanting to cruise Main Street or being honest comes from such experiences being paired with things the child already likes. Isn't there a better, more psychological way to develop values in children?

A. No matter what gimmicks or fancy sounding psychological shortcuts you may be told about, there is no better or faster way. Those shortcuts or "easy ways" to develop values which some people advocate are as effective as those shortcuts and easy ways to lose weight. This unit gives you the best shortcuts and tips available anywhere. Use them and you will find they work—and often quicker and easier than you expect. But remember, values take longer to develop than simple actions of a child.

Tips in Solving Parental Problems

Solving the problems of parenting should do two things. First, it should help develop happy and content children. And second, parents themselves should continue to grow and progress as individuals. This unit pulls together information from all the preceding units and shows how the problems of parenting can be turned into strengths for both the child *and* the parent.

DEVELOPING THE "MUSCLES" OF THE MIND

If you were asked how to go about developing physical strength, could you give some good suggestions? Of course. The fact that muscles develop and grow because of situations where those muscles must work against some resistant force is no secret. Our lives are full of resisting forces which challenge our muscles. Our day-to-day routines require us to stand up against the force of gravity, lift objects, run, and carry things. And if we want to maximize muscle development we can prepare a special weight training program and diet. **Creating physical stress provides the avenue for developing physical strength.**

Did you ever stop to think that the same principle holds true for mental strength? **Creating mental stress provides the avenue for developing mental strength.** Problems are a natural part of life. Everyone has them—**everyone!** They are the mental hurdles designed to develop our mental skills. Human beings were not born with instincts to tell us what to do in different situations. Born with the ability to learn and make decisions, we are given opportunities for solving problems that sharpen our mental skills and mold our abilities.

Perhaps you had not thought of a problem with your child as an opportunity to develop your mental skills. But that is what it can be. Now, that doesn't mean that every parent/child problem you have had or are going to have will strengthen a parent's mental abilities. It means that every problem situation provides the opportunity for self-improvement. (Remember, the NAP

PHYSICAL STRESS PRODUCES PHYSICAL STRENGTH.

MENTAL STRESS PRODUCES MENTAL STRENGTH.

Problems are a natural part of life.

183

System supports the idea that not only should parents help their children to grow, develop, and mature, but also that they, themselves, should consider their own continued growth and development.) Just as a father may injure himself by incorrectly using body-building equipment, so may parents weaken, rather than strengthen, mental skills by using incorrect problem solving techniques with their children.

The purpose of this unit is to (1) point out the things parenting professionals do when solving problems, and (2) suggest how the units in this handbook can best be used to solve problems parents encounter. Besides bringing together material from all the previous units of the handbook and suggesting how the information from those units can be used in the problem-solving areas of parenting, this unit points out the steps parenting professionals go through in solving parent/child problems.

Each of our lives will include literally hundreds of problems to solve. The degree to which we can rely on ourselves to solve them is one of the key dimensions that distinguishes us from all of Mother Nature's other creatures. We have the ability to create solutions to the problems children may bring into our lives. The more problems we solve, the better we can handle future problem situations.

So what can parents do to improve their problem-solving skills? One of the best things to do is **do what the pros do.** Approach problems the way child-rearing professionals do. There are four main things professionals look at to improve problem solving:

1. Analyze the situation carefully and completely.
2. Use all available sources in developing a solution.
3. Remember, there are things to do **after** the problem is solved.
4. Learn to use what you have to solve problems.

Thoroughly analyze
the problem.

ANALYZING SITUATIONS: Tell yourself about it.

The first step in problem-solving is to take the time to tell yourself all about it. If you've ever been to a doctor's or psychologist's office or met with a lawyer or other professional person, you'll remember that they spent the first portion of their time with you in asking questions. Asking questions is an important part of what psychologists do. Those questions help identify what the problem really is and why the problem seems to exist. When asking questions, psychologists are like police detectives who are trying to get a clear picture of the real situation they are facing. So, instead of paying $90 an hour to psychologists and psychiatrists to ask you questions, ask yourself the questions and save the money.

The questions to ask yourself are really quite basic. You do not have to have a degree to ask them. What you want to get clear in your mind are three basic things:

WHAT?   WHEN?   WHY?

WHAT is the real problem?

Frankly, in most family situations parents do not take the time to get a clear picture of what the problem really is. Satisfied that they have a general idea as to what is wrong, parents begin trying to correct it. Usually, when their attempts fail, it is because they did not have a complete enough understanding of the whole problem. By asking "**What** exactly is my child doing?" parents can get a better picture of **what** the problem really is. The *Outlines for Action* for the four types of misbehavior (explained in Unit Seven) list some of the questions psychologists would ask.

WHEN does the problem occur?

What parents really want to search for in answering this question is: *"Under what conditions does the problem exist?"* Does Johnny lie to get out of work or does he lie (tell tall stories) to get attention? Does Amy get nervous around everyone or just one particular person? Does David do what dad tells him, but not what mother asks?

WHY does the problem exist?

People do things for reasons. And problems do not just happen. There are reasons for them. Johnny does not save money because dad gives it to him whenever he wants it. Beth does not keep her room clean because mother comes along and does it. Keri sits quietly and is withdrawn in class because the teacher gives her more attention when she acts that way. These are examples of "why." Look for the "why" in your problem situation. They are always there. There may be more than one plausible "why" that could explain a problem's cause. By sitting down and thoroughly examining the problem, parents can usually determine the "why."

When you begin telling yourself all about the problem, be specific. Go into great detail, for in the details you will find the key to solving the problem. *Exactly what does the child do or not do? Where does the problem occur? Is there any particular person around whom it occurs? What do you, the parent, do?* Parents can ask themselves good questions just as psychologists do. Try it! Write it all down on paper. After describing the problem to yourself, over and over several times, start looking for a pattern.

> *"Every time Billy yells, I give him what he wants."*
> *"Michelle does most of her complaining when she misses her nap."*
> *"I do not follow through with my threats and promises, so Andrea ignores what I tell her to do."*

DO WHAT THE PROS DO.

ASK: *WHAT?*
      WHEN?
      WHY?

BE SPECIFIC.

LOOK FOR PATTERNS.

185

After going through this process parents are usually amazed at how clear the problem becomes to them, how the reasons for the problem become more obvious, and how several solutions to the problem begin to emerge. Eighty percent of the time parents can solve problems as well as professionals by just taking the time to analyze the situation more thoroughly.

After analyzing the problem situation(s), parents should have a better idea of what the problem is and why it exists. This step usually includes one or more of the following:

Thoroughly analyzing a problem is the key to its solution.

1. There are some negative behaviors in the child that need to be **decreased**.
2. There are some positive actions that need to be **increased**.
3. The child's values need to be strengthened or changed.
4. The child's self-esteem needs to be improved.
5. Better communication skills need to be developed between parent and child.

In some cases the problem is only one of these five. In most cases, however, it is more than one. Whatever the total problem is that you identify, the next step is to develop a solution.

USE ALL SOURCES FOR DEVELOPING A SOLUTION

Having a pretty good idea about what the problem is and why it exists, the parent is ready to determine what steps should be followed to remedy the problem, and what alternatives are available to do so. One or more of the following should be considered:

1. **Decrease** some negative behavior.
2. **Increase** some positive actions.
3. **Influence** the child's values.
4. **Influence** the child's self-worth.
5. **Develop** better communication skills.

As you will already have noticed by reading the previous units of this Handbook, these five issues have already been discussed in some detail. Figure 12.1, on the following page, reminds you which units relate most specifically to which types of problems. As a result of your problem-analysis you should be able to determine which units best address the particular problem you are concerned with.

By studying the suggested units, parents can determine which is the best method to follow. Suppose, for example, a parent wants to stop certain misbeaviors of their child. By reading Unit Two that parent should get an idea why the child misbehaves. Unit Three tells the parent three basic techniques that can be used to get rid of misbehavior. Unit Five gets even more specific and outlines six methods for treating misbehavior. Unit Six explains to parents what the basic types of misbehaviors are, and what methods work best in changing them.

	DECREASE NEGATIVE BEHAVIOR	INCREASE POSITIVE ACTIONS	INFLUENCE CHILD'S SELF-WORTH	INFLUENCE CHILD'S VALUES	DEVELOP COMMUNICATION SKILLS
UNIT 2 — What motivates a child?	●	●	●	●	●
UNIT 3 — Putting motivational forces to work in the family.	●	●	●	●	●
UNIT 4 — Developing positive thoughts and actions in children.		●			
UNIT 5 — Six ways to handle misbehavior in children.	●				
UNIT 6 — The four main types of misbehavior—what to do about them.	●				
UNIT 7 — Outlines for Action: The key to behavior change.	●	●			
UNIT 8 — Communication: Using the power of language.					●
UNIT 9 — Communication: Developing a good climate.					●
UNIT 10 — Improving your child's self-worth.			●		
UNIT 11 — Helping children develop values.				●	

Figure 12.1 A list of five basic types of problems parents may need to deal with, showing the units specifically designed to provide information for handling each type of problem.

If the child has poor self-worth, the parent can focus on Units Two, Three, and Ten. Units Two and Three explain the basics behind why a child acts and feels like he does. Unit Ten explains what the *self* is, how it develops, and several things a parent can do to influence a child's self-worth.

It is important to remember that a parent is most likely facing more than one problem at any given time. So how does the parent deal with more than one? The answer is similar to what you would do with physical health problems. If you have a runny nose, clogged sinuses, a headache, and so on, you take a multi-ingredient capsule that includes a combination of medications which focuses specifically on each problem.

The same is true for parent/child problems. Figure out the solutions to each of the problems individually, then combine them into an overall plan of action. Seldom does the remedy for one problem contradict the remedy for a second one. For example, if your child misbehaves and has a poor self-worth problem, the remedy for handling misbehavior will not usually undermine the remedy for improving the child's self-worth. In fact, successfully treating one of the problems usually helps the others. Developing better communication skills, for example, often has the effect of reducing misbehavior.

Working on one problem usually helps correct another one.

Most parents will find it best to tackle only one type of problem at a time. Start with the one you feel most confident about handling, then tackle more difficult ones. Then, like a circus juggler, you will find your ability to handle more than one problem at a time will increase.

AT FIRST, TACKLE ONE PROBLEM AT A TIME.

There are four steps to solving any problem:

1. Define the problem.
2. Study the units pertaining to the type of problem being handled.
3. Develop a plan of action.
4. Consider all possible factors that might affect the plan of action.

Steps one and two have just been discussed. Step three is quite important. Units Four and Seven explain how to fill out and use various *Outline for Action* forms. If you feel the need for more specific help, audio-cassette tapes (each of which has an *Outline for Action*) are available which give even more detailed advice. (See the last page of this handbook for ordering information.) These *NAP Practical Problem Series* tapes include:

How to Handle Fears
How to Handle "Goal-Getting" Misbehavior
How to Handle Indolent Misbehavior
How to Handle "Reaction-Seeking" Misbehavior
Lying and Stealing
Bedwetting and Arguing
Sexual Problems
Drug Problems
Do's and Don't's of Discipline and Punishment
Options for Handling Conflicts
Communication and Caring
Getting Children to Do It for the Right Reason
Developing Positive Thoughts and Actions in Children

Step four suggests you consider the following ideas that can make your plan of action easier to put into action and more useful in its results:

It takes time—the right time.

1. Pick the right time to start.

Don't start until you can give the needed time to follow through with what you plan to do. Pick a time when other things will not get in your way.

Be considerate and understanding.

2. Do not demean a child when treating a problem.

We tend to chastize or criticize the child rather than the child's actions.

There's nothing as constant as change.

3. Do not expect permanent change in the child.

Often parents expect their remedies to change a child permanently. Think what that really implies. What if a child of fourteen were made so he could not be changed once he was a certain way. Being "set for life" is not something we should really want for anyone. We should be able to change—to grow and develop every day.

Consistency and Completion are the C's of suCCess.

4. Follow through.

Not following through with a particular plan of action can often reinforce the problem or misbehavior and make it worse. You may need to back up, make some adjustments in your plan, and continue until completion. Parental inconsistency and not doing what you tell a child you'll do strengthens misbehaviors.

Nobody's perfect.

5. Expect to make mistakes.

As you actively work to correct problems, you're bound to make some mistakes. Make adjustments in your analysis and plan of action and continue on.

188

By way of review here is a list of **do's** and **don't's** of problem solving:

DO'S AND DON'T'S OF PROBLEM-SOLVING

★ **Don't** try to change everything at once.
★ **Don't** blame deep psychological causes for the problem.
★ **Don't** go off half-prepared to solve a problem.
★ **Do** believe you can do something about the problem.
★ **Do** remember that actions are changeable through consequences and developed expectancies.
★ **Don't** forget that environmental cues have power and can change actions.
★ **Don't** expect problem-free parenting—there will be unpleasant times.
★ **Don't** expect your child to act mature and reasonable all the time.
★ **Do** mix the elements of positives, negatives, and mistake correction.
★ **Do** focus on actions rather than character when disciplining.
★ **Do** expect to make mistakes.
★ **Do** what you say and say what you'll do.
★ **Do** remember that "good" and "bad" are relative.
★ **Don't** be scared off by a child's attempt to stop what you are doing.
★ **Don't** expect permanent change. We really wouldn't want that.
★ **Do** write out your plan of action.

If there is anything that we wish to change in a child, we should examine it and see whether it is not something that could better be changed in ourselves.

C. G. Jung
Psychological Reflections

Following the instructions laid out in this NAP Handbook can help parents develop solutions to problems. But don't forget that help is also available from other sources, too. For example, use friends to help evaluate any plan you devise. Have you ever noticed how confident you feel in knowing what your neighbor should do to handle **his** child? Well, it is true that parents are often so close to a problem that they cannot see what needs to be done. Parents often make unwise allowances and excuses for their own child's action that they won't for someone else's child. So ask your friends for advice. And do not be too sensitive if the suggestions you get do not coincide with what you feel about the situation.

Ask other parents what remedies they use. Psychologists, psychiatrists, and doctors always ask each other for advice. No one person has all the answers.

189

WHAT TO DO AFTER THE PROBLEM IS SOLVED

What should a person on a diet do after he or she reaches a desired weight? They need to move from the diet plan to a maintenance program to keep the weight off. The same principle is important in problem-solving situations. Mother Nature never intended parents to be continually running around, trying to keep problems with their children under control. The natural plan of life is designed so each child can come up with solutions to life's problems without parents needing to become too involved. The natural consequences of life are usually adequate to help the child progress.

DON'T LET HIM KICK HIS BROTHERS OR SISTERS FOR AT LEAST SIX WEEKS.

KINGSLEY 83

The physician operates on a child to help the child get back on the natural, healthy track. After surgical corrections, the physician slowly withdraws himself from the picture and lets nature continue to take its course. The parent should expect to do the same—solve the problem, then make adjustments so everyday consequences are strong enough to keep the problem from re-occurring. Parents are not there to control everything. They are there to help bring a child's actions under control of nature's plan when the natural forces are not strong enough to make the necessary corrections. Sometimes children get off track and misbehave. They may turn to lying, stealing, throwing tantrums, or being self-centered. Sometimes the natural conditions are not strong enough to get a child to save money, to do things for others, to be patient, or want an education.

Parents often have to implement special conditions to change the child. And often these special conditions may be detrimental if continued for too long. For example, in order to get James to clean his room, his parents may need to give extra rewards and attention. But later, when he has been consistent in cleaning his room, less reward and attention should be given. Units Four and Eleven talk about how parents should fade out the use of extra rewards once positive actions are occurring. They also talk about how to shift the control of actions from material rewards to internal feelings of satisfaction in the child (value shifting).

INSTILL CORRECT PRINCIPLES IN CHILDREN SO THEY CAN RULE THEMSELVES.

Parents should keep in mind that solving problems may be more than just coming up with a solution for changing an action in a child. If often includes arranging conditions so that changes in the child can be maintained by the natural functions of daily life with little special attention from mom and dad. They won't always be there. The plan of life expects the child to eventually not need mother and dad's help. The whole idea behind parents helping solve their children's problems is to **instill the correct principles in children so that, as adults, they can properly rule themselves.**

USING WHAT YOU HAVE

One of the most important parts of solving problems is learning to use what you have—your own resources. Common complaints child-rearing professionals hear from parents are:

"But I don't have anything I can use to influence my child."
"The Browns have lots of things they can do to handle problems with their children, but I don't have the money or the time."

The secret to success in life is not to wish you had the talents or assets of others. The secret is to recognize your own talents and develop them. Likewise, parents need to learn to solve problems using what is at their disposal. It is surprising what you can do, when you begin to put your mind to it. All of us suffer from what psychologists call "functional fixedness." We see things around us as having only one certain function when, in fact, those things could be used in other ways.

- *Have you ever thought a pretty rock could be a paper-weight?*
- *If you ran out of water on a desert road, would you think to use the liquid in a cactus?*
- *Could you use a belt to make a tourniquet to stop bleeding?*
- *Could you use nail polish to stop runs in nylons?*
- *Could you use powdered potatoes to make a glue?*

Few things in life can be used for one thing only. Most have several uses, if we would but think about them for a moment. Is this also true in solving parent/child problems? It certainly is.

An infant programmed to cry when in pain can learn to use that same cry to get attention.
A mother who cooks daily can use her cooking skills not only to satisfy the hunger of her family, but also can use such skills to increase positive actions or decrease misbehavior in children.
Parents can use bedtimes as a method of influencing a child's actions.
The weekly chore of cleaning the family car can be turned into a postive time for interaction between father and son.

Happy and successful children can come from rich or poor families, from single or two parent families, from families in Brazil or Alaska, from large or small families. The ingredients for successful parenting seem to be available to all. The key is to be able to learn to use what you have.

USE YOUR OWN RESOURCES.

Recognize your own parental talents and develop them.

Any home can have happy and successful children.

191

TURN LIABILITIES INTO ASSETS.

Mother Nature has not given us a problem that cannot be solved.

Mother Nature has given us everything we need to be happy.

There are two main ways of doing this. First, is to learn to recognize how things can be used. Unit Three explained how a particular item can be used by parents to develop positive actions or get rid of misbehaviors. Unit Three also pointed out how parents can re-arrange home situations to influence a child's actions. Reading the NAP Handbook and asking other parents what they do are ways to become better at doing this.

The second way is to learn to turn liabilities into assets. There are many dimensions in our life that appear to be problems, that can, in fact, be turned into benefits. A third grade teacher complained that she had a very difficult time in her class because her students were not all at the same level of achievement. Some were at kindergarten level, while others were above a third grade level of performance. This problem was turned into a benefit. A program was designed in which she used a more able child to teach another child who was on a lower vocabulary and reading level. This method would not have worked had all students been at about the same level. In families with many children, parents can use older children to help teach their brothers and sisters. Most parents fail to take advantage of their children as a force to help others in the family. It can be done!

A mother without a husband complained that she had a difficult time raising children alone. Certainly this was true, but a possible benefit she enjoyed was that she did not have a mate contradicting her methods as many two-parent families do.

Judo and other martial arts are strongly based on turning an opponent's strengths to one's own advantage. The science of child-rearing is only beginning to realize how this can be done in family situations. We are learning more and more how to help parents turn the weaknesses of a family into strengths.

Mother Nature has allowed problems to be a part of our lives. But she has also endowed us with problem-solving skills. The solutions to our problems are within our grasp. Often, however, we are looking in the wrong place and in the wrong direction for the solutions. The intent of this NAP Handbook has been and is to help you and all parents to identify and solve individual and family problems using the natural procedures and guidelines Mother Nature has given us. We all have the potential to be either happy children or happy parents (depending upon our relationship to those ahead of or behind us on life's continuum), residing together in happy, loving homes.

SO, WHAT NEEDS TO BE CONSIDERED
WHEN SOLVING PROBLEMS?

Solving problems with children can be more effectively and easily done if parents keep a few things in mind. First, sit down and analyze the situation thoroughly. Child-rearing professionals start by asking dozens of questions to get a clear idea as to what is involved in the problem situation. Parents can do the same. Instead of having a rough idea about what problem exists, parents should look more deeply and thoroughly at the situation.

Second, keep in mind that there are five basic types of problems parents have with their children: (1) problems of **decreasing** misbehaviors, (2) problems of **increasing** positive actions, (3) problems with a child's self-worth, (4) problems with a child's values, and (5) problems in parent/child communication. In most instances parents have children with more than one type of problem.

Third, learn to use several units in this handbook to deal with a particular type of problem. Figure 12.1 gives the reader a quick indication which units focus on each of the five types of problems.

This unit also refers to additional material (audio-cassette tapes) which parents can turn to for more in-depth coverage of specific types of problems. (Ordering information is on last page.)

The unit ends with four things to remember about problem solving. First, keep in mind the importance of picking the right time to start. Second, consider the sixteen **do's** and **don't's** of problem solving. Third, keep in mind that things need to be done after the problems are solved. Four, parents should focus more on using what they do have to solve problems than wishing for things they do not have.

TIPS FOR SOLVING PARENTAL PROBLEMS
Exercise 12.1

1. Pick a problem you child has and answer the following questions:

What is it? _____

_____

_____

When does it happen? _____

_____

_____

Why does it happen? _____

_____

_____

2. From question one above, which of the following to you see you are dealing with?

    a. Decrease some negative behavior.
    b. Increase some positive behavior.
    c. Influence the child's self-worth.
    d. Influence the child's values.
    e. Develop better communication skills.

3. List the units in the NAP Handbook that you should focus on in using the problem-solving approach you identified in question two.

_____

_____

_____

4. In the section entitled "Using What You Have" several suggestions are made of things parents can use to help solve problems. List two things you have in your home routine that you could use to help solve a problem with your child. (Try to pick ones not mentioned in the section.)

Problem	What You Have
Example: *Tammie is poor in math*	*Tammie could help her younger sister with basic math. This way the need in the home for younger sister to do math can help Tammie get experience.*
_____	
_____	

Question four continued on next page.

Continued from previous page.

Problem	What You Have
a._____	_____
_____	_____
_____	_____
b._____	_____
_____	_____
_____	_____

5. Pick a problem area in your home and explain how you can or did turn that problem into an asset.

Example: *Washing dishes (an unpleasant family chore) can be turned into a positive time to interact with a child.*

_____

_____

_____

_____

_____

_____

QUESTIONS and ANSWERS

Q. I am not sure I can ask the right questions to myself in trying to solve my child's problems. Any additional suggestions?

A. Pretend you are a detective trying to solve a crime. Try to ask yourself at least 30 questions. Some will be irrelevant, but you may be surprised with what good questions you can ask. Also, try talking it out with someone else. That often helps.

Q. I often have difficulty figuring out what kind of problem I am dealing with. Do other parents?

A. Yes. It often is not easy to get a quick, clear picture of what the problem is. Many times this happens because there are two or three intertwined problems. When this happens, keep in mind the five basic problems mentioned in this unit and try to classify your situation into one of these five areas.

Q. Do different families have similar types of problems? It seems like each family would be different.

A. Over the years perhaps the biggest unexpected surprise I received from working with children is realizing how common most family problems are and how different family situations can have so many things in common. That is why I wrote *Manipulating Parents* and the *NAP Handbook*. By helping parents see the common elements in dealing with children, the solution should become more apparent. Parenting can be fun when parents become better at solving problems.

Q. What is typically the most difficult part of solving problems with children?

A. The most difficult part for most parents is wondering if they have defined the problem correctly. Most feel comfortable with implementing the methods explained in the *NAP Handbook*. But parents begin wondering if they have diagnosed the problem correctly in the first place. Here again, it might be well to ask the advice or opinion of a friend. Often they can see something more clearly from their perspective outside your family circle.

Q. What is the most common mistake parents make in handling problems with children?

A. The most common mistake is believing the problems they have with their children stem from some unknown and deep psychological disturbance in the child. When looking at the children of neighbors and friends, we can spot the problem quite easily. The child is asking for too much or the child is throwing a tantrum just to get her way. However, when it comes to our own children we parents seem to lose our clear vision and our child's problem cannot be explained so simply and logically.

Q. Figure 12.1 shows which units are more specifically designed to deal with each of the five basic types of problems parents may have with children. It seems to me that Unit Eleven on values would be helpful in dealing with problems with a child's feelings of self-worth. Isn't self-worth a value problem?

A. It certainly is. And I agree that reading Unit Eleven would help a parent deal with increasing a child's feelings of self-worth. I also believe reading all the units in this handbook will help a parent handle any of the five types of problems. All units should contribute valuable information to parents.

Becoming A Better Person Through the Family

> This final unit tells how the family can help individuals become better and, as a result, happier. Through family organization, activities, and experiences, individual family members learn to increase positive actions, decrease negative behavior, improve feelings of self-worth, develop strong values, and improve communication skills—all things that improve the quality of life.

HOW TO MAKE A BETTER YOU

Through the ages philosopher after philosopher has attempted to answer the question: *"What is the reason for living?"* Some have claimed that living is nothing more than a figment of someone's imagination. Others have said that mankind's existence is nothing more than a mechanism for chromosomes in our bodies to propagate themselves. Such philosophical explanations may be interesting, but not very practical. On the practical side most would agree that the reason for living could be **to become a better you.**

So what makes a better you? There are five basic ways in which people can become better: (1) increasing positive actions, (2) decreasing misbehavior, (3) improving self-worth, (4) developing positive values, and (5) improving communication skills. Do these five sound familiar? They should, because they represent the five main types of problems parents have to deal with that were discussed in Unit Twelve. But these five important aspects of life do not have to remain problems. A family, working together, can turn them into strengths that will help build a better you.

Increase Positive Actions. One of the main dimensions of life is to become better at doing the things we do. Most of us want ourselves and our children to become better at such things as being helpful and efficient, friendly and appreciative, honest and gracious, and clean and healthy. We want to become better at giving advice, leading others, obeying laws, making decisions, solving problems, and getting things done.

THERE ARE FIVE
EVEN BETTER WAYS
OF BUILDING
A BETTER YOU:

Increase positive actions.
Decrease misbehavior.
Develop positive values.
Improve self-worth.
Improve communication skills.

197

Decrease Misbehavior. Mother Nature gave us the ability to make choices, but not all of our choices will be correct. Each of us misbehaves or makes mistakes thoughout our lives, either intentionally or unintentionally. We often build bad habits that we want to get rid of. One avenue for improving ourselves and our children is to reduce the frequency of misbehaving and making mistakes.

Develop Positive Values. Life provides us with the opportunity to develop values. We can learn to enjoy music, work, or learning; to develop a feeling for honesty and neighborliness; to value books, athletics, dancing, or any of thousands of other things. People can become better through developing positive values— values about objects, actions, or people.

Improve Self-worth. Self-worth is a value or feeling people have about themselves. How we feel about ourselves has a great impact on what we do and on other things we value. Better self-worth results in a better you.

Improve Communication Skills. Each one of us could become better by improving our communication with others. Knowing what to say, how to say it, and when to say it is something both parent and child can benefit from.

MAKING THE FAMILY A MUTUAL DEVELOPMENT SOCIETY

THE FAMILY:

The world's best mutual development system.

The family is perhaps Mother Nature's greatest invention. No society or government has developed a system that even comes close to the family system for helping individuals become better persons. The family system is a *mutual development* system where both parent and child are learning and growing.

As a helpless infant we enter this world dependent on our new family for everything. Over the years we learn who we are and what we are, and we develop ideas about what we can become. We must learn to use the intellectual potential we were born with. We must build up our experiential background so we can effectively make decisions. Family experiences are the main determiners of what we learn to do, what we think of oursleves, what communication skills we develop, and what values we accept.

As parents we are allowed to set up our own home based on the values we choose. Having children gives us the additional opportunity to be teachers and leaders. We have the opportunity to learn from interesting experiences with our children. We have the right to preside in our homes and reap the rewards (or penalties) of deciding how our family will be run.

Shared family experiences—working and playing, happiness and sadness, cooperation and conflict—are areas where both parent and child can develop in the five dimensions of life. The family system is intended to be a source for positive development of both parent and child. Both are to benefit from family experiences.

Keep in mind that a family structure is not enough. Mother Nature, giving us a family structure, has allowed us to decide how to make such a family grouping work. No two families are expected to function in the same way. One way may work better for one family than for another. However, a family plan is needed to give guidance and direction for developing the family and family members. Parents should be concerned about finding ways to help make families become *mutual development societies.*

CHARACTERISTICS OF AN EFFECTIVE FAMILY

There are five action-oriented characteristics of effective families. Such families (1) emphasize family identity, (2) set rules, (3) set goals, (4) actively develop methods for reaching goals, and (5) work on developing a balance of satisfaction.

Family Identity. Each of us needs to feel a part of something bigger than ourselves. Teenagers seek gangs and attention-getting exploits when they cannot identify with a strong family. Adults seek clubs and causes when a family identity is weak. Effective families generally have something which individual family members can identify with. Some families stand out because of ethnic background, family traditions, religious convictions, or unique family ties. Emphasizing these unique aspects of your particular family can go a long way toward helping family members develop and grow. Things a family can do to increase family identity include:

EVERYONE NEEDS TO BELONG TO SOMETHING.

1. First, write down what your family stands for. A family charter may be drawn up and decoratively posted stating several things that sets your family apart.

2. Decorate your homes with pictures, plaques, and other visual objects that represent the values and beliefs of your family. This could include such things as ethnic or religious pictures and objects, or pictures of well-known people your family admires. Visual cues in your home, such as objects that represent family vacations and memories, can act as prompts for family members.

3. Have photo albums, personal and family journals. Be sure to reflect weekly or monthly on past experiences and accomplishments. Talk about past fun times.

4. Do things together as a family. Have at least one family activity a week. Rotate which family member gets to choose the activity.

5. Make things which reflect family togetherness. Do things such as making a special family crest or logo or getting family T-shirts.

6. Have parents talk about their childhood, and talk about grandparents and their experiences.

7. In a positive way parents could talk about what they like and dislike.

8. Eat at least one meal together each day and communicate with each other during the meal.

Set Rules. All organizations need rules, and families are no exception. Wisely choosing rules has a stabilizing effect in a family. Some important points to remember when setting family rules are:

1. In a family based on presiding structure, parents have final say on the rules in their home. However, children, as family members, play an important role in giving input concerning these family rules.

2. Rules which family members might have difficulty with should be clearly spelled out and written down.

3. Family rules should be open to change. Family members should be able to question the value of any family rule and make suggestions for change.

RULES SHOULD BE FLEXIBLE.

4. In a presiding structure, parents are sensitive to any family member's request to review family rules.

5. Family rules are based on benefitting individual family members. For example, bedtime for twelve-year-olds and older may be 10 p.m. Later bedtimes may be allowed *if* the child can get up on time and not be grumpy.

6. Developing rules should also involve determining the consequences for breaking those rules.

7. Some method should be used to check up on all family members' adherence to the rules. (Rules made and not checked soon do not influence positive action.)

Set Goals. Without goals, families lack direction in their growth. People are much more successful when they define their goals. Some important points to remember when setting goals are:

1. Set both family and individual goals. Such goals should be growing experiences for the family and could include things like planning next year's summer vacation (where all help earn money and perhaps learn a foreign language to use) or setting up money-making family projects (Dad helps buy a mower and the kids share the profits from mowing lawns after expenses are met). Individual goals may involve getting better at something, learning a skill, learning to communicate more effectively, learning patience, etc.

2. Break down goals into steps that can be accomplished in weekly or monthly steps. High places are easier to reach if you can climb a step at a time.

3. Determine payoffs for reaching weekly or monthly goals. Recognize and reward each other in the family for reaching goals.

4. Provide some means to monitor progress toward goals. Checking progress is important.

Develop Methods for Reaching Goals. *Answers: A Parents' Guidebook for Solving Problems* is full of methods parents can use to help both their children and themselves improve in the five main dimensions of life. The wise parent should use this NAP guidebook as a source of alternative methods to use. Besides using the previous units of this book, parents can become better at developing methods if the following points are kept in mind:

1. Take the information in this book and design a personal plan to follow. This guidebook has discussed alternative ways to develop positive actions and remove misbehavior and bad habits. It has suggested what to consider for improving self-worth, developing values, and improving communication skills. Use the Outline for Action forms and personalize a plan for you or your child.

If one plan doesn't work, try another.

2. If your plan does not work, analyze the situation, and try again, perhaps with some new alternatives.

3. Use methods that "kill two birds with one stone." If dishes need to be washed and talks need to happen, combine dishwashing with communicating with your child. Communicate in driving to and from school. Use vacations to teach lessons of life. A goal to learn patience could be worked on while trying to teach your child to read. Set up goals to accomplish more than one thing at a time.

Develop a Balance of Satisfaction. Life is full of positives and negatives. Some families set goals which produce more adversity and pain than satisfaction. Others try to make life nothing but fun. Life is a mixture of both the sweet and the sour. We cannot eliminate either. Effective families work for a balanced situation where life produces more sweet than sour, though some of both. To do this, several hints may help:

1. Emphasize in your family that more worthwhile goals often take greater effort and require one to wait for payoffs.

2. Although life may have many unpleasant aspects, families still need to remind themselves of the positive dimensions. Keep family members from dwelling on the negatives of life.

3. Teach family members to turn liabilities into assets. If a child has a bad experience, help him/her focus on what the experience taught. All families have conflicts and bad times. Effective families do not necessarily have more positive experiences than ineffective families. They are just better at finding the good in bad situations.

4. Make the best of what you have rather than spending time wishing for things others have. Most families have the ingredients for success, if those ingredients are used properly.

WE CAN TURN NEGATIVES INTO POSITIVES.

NAP—AN EFFECTIVE FAMILY PLAN

One of the most common questions asked by parents is *"How do I change my family environment to produce a better family?"* Parents often want specific suggestions that will help their family become more effective. The NAP Family Plan is developed for that purpose. It is designed to: (1) help beginning families develop a proper organizational format that can be adjusted and modified as the family acquires new members, and (2) provide a format that can be introduced into an already-established family so that the problems that have already developed can be corrected.

THE BASIS OF NAP: THE FAMILY MEETING

The key to successfully implementing the NAP Family Plan is to have family meetings. Although Mother and Dad may establish the general goals and activities for the family, full family participation is important for a number of reasons. Children are apprenticing and need the experience of helping make decisions. Family meetings help children learn how to work together as a family. Such meetings help establish a family identity; they help family members more fully understand the needs of others; and they provide times for positive family communication so children are not talking to parents only during conflict situations. Family meetings help Mom and Dad be more consistent in planning family interaction and activities. The NAP system has found nothing that can help people develop in all five dimensions of life better

FAMILY MEETINGS:
The foundation for a successful family.

than well-run family meetings. Although Mother or Dad presides at each meeting, the children should have their turns at conducting (being in charge of making up the agenda and carrying it out).

MAKING THE NAP FAMILY PLAN WORK

How do you work the plan? By planning the "work"— writing it down.

There are four main written parts of the NAP Family Plan: (1) *the Family Charter and Rules*, (2) *the Family Chore Chart*, (3) *the Monthly Activity Calendar, and* (4) *the Weekly Planning Form.*

Family Charter and Rules. In a conspicuous place in the home a family charter with rules should be posted to remind family members. Newly starting families will find this useful, but it is particularly important in re-establishing family identity in families having problems. In such families, a counselor may assist the family in redefining what the family stands for, and what the rules of the family should be. During family meetings, family rules can be reviewed and changed when necessary. Family meetings should also consider suggestions relating to improving family identity. Possible suggestions were included earlier in this unit.

Family Chore Chart. Accountability and responsibility are two important dimensions of family life. Each member of the family should participate in chores that are part of every family. Three-year-olds can pick up toys and clothing. Five-year-olds can empty wastebaskets. Six-year-olds can set the dinner table. Figure 13.1 shows a blank Family Chore Chart.

At the beginning of each week a parent puts small horizontal dashes or marks on the chore chart. The child needs to do the chore on the days a dash is present in the box on the chart:

	Wash Dishes	—		—		—			
Roger	Clean bedroom	—	—	—	—	—	—	—	
	Put away clothes	—	—	—	—	—	—	—	
	Keep articles picked up	—	—	—	—	—	—	—	
	Vacuum *family room*		—		—		—		
	Dust and pick up ___								
	Clean cars						—		
	Water outdoor plants	—		—		—			
	Wash dishes		—		—		—		
Amy	Clean bedroom	—	—	—	—	—	—	—	

At the end of each day the parent takes ten minutes and checks to see what chores were completed. The dashed line is made into a "plus sign" and those chores that are not completed are circled:

Roger	Clean bedroom	+	+	⊖	+	—	—	—	
	Put away clothes	+	+	+	+	—	—	—	
	Keep articles picked up	+	⊖	+	+	—	—	—	
	Vacuum *family room*		+		⊘		—		
	Dust and pick up ___								
	Clean cars						—		

FAMILY CHORE CHART

ASSIGNED TO:	CHORE:	MON	TUE	WED	THU	FRI	SAT	SUN	COMMENTS:
	Clean bedroom								
	Put away clothes								
	Keep articles picked up								
	Vacuum _____								
	Dust and pick up _____								
	Clean cars								
	Dust/sweep shop								
	Wash Dishes								
	Clean bedroom								
	Put away clothes								
	Keep articles picked up								
	Vacuum _____								
	Dust and pick up _____								
	Clean cars								
	Water outdoor plants								
	Wash dishes								
	Clean bedroom								
	Put away clothes								
	Keep articles picked up								
	Vacuum _____								
	Dust/sweep garage or carport								
	Clean patio								
	Dust blinds								
	Help cook								
	Clean bedroom								
	Put away clothes								
	Keep articles picked up								
	Vacuum _____								
	Clean windows								
	Take out garbage								
	Clean bathrooms								
	Help cook								
	Clean bedroom								
	Put away clothes								
	Keep articles picked up								
	Vacuum _____								
	Clean windows								
	Take out garbage								
	Wash dishes								
	Laundry/iron								
	Clean bedroom								
	Put away clothes								
	Keep articles picked up								
	Vacuum _____								
	Water indoor plants								
	Feed animals								
	Wash dishes								
	Laundry/iron								

Figure 13.1 Family Chore Chart

This example shows you some of the types of chores that might be put on a chore chart. Page 210 has a short version that is blank and can be tailored to your needs.

The Family Chore Chart becomes a record of how well family members are meeting their chore responsibilities. In families where allowances are given, penalties can be determined for missed chores: for example, 15 cents is deducted for each of the first three missed, 25 cents for the next three, and loss of the whole week's allowance if there are more than six uncompleted chores. During family meetings the assignment of chores could be discussed and agreed upon. Past experience has shown that children can be given too many or too few chores. Five to seven daily chores has proven to be the best. Be sure the Family Chore Chart is kept posted in a conspicuous place.

Monthly Activity Calendar. A large calendar with room to put notes on each day should be posted next to the Family Chore Chart. Family members should pencil in future activities on the calendar as soon as they know about them. This helps to plan ahead for family needs (money, transportation, scheduling). Weekly family meetings can review the proposed activities and how they can fit individual goals and the functions of the family. A suggested family rule is that people who plan ahead first, get first priority on family facilities and support.

Weekly Planning Form. Figure 13.2 shows a Weekly Planning Form. It has two sides. On the first side is an agenda for the weekly family meeting. A parent or one of the older children is assigned to conduct the meeting. Old business is covered first. Moving on to new business, a sergeant-at-arms may be voted in to be responsible for keeping the family chore chart up to date and checking on completion of chores by family members. This is an excellent way of teaching children the value of authority combined with responsibility and accountability. Next, lingering problems and arguments between family members could be discussed. Such discussions should require participants to not only point out problems, but also propose realistic solutions. Family disputes over chores, use of car, use of T.V. and the like could then be covered. (Be sure suggestions for improvement are included.) Any sort of general issues or concerns could then be addressed.

The opportunity for family members to discuss and change family rules should be included. In many families, rules are often discussed in moments of emotional conflict. It is surprising how reasonable and realistic children can be in "non-combative" family meetings.

Family and individual activities are a very important part of personal growth. Discuss the activities of each family member. Talk about the reasons for the activities, and try to identify which goals of life these activities help. This helps get children thinking about why they should and should not do things.

The last part of side one of the Weekly Planning Form is the family weekly journal entry. Whoever conducts the meeting should lead the family in reviewing what happened during the past week. Those family events of note, i.e., winning awards, camping trip disasters, moving into a new house, should be recorded. This Weekly Planning Form should then be put in the family journal binder at the end of each week.

Keep a record of memorable family activities and happenings.

WEEKLY PLANNING FORM

Person conducting: _____   Date: _____

OLD BUSINESS: _____

_____

_____

NEW BUSINESS:

Sergeant-at-Arms selection: _____

Family communication problems or suggestions: _____

_____

Family disputes and suggestions: _____

_____

General issues: _____

_____

_____

Family rules review: _____

_____

_____

Family and individual activities:

Description   Reason for doing

_____   _____

_____   _____

_____   _____

WEEKLY FAMILY JOURNAL ENTRY

_____

_____

_____

_____

_____

Figure 13.2 Weekly Planning Form (side one)

205

WEEKLY PLANNING FORM
(side two)

DEVELOPING POSITIVE ACTIONS

What was planned   What occurred

_____   _____

_____   _____

_____   _____

ELIMINATING MISBEHAVIOR

What was planned   What occurred

_____   _____

_____   _____

_____   _____

INFLUENCING SELF-WORTH

What was planned   What occurred

_____   _____

_____   _____

_____   _____

DEVELOPING VALUES

What was planned   What occurred

_____   _____

_____   _____

_____   _____

INCREASING COMMUNICATION SKILLS

What was planned   What occurred

_____   _____

_____   _____

_____   _____

Figure 13.2 Weekly Planning Form (side two)

The second side of the Weekly Planning Form provides space to write down family or individual goals for any of the five main areas of development that concern parents. If a particular child has difficulty keeping his room clean and doing family chores, this could be discussed by the family, and an Outline for Action (on indolence) filled out. In some cases parents may use this side of the planning form on a child without bringing the rest of the family into the issue. This side of the planning form should help stimulate parents to keep working toward at least one of the five goals each week.

WHAT TO DO WHEN YOUR FAMILY DOES NOT FIT THE MOLD

"But my family is different." This is a common concern heard from parents when they cannot seem to get a family plan going. Some cannot get all family members together for a meeting because of conflicting schedules. Some families have only one parent. Or it takes too much time.

Although there may be many good reasons why families do not get an effective family plan going there is an even better reason to make it work—**most families will fail without it.**

For those families who do not seem to "fit the mold," but desire to get a family plan going, here are a few suggestions:

1. Keep in mind that *every* family has to make some concessions and adjustments to get a plan going.

2. Family plans actually save time. Family Chore Charts and the like cut down on what the parents have to do. The few minutes required to check daily and keep up a chart are less than the time of doing the chore for the child.

3. The same NAP plan can be used for both single and two-parent families. The aim of the plan is to get all family members pulling their "family weight," while still meeting individual goals.

4. Even if you cannot formally set up the complete NAP Family Plan, do as much as you can. Doing some things is better than nothing.

5. While weekly meetings are best, monthly meetings can still help.

6. Make meetings enjoyable. If family members hate to come to the family meetings, things need to be changed. Arrange it so having meetings pays off.

7. Short meetings (20-30 minutes) are better than long ones.

8. If one parent is not willing to join family meetings, the other could do it and still be quite successful.

9. Have surprise (brief) activities at meeting; have special food treats.

THE NAP FAMILY PLAN—

The remedy for failing families.

GET IT ALL TOGETHER IN FAMILY MEETINGS.

THE FAMILY—WHAT'S IT ALL ABOUT?

There is strength in numbers. It is easy to break one pencil in half, but trying to break a handful is very difficult, if not impossible. It is the same with people. By themselves, they "break." Together, they become strong.

Everything in this unit involves two or more persons helping each other to grow and develop in the five basic areas. That's what a NAP family is all about—doing things TOGETHER, helping each other.

We believe that by using the information in this and the other units of this NAP guidebook you can make your family one that grows, develops, and has fun—TOGETHER.

MAKE A COMMITMENT

It is difficult to be successful at anything without first making a commitment. Surely the most important commitment we should make is to have a successful, happy family. We offer the following statement by W. H. Murray on making commitments. It works! This book is the result of following such advice. Try it! Make it work for you.

. . . Until one is committed there is hesitancy, the chance to draw back, always ineffectiveness. Concerning all acts of initiative (and creation), there is one elementary truth, the ignorance of which kills countless ideas and splendid plans: that the moment one definitely commits oneself, then providence moves too.

All sorts of things occur to help one that would never otherwise have occurred. A whole stream of events issues from the decision, raising in one's favor all manner of unforeseen incidents and meetings and material assistance, which no man could have dreamt would have come his way.

I have learned a deep respect for one of Goethe's couplets:

Whatever you can do, or dream you can,
begin it.

Boldness has genius, power and magic
in it.

—W. H. Murray

Special Helps

This special helps section includes additional insights on two issues, punishement, and foreward and backward chaining.

PUNISHMENT

For the past thirty years many professionals in child-rearing have been telling parents that punishment is not only an ineffective method for controlling a child's behavior, but that it also causes irreparable psychological harm. In some cases one or two psychological studies are quoted to verify these ideas. It is often claimed that "new psychological evidence has shown that punishment is harmful and ineffective." Actually, just the reverse seems more true. Psychological research suggesting punishment has no positive effects were found mostly in the 1930's, 40's, and 50's. Punishment studies in the 1960's, 70's, and 80's have overwhelmingly indicated it is effective (and does not produce everlasting psychological trauma). In the book *Manipulating Parents*2 (pages 163-64) several references are given to support this claim. One of the better references given for parents and child-rearing professionals to look up was Gary Walter's and Joan Grusec's book entitled *Punishment* published in 1977. This book does a good job of addressing the issues for and against punishment. Two additional and somewhat more technical references reviewing punishment research are: Richard Solomon's 1964 article in the *American Psychologist Journal*, and a 1983 book entitled *The Effects of Punishment on Human Behavior* edited by Alexrod and Apsche (Academic Press).

While evidence has been piling up that punishment is effective in changing a child's behavior, most state social service programs (including foster care) and institutional care programs forbid the use of punishment. State policies on punishment arose because of four main reasons: (1) incorrect professional advice as to the effectiveness of punishment, (2) concern about potential lawsuits from incorrect use of punishment by foster parents, etc., (3) the actual misuse of punishment in institutions, and (4) claims that misbehavior in children can be controlled in all cases without having to resort to punishment.

The Natural Approach to Parenting System agrees with Axelrod and Apsches's review of the literature indicating punishment is necessary in some conditions. Not letting foster parents and child-rearing professionals use punishment because they may abuse it or because they have abused it seems to be like banning the driving of cars because some could or do drive unwisely.

NAP proposes that the same approach for allowing policemen to use controlled force be instituted with child-rearing professionals. Teach foster parents and institutional attendants how to properly use the variety of potential punitive methods; give them the authority to use it; then review any use of it.

NAP also provides more information about punishment on a tape entitled "The Do's and Don'ts of Discipline and Punishment" and a booklet entitled "The Value of Punishment: Several Perspectives."

FOREWARD CHAINING

Just as a chain is composed of many links, so can many tasks be broken down into a number of separate parts (*sub*acts). Take tying shoes, for example. Tying a shoe actually involves a chain of actions. Conventional or forward chaining might involve the following steps:

Step 1   place a shoelace in either hand.

Step 2   fold one shoelace over the other, tucking it through, and pulling tight

Step 3   make a loop with the shoelace in the left hand

Step 4   circle that loop with the shoelace in the right hand and tuck it through while forming the second loop

Step 5   grasp both loops with separate hands and pull them away from each other, thereby drawing the knot tight

Notice that the task of tying a shoe could actually be broken down into more than five separate actions. So, if five divisions produced too big of steps for the child, then smaller actions or steps should be worked with.

BACKWARD CHAINING

There is a special technique for making it easier to learn an action that experts in action development use all the time. Generally speaking, parents may find this technique somewhat surprising because it goes against some of the habits they have been taught all their lives. However, this technique is so valuable and more effective than the traditional approach that perhaps you should be introduced to it. It is what has been labeled the *Principle of Backward Chaining*. In essence, it says that **once you break down some task into a chain of actions, start teaching that chain from the end and work towards the beginning.** Teach the child Step 5, then Steps 4 and 5, then Steps 3, 4, and 5, and so on.

Let's compare the two approaches, foreward and backward chaining, and analyze what happens. First though, to better understand what is taking place, it is necessary to know something about *bonding*. When the mind relates an action to its consequence a *mental bond* is formed. In dealing with positive actions we want to maintain a strong bond. (To change an action or break a habit, a bond needs to be broken, weakened, or changed.) Let's look at the front chaining methods for teaching tying a shoelace. As the child performs Step 1, he is rewarded with praise and recognition. A mental bond takes place—he relate the act (Step 1) with a pleasant consequence (praise). Step 2, when introduced, breaks the previous bond and a new bond is formed—a bond between Step 2 and the reward (praise). Each time a new step is added, a previous bond is broken and a new one is created. Eventually, after breaking several mental bonds, the child realizes the satisfaction of completing the task, and the final bonding between the completed task and the positive consequence takes place with no more breaks. There is a greater chance of frustration and delay in learning how **to finish** a task using this approach.

Now, let's look at the backward chaining method. The child performs Step 5 and receives praise and recognition. At this point the bonding is no differnet than that of learning Step 1 with foreward chaining. The act and the consequence are mentally bonded in the child's mind. There is one additional and immediate result, however—*the child has completed the task*. In this case, the shoelace is now tied. He can, after only one step, feel a sense of accomplishment—he has participated in the completion of a task.

As the process continues, Step 4 is put in front of Step 5. He receives a positive consequence. No bond is broken, no new one is formed. The previous bond is strengthened **and** he again experiences **finishing** a task. This process continues until he is able to move through Step 1 to 5.

In backward chaining, then, the mental bond between action and positive consequence is strengthened with each additional step, and the child experiences the **completion** of the job—in this case, at least five times. In foreward chaining, bonds are broken and re-formed and the child experiences the completed task only once.

Backward chaining can be a time-saver. In many cases a child develops a chain of actions using this chaining technique in one-third the time it would take to develop it by starting from the front, as it is traditionally done.

Besides economy of time, backward chaining provides a second (very important) advantage. Already mentioned earlier, it deals with task completion. When parents attempt to develop chains of actions in their child using the usual foreward chaining method, the child often fails to continue with the training until the complete job is learned. In such cases, that child often develops the habit of starting tasks but not finishing them. That tendency is greatly reduced when parents use backward chaining techinques.

To illustrate with dishwashing, have the young child help do the last one-fourth of the dishes to receive the satisfaction of the job completion rather than helping with the first quarter of the dishes. Then have the child help with the last half, then the last three-quarters, and so on until he or she can do them all.

For some tasks, starting from the back is only mildly more effective.

The Family Chore Chart is similar to the one on page 203, without specific chores being listed. You might make several copies of it, depending upon the size of your family or simply use it as a guide to make your own.

FAMILY CHORE CHART

Assigned to:	Chore:	MON	TUE	WED	THU	FRI	SAT	SUN
	1.							
	2.							
	3.							
	4.							
	5.							
	6.							
	7.							
	8.							
	9.							

Assigned to:	Chore:	MON	TUE	WED	THU	FRI	SAT	SUN
	1.							
	2.							
	3.							
	4.							
	5.							
	6.							
	7.							
	8.							
	9.							

Assigned to:	Chore:	MON	TUE	WED	THU	FRI	SAT	SUN
	1.							
	2.							
	3.							
	4.							
	5.							
	6.							
	7.							
	8.							
	9.							

Assigned to:	Chore:	MON	TUE	WED	THU	FRI	SAT	SUN
	1.							
	2.							
	3.							
	4.							
	5.							
	6.							
	7.							
	8.							
	9.							

INDEX

Dr. Paul Robinson is Professor of Psychology at Brigham Young University. He is the author of twelve books, including the best-selling *Manipulating Parents*. His *Fundamentals of Experimental Psychology* with an emphasis on teaching future psychologists how to analyze situations was the number one best-selling college textbook. For over fifteen years he and his wife, Carol, have taken in and worked with problem children in their home. In 1983, the State of Utah presented Dr. Robinson with the Maurice Warchaw Award for distinguished service in the foster parenting field. Dr. Robinson has been a guest on over 100 televison and radio talk-shows in major cities throughout the U.S. He is also a contributing author to many scientific journals and magazines including: *Journal of Psychology, Journal of Applied Behavioral Analysis, Journal of the Experimental Analysis of Behavior,* and the *Journal of Advertising.* Dr. Robinson was recently voted one of the most interesting professors at B.Y.U. by the graduating senior class.

Leo Hall is one of those rare individuals who follow their convictions and dreams. After receiving his Master's Degree in Education, he taught in schools in Oregon and New Zealand. Throughout his travels, he and his wife, Charlotte, have raised ten children, many of whom have distinguished themselves in state and national competitions in such categories as speech and graphic art. The four oldest are currently attending university on various scholarships. Leo and his wife, who is a professional in nursery and pre-school training, reside in a community south of Portland, Oregon, where he is pursuing his career in writing and consulting.

Any inquiries about the NAP materials or services mentioned in the introduction at the front or elsewhere in this guidebook should be directed to the address below. Some items may not yet be available or temporarily out of stock. We will endeavor to meet your requests as soon as possible and keep you informed of other materials and programs to be developed in the future.

LION HOUSE PRESS
P.O. Box 791
Canby, Oregon 97013